NOT TACO BELL MATERIAL

NOT TACO BELL

MATERIAL

A MEMOIR

ADAM CAROLLA

THREE RIVERS PRESS • NEW YORK

This book is dedicated to my twins—Sonny and Natalia.
But this is the only page of it they'll be allowed to read.

INTRODUCTION

This is a book of stories. My stories. They range from pathetic to infuriating to disgusting to absurd. But something important I want to make clear right at the top is that *all of these stories are true*. There is not one ounce of hyperbole. I've not exaggerated or fabricated any of the details. In fact it was probably worse than I remember, but my psyche has dimmed it down for my own protection.

Let's talk houses. As a kid the places I called home were cracked stucco, dirt lawns, and furniture raccoons wouldn't fuck on. But there's another way of looking at homes. They are where you create memories with your family, good and bad, and the pad you launch from when you start your own life. If you want to know where someone is at physically, mentally, financially, and spiritually, look at where they're living.

So I've decided to start each chapter by telling you a little bit about the different abodes I've called home. This book will be a journey from the plethora of dumps I was raised in, through the shithole apartments I rented in my twenties, to the homes I purchased and personally renovated when I found some success.

1

A CRACKED FOUNDATION:
MOM'S HOUSE

NORTH HOLLYWOOD, CA

YEAR BOUGHT: 1951

PURCHASE PRICE: $10,000

                 875 SQUARE FEET

                 TWO BEDROOMS

                 ONE BATH

                 ZERO HOPE

THE photo on the previous page is of the first of many dumps I grew up in. Technically there were a couple of stops in Philly and New Jersey when I was a baby and a couple months in a rental house in Chatsworth as a toddler, but this is the house I consider my childhood home. The roof was falling off and the porch was falling apart. At some point my grandfather decided to rebuild the front porch. But in the penny-wise, pound-foolish Carolla tradition, he bought used lumber that had been salvaged from a pier fire. The boards were warped, charred, and had termite damage. That porch stayed on the house for fifteen years. It was humiliating living in this place. It was called "the barn" by the neighborhood kids.

It had one bathroom, no dishwasher, no air-conditioning, one washing machine but no dryer, yet it had two front doors. *Two* doors right next to each other at ninety degrees. I never thought that was strange until I dug up the picture below some years later. There is symbolism to it. It made no sense and didn't conform to any

1977—The barn. Family photo or police lineup? You decide.

standards, yet was accepted as if it was completely normal and did not need to be fixed. Just like my family.

My dad is the white guy in the dashiki who looks like the lead singer from Boston. My parents had just gotten divorced and my dad was ready to swing. It was time to put on a medallion and hit the disco. My mom is the one in the back looking like a depressed, lesbian Moe Howard. Next to her, hiding from the world, is my older sister and only sibling, Lauren. That's me, second from the left, standing next to my step-grandfather, Lazlo Gorog, the one sane person in my clan. More on him later. My grandmother is behind the camera. I could fill the rest of this book with details about the other dead-eyed people in this picture, but I won't. What I want you to notice is that these are the expressions they have when a picture is being taken. Imagine the complete lack of joy being expressed when the camera was put away. That's what I grew up in.

My mom was a full-blown hippie. Everyone thinks being a hippie is all free love and tambourines. But my mom was the paranoid-bummer version of hippie. There was constant hand-wringing and worry about the atomic bomb and the ozone layer and pollution in the streams and how we're oppressing the indigenous peoples. Her message was basically, "Good luck enjoying your childhood while other people starve, the planet goes to shit, and we nuke each other. Oh, and it's all our fault because we're evil greedy white people." Being a depressed hippie is a lose-lose. It would be like if a rice cake had the caloric content of a MoonPie.

My mom hung out with some world-class longhairs. She had a friend named Happy, one named Sunshine, another named Axis, and one guy named Zorback. His name was probably Gerald but he went by Zorback as a fuck-you to the Man. Take that, Nixon! I'm not sure if they were dating and I don't want to know. But he was one of those guys that was always hanging around after my folks split up.

Zorback drove a customized (using plywood, duct tape, and a jigsaw) microbus. The kind you might find up on blocks in front of a commune. It was essentially a mobile raping unit. The streets in the San Fernando Valley in the early seventies were filled with custom vans, three-wheeled Harley choppers, Army jeeps, Baja bugs, and sand rails—everything except normal cars. Picture the bad guys from *The Road Warrior,* minus the super-homoerotic overtones.

One time when I was eleven, Mom, Zorback, and I piled into the *'Back*mobile to go camping. I was sitting next to the rear window, which was fashioned out of an old screen door. This created a vacuum that sucked all the exhaust into the back of the bus. I thought I just fell asleep, but later I figured out that I had gotten carbon monoxide poisoning. Thank God the adult supervision was baked and decided to stop for munchies and left me in the back. Parents, I know what you're thinking: "They just left you alone?" But you have to remember it was a different time. If your kid was asleep in the car, you wouldn't wake him up unless you needed him to go into the liquor store and get you a pack of smokes. I woke up, left the bus, and wandered around the grocery store. I grabbed a can of Coke that I wanted them to buy for me, but I kept dropping it. I was so loopy from the carbon monoxide, everything was dark and echoey and I couldn't get my feet under me. I stumbled into the bathroom and thought it would be a good idea to take a nap on the cool tile floor. Eventually an employee came in and told me to move along. To add to my tripped-out confusion, a woman came up to me, handed me a packet of beef jerky, and asked me to open it for her. How often does that happen, some stranger coming up to you in a store and asking you to open a bag of jerky for them? Yet it happens to me when I'm eleven and fucked-up on carbon monoxide. I was wrestling with it like an alligator. I don't know if I ever got it open. I staggered out of the place and back to the bus and became more coherent as the minutes wore on. But I was nauseous and had a headache and was fucked-up for the next forty-eight hours. (Eventually Mom and

Zorback did figure out I had carbon monoxide poisoning and attempted to remedy it by sitting me next to a campfire and bathing me in secondhand pot smoke.) I know that this has caused me some brain damage. I'm convinced if it hadn't happened I would have ended up going to college, then grad school, and eventually creating Facebook. Nice going, Zorback.

Everything in the house was secondhand. If there was such a thing as thirdhand, the Carollas would have jumped on that train. It wasn't just furniture and retreads on the car. It was intimate items: pillows, blankets, coffee mugs, tampons, maxi pads. My sister's favorite drinking glass was a graduated cylinder from the turn of the century that looked like it was part of an old-timey chemistry set. We later found out it was a jar for urine specimens.

Like any decent hippie, my mom shunned material possessions and waste and the consumer society and blah blah blah. Some families have lasagna night and family board-game night. For the Carollas, Thursday night was trash-picking night. Mom, Sis, our neighbors—the Gravitches—and myself would scour the neighborhood in search of stuff we wouldn't throw away. You've heard the old adage that one man's trash is another man's treasure. Unfortunately, I was raised by the second guy. So my idea of a good weekend growing up was to head to the Schwinn shop and do some dumpster diving. If I was lucky, I might find some handlebars that were bent because the previous owner was unlucky and got hit by a truck.

My family was cheap and poor but they were also honest. Maybe a little too honest. A lot of kids, especially nowadays, are raised with a go-out-and-get-yours or screw-him-before-he-screws-you mentality. My family's battle cry was "What about the other guy?" All other people, especially if their skin was darker than mine, were to come first. Here's a little story that predates this house but perfectly illustrates this line of thinking. I was about five years old and living in Cherry Hill, New Jersey. I was at the Cherry Hill Mall with my mother and I found a fifty-dollar bill. Not a wallet with a fifty in it, just a loose crumpled-up bill. I used to find a lot of shit when I was a kid, but I just recently realized that was because I was only two feet off the ground. Sadly, my five-year-old twins never find anything on the ground because they're too busy staring up at the forty-two-inch flat-screen mounted on the wall of their room. Anyway, I showed my mom what I'd picked up and she told me we had to go to the lost and found and report it missing. Even at five years old I was thinking, "Bitch, are you nuts? The guy at the lost and found is just going to pocket it." I should have grabbed a barstool, climbed up, and slapped some sense into her. When we brought it to the desk, the guy said, "We'll keep it for two weeks. If no one claims it, it's yours."

I was at my house waiting impatiently for the two weeks to expire like a prison convict scratching lines into his cell wall. You have to remember this was fifty bucks in 1970. At the time, gas was twenty-two cents a gallon. And we were Carollas: I didn't even know fifty-dollar bills existed. I thought they stopped at ten.

The bounty was claimed, to my mom's self-hating white delight, by a heavyset woman of color. To the woman's credit, she found out I had returned the bill and came to our house to give me a reward. Ten bucks. Then for some reason my mom made me split it with my sister. My fifty dollars cash got whittled down to five dollars and a hug from Nell Carter.

The perfect storm of poor meets atheist—with an unhealthy dose of "What's in it for me?"—formed the holy trinity of pathetic Carolla Christmases.

One of the most memorable holidays was the year my mom cut

down a branch from a pine tree and leaned it against our living-room wall. That's a step down from Charlie Brown.

Christmas at my grandmother's house was even worse. She never purchased a tree, opting instead to decorate the potted rubber-tree plant that was in her living room. She just threw a little tinsel on a houseplant and called it a holiday.

Two of the people in the photo at the beginning of this chapter are my uncle and step-aunt. They were named Gobbi and Bueshi and they were from Hungary. We used to spend Christmas Eve over at their house. This provided the setting for the only Christmas tradition we had—the family grab bag. Imagine this scene: All the grown-ups would bring a gift costing no more than five dollars. The gifts would get wrapped and piled in a corner, everyone would get in a circle and draw numbers, and when their turn came up, they grabbed a random gift.

One year my dad drew his number, took his turn at the grab bag, and got a gift fit for a king. A shrimp de-veiner. It was a little plastic shrimp on a weird hook thing, used to pull the veins out of shrimp. It

1965—Grandma's house. Moments before singing the traditional Christmas carol "Oh, Rubber Tree."

could not have cost more than a buck twenty-nine and was definitely purchased at the grocery store on the way to the party. That's if it was purchased at all. It might have been stolen from an all-you-can-eat seafood joint. What is for sure is that there was zero thought put into it. A moment of contemplation is all it would have taken to realize that no one in my family could afford shrimp. Shrimp were far too expensive and delicious to grace the Carolla dinner table.

A *fucking shrimp de-veiner*. If someone gave that to me today as a gift I would dive across the table and stab them in the neck with it.

In my family, the cheap jab was always followed by a haymaker of laziness to deliver the knockout blow. Average garden-variety laziness might prevent someone from accomplishing a goal for a couple of months, but in an ironic twist, the Carollas really stepped it up when it came to not stepping up. I'll give you two examples, both over forty years in the making, and in keeping with the holiday theme, the first one takes place on Thanksgiving. My grandmother's house had a piano; I know that sounds upscale, but like my grandmother, it was weathered, old, and barely upright. Before I was born some roofing tar dripped onto its arm—think wax drippings from the world's shittiest candle. And there it stayed until I grew up. We were at my sister's house six years ago for Turkey Day. My grandfather had died and my grandmother was fading fast, so the piano had made it to her house. I was sitting there eating my stuffing and cranberry sauce when I glanced over at the piano and noticed something. The tar. The goddamn tar was still there. I asked why it hadn't been removed. Not one member of my family could give me an adequate answer. It wasn't like they tried solvents and a wood chisel but it was too mighty a foe. Nope. No one had bothered. But I was bothered, so I got up, walked to the kitchen, grabbed a butter knife, and easily popped the tar off. I did in one single motion what my whole family couldn't—and more importantly didn't—attempt to pull off in my entire life span leading up to that moment.

The second incident occurred just last year when I went to visit my mother. I hadn't been inside the house in quite a while and poked my head into my stepfather's room, which was also our den. My mom and stepdad sleep in separate rooms—don't ask. I looked up toward the ceiling and saw something very pathetic and telling. In 1973, my cousin Greg was visiting and we were eating Fruit Rolls (the cheap generic precursor to Fruit Roll-Ups). We were fucking around and decided to see if we could stick a piece of Fruit Roll to the ceiling. This was an old colonial house from the 1880s and for some reason back then they built houses with super high ceilings. Which is ironic since the average height at that time was five foot six. Most ceilings now are down to eight feet while we're all getting taller. At this rate my grandkids are going to get brain damage from a ceiling fan. But what makes it even nuttier is that the footprint of the room is seven by nine. My stepfather's room/den was built like a shoe box standing on its end.

Despite this we managed to pull it off, and thirty-nine years later that quarter-sized piece of jelly flypaper was still affixed to the ceiling. My stepfather has been in that room staring at the ceiling as he drifts off to sleep with visions of strawberry Fruit Roll-Ups dancing in his head for forty years. He's now officially a Carolla.

Final thought on how lazy my family is: I don't even have a middle name. There is a blank spot on my birth certificate where a middle name should go. Somewhere in the mid-eighties I was renewing my license and the middle-name spot was blank, mocking me. Thus Adam "Lakers" Carolla was born.

About six years ago I asked my dad why I don't have a middle name. He gave the worst answer a father could give his son. He thought about it, scratched the back of his neck and said, "I don't know." He

followed up with, "Ask your mom." When I asked my mom, she gave me the worst answer a mother could give her son: "Did you ask your dad?" I'm more offended at the lack of excuse than the lack of a middle name. It wasn't like, "You were born premature in the back of a cab and we didn't have time to fill out the paperwork." Nope, just "Ehh." And here's the worst part, my dad's dad's name was Giacomo. I could have been Ace Giacomo Carolla. It's such bullshit.

You'll read more, much, much more about my friends Ray and Chris in future chapters, but I thought it was worth pointing out that it was at this stage of my life I met the two guys who would become my best friends and occasionally my worst enemies. I met Ray at Colfax Elementary and Chris while playing Pop Warner football.

I started on the farm team, then moved up to Gremlins, then two years of Mighty Mites, Pee Wee, Midget, then Bantam. My hippie mom hated that I played Pop Warner. The only thing she liked about it was that it exposed me to people of color so I could learn first-hand how horrible white people are. As I said, race was an issue for my mom. She was a Chicano Studies major at Valley Junior College despite being slightly whiter than Tom Petty. *Really,* that was an actual major. We didn't watch a lot of TV when I was a kid but we did see every second of *Roots.* My mom sat there staring at it with a disgusted look on her face and then every ten seconds she'd look at us and say, "Do you see how bad we are? Do you see what we did?" I was thinking, "I'm twelve. What the fuck did I do?"

(Throughout this book I won't be able to stop myself from going off on a few tangents. These will be signaled by this dapper fellow—a Tan Gent. Get it?) I've spent the better part of my life in a society that's trying to make me feel guilty for a crime I did not commit. My dad's family was in Italy during the time of slavery. And forget about owning people, those losers would be lucky if they owned a donkey. Once on *Loveline* when I was trying to plead my case about the Carollas and slavery I made the mistake of using my sister's children as an example. They're not black, they're the opposite. They're German. I said, "These kids were born in Germany, their father is full-blooded German, and they arrived on this planet a lot closer to the Holocaust than I did to slavery. Does that mean they should be held responsible for the Holocaust or bear the guilt associated with it?" Of course that would be an insane notion. But somehow this same math doesn't apply to many Americans when it comes to slavery. On a happy note, some cunt my sister carpools with told her that I called her kids Nazis.

Side note to my side note. I'd like to address this to the people who feel the need to pass along hurtful information, especially when they have to bedazzle it with bullshit. You should kill yourselves. Please kill yourselves. You're driving me fucking crazy. It's profoundly disappointing to me that people feel the need to invent "facts" to bolster their incorrect arguments. Your motives are worse than a serial killer's, you're going out of your way to hurt someone, but you stand to gain nothing from it. At least the serial killer gets to go home and beat off.

But back to Mom. When I was nine or ten she used to ship me off to hang out with the Boyd brothers, black twins who were on my Pop Warner team. Henry and James Boyd lived in a ghetto on the edge of Los Angeles called Pacoima. I was the only white guy amid a sea of black faces. Their dad wasn't around, their older brother was in trouble with the law, and Mama was morbidly obese. We used to eat grits and collard greens. Think Steve Martin's family from *The Jerk*.

One semi-awkward moment came when I was spending one of many weekends there and we were playing football on the front lawn. At this point in my development I couldn't be tackled by someone my own age. I had supernatural balance. Even the Boyds couldn't take me down. I got the ball, did a little shake on Henry and a little bake on James, and scored a touchdown. And I followed

1973—Pop Warner. With Henry or James
(I can't tell those people apart—twins, not blacks).

it up with a hearty "How do you like me now, nigger!" Before you call Al Sharpton, you have to remember a couple of things. This was the mid-seventies, the height of Richard Pryor's fame. That word was used liberally at the time, especially by the Boyd brothers. I didn't even realize I was doing it. I was just fitting in. They'd been saying it all day. And more important, they weren't offended. In fact they were kind of impressed. It was like that scene in *Goodfellas* where Spider tells Tommy to go fuck himself and everyone is proud of him. Of course Spider ends up getting shot in the chest seconds later.

But Pop Warner was the most important thing in my childhood. I think everything that's wrong with our kids today could be corrected with just a few seasons of Pop Warner. Teamwork, discipline, and, most important, a fat guy in a maroon windbreaker screaming at you. Dig this notion for just one minute. I played seven years of Pop Warner football, ages seven to fourteen. I played offensive tackle or guard every single one of those seven years. I never scored a touchdown or even touched the football. All I did was block for the guys who did get to do that. And I liked it. It felt good to be lying on the ground and look up to see a guy run through the hole I just opened. I can't imagine your average nine-year-old feeling that way today. But my mom just saw it as violence and completely ignored the self-sacrifice, drive, and discipline it taught me. She didn't have enough energy to stop me from playing, so she adopted basically the same stance a Buddhist would have with the Vietnam War. To put it another way, Arianna Huffington has more interest in tractor pulls than my mom has in football.

In ten years of football and six years of baseball, I accumulated a closetful of participation trophies. None of them means as much to me as a little cup the size of a soft-boiled-egg holder on a piece of imitation marble with a plaque that didn't contain my name. It was awarded to me by the opposing team at the 50-yard line following a bowl game and simply said BEST DEFENSIVE PLAYER. The fact that a group of athletes we'd just finished competing against decided that I was the best on the defensive side of the ball means more than any participation trophy ever could. (Unless it's the one they gave out to those guys who set the world gangbang record.) The criteria for a trophy should be more than being born and having a mom who owns a minivan. Without distinction and achievement, it's not worth the plastic it's molded out of. The handful of brave souls who attempted to take out German pillboxes on Omaha Beach weren't lumped in with the guys stateside setting up folding chairs for a USO show. In the past, we never confused stepping up with showing up. Now if you'll excuse me, I have to present my son a plaque for making a solid BM.

The following story demonstrates just how nuts I was about football. In my fourth season, I suffered a freak injury. I broke and dislocated my right shoulder during a game. The injury was so severe that they called an early halftime and let me lie there in the middle of the field until an ambulance arrived. I don't think any of the dads were up to moving the kid with his shoulder dangling out of its socket. So we just sat there and waited. The separation was so bad that my shoulder was out of its socket for the following four days. That's got to be some kind of record. How was my shoulder out of its socket for four days? Day one: took an ambulance to the emergency hospital, shot my shoulder up with God knows what, and the poor ER doctor tried to pull it back into place. It didn't go, and you only get one attempt because the screaming and writhing in pain is too much for a second round. Day two: went to the orthopedic specialist, he shot it up with something, and he got one try. Day three: checked into a hospital and waited for day four. Morning of day four: I was put under general anesthesia, and that's when they were able to put my shoulder back where it belonged. Now how does this illustrate my resolve when it comes to Pee Wee football?

The next year rolled around and I was excited for my fifth season. My parents took the only stand I could ever recall. They were separated and didn't agree on anything. But on this topic, they were a unified front. No more football. My injury from the year before had been so severe that the doctor said my arm might not grow correctly. The orthopedic surgeon wanted to put a permanent pin in my shoulder. My mom fought against it, and I ended up with a cast for three months instead. Either way, if my shoulder was injured again it would have been catastrophic. I told my parents I was playing and that was that. The only upside to having a family that took a laissez-faire approach to child rearing was that you could call the shots. Them not saving for college or preparing meals was the downside. They, in a very uncharacteristic burning of calories, said absolutely not. I said, "Either I play football this year or you don't have a son." I proceeded to not talk to them for more than two weeks. Although I'm not sure if my dad noticed. Finally they gave up and said go ahead. I played six more years including high school and a year of college and never injured that shoulder again. When I think back on that experience, I now realize my motivation wasn't so much a love of football but a hatred of my life off the field.

My freak shoulder injury sidelined my first love of football and was about to sideline my second love, riding a unicycle. Contrary to popular belief, Julianne Hough didn't teach me to ride the unicycle in my early forties. I, in fact, mastered that discipline by my tenth birthday. My dad was dating a woman whose son had a unicycle.

One day when we went to her house on the west side, I decided to spend several hours teaching myself to ride it. I went out into the street, propped myself up on a car fender, and refused to quit until I could take five pedals away from the Pontiac. The first time I did it, it felt transcendent. That night on the ride home I could think and talk about nothing else. But how was I going to get my hands on a unicycle? My family was the opposite of the Make-A-Wish Foundation: They took able-bodied kids and did nothing for them. This was pre-eBay, pre-Craigslist, and North Hollywood wasn't exactly Sarasota, Florida (headquarters of the Ringling Brothers). And then it hit me. Dave Lewis, son of the Munsters' Grandpa Al Lewis and older brother to my former best friend Teddy Lewis, had a unicycle, albeit covered in rust and duct tape in his backyard. He was willing to part with it for $10. I washed a bunch of cars at my dad's apartment building that weekend, and the next thing you know, that unicycle was tucked neatly between my ball sack and asshole. I polished the chrome with a Brillo pad, oiled the only moving part it had, and even sewed a denim seat cover from the part of cutoffs they never talk about. In a few days I was getting on and off it without the aid of a car fender. Within a few weeks I was riding off curbs and park benches, and by the end of the year I was dropping off picnic tables and riding away. Even the huge cast on my right arm from shattering my shoulder didn't slow me down. Unfortunately, a kid with a broken arm on a unicycle was a rolling billboard for my mom's "don't ask, don't tell" parenting approach. She put her Birkenstock down and said no unicycle. Since my unicycle license had been revoked, my friend Chris Shipman decided that as long as it was gathering dust, I should let him borrow it. I did, and it was a mistake. When my cast came off, I asked for my unicycle back. Chris said that he had returned it to my backyard, and that if it wasn't there someone must have stolen it. Chris's mother immediately snapped into action by doing nothing. This led to a standoff. She was too busy creating a self-entitled monster to make him return something that wasn't his, and my mom was too apathetic to go and demand back something that was stolen from her kid. It was like Ali–Frazier. Two great warriors going at it in a "Well, that's that. What are you gonna do?" grudge match. Ultimately my mom retained her belt when Chris's mom did not return my unicycle.

I'll never know for sure if Chris put that unicycle in my backyard or not. He died at twenty-five from what most people think was AIDS. His older brother Jesse had already died at nineteen in a car accident. My guess is his mom doesn't think about the unicycle nearly as much as I do.

Through most of my life I had a large unicycle-shaped hole in my soul. It wasn't until I was in my early thirties that I finally got my next unicycle. I went out, bought myself one, and got back on it. Riding a unicycle is just like riding half a bicycle: you never forget. My point is this. You can see that life did not start well for me, and for a lot of you reading this, it didn't start well either. But that doesn't mean it's too late to go out and get back in the saddle of your proverbial unicycle.

That said, I had several more years of purgatory to wade through before I could even consider achieving my dreams. My dad had just closed escrow on a $15,000 A-frame with a dirt driveway, so it was backward and downward.

2

SAME SHIT, DIFFERENT PLACE: MY DAD'S FIRST HOUSE

NORTH HOLLYWOOD, CA

YEAR BOUGHT: 1977

PURCHASE PRICE: $15,000

ONE BEDROOM

ONE BATH

650 SQUARE FEET
*(NOT COUNTING FUNKY
SWEATBOX LOFT ON TOP
AND BOOTLEG GUEST
HOUSE/GARAGE WITH
ROOTS GROWING UP
THROUGH THE SLAB)*

WHILE I was shackled to my mom's shitbox house, my dad spent a couple of years in a one-bedroom apartment on Laurel Canyon Boulevard. When I was twelve, he managed to scrape together enough money to buy a shitbox of his own. Fifteen thousand dollars. I know this seems like an unobtainable sum for my dad, who at the time was a substitute schoolteacher. So how did he do it? Well, he got into a car accident, and a friend of a friend who happened to be a lawyer told him he could make five grand, and that was more than enough to cover the 20 percent down payment.

One day it came up that I was going to go live with Pops. There was no discussion, but there was also no drama. People tend to view a moment like that through the prism of their normal family and have notions of being "torn away" from their mother. But with mine it was not a big deal. There was as much tearing away as a glass pancake in a Teflon pan filled with talcum powder. My mom was glad to get me out. Actually, my mom is glad to do anything that makes her life easier. So dodging the bullet of raising children was great as far as she was concerned. Don't get me wrong, she liked seeing us kids on weekends and taking us out to eat, but the nuts and bolts of parenting were not something she enjoyed. And who'd blame her? I'd like to have a dog that I could take to the beach once a week and throw a ball around with, but not have to deal with trips to the vet and buying sacks of kibble.

As far as the house went, it would be tough to tell which was worse, my mom's place or my dad's. You could take a thousand people to both houses and they would split fifty-fifty on which was the bigger dump. Or, to be more accurate, the smaller dump.

My dad's house was an A-frame, and I slept in the loft. My bedroom was up a very steep and uneven flight of stairs covered with bad green shag. The ceiling at its high point was about six feet high but quickly dropped from there. If you took a half step to your left or right, you'd bang your head on the bottom side of the roof sheathing. The only insulation was my seventies Jewfro. My bedroom was more like a rec room for bats and hunchbacks. And damn, did that loft get hot. It would still be 100 degrees, even at night. The heat rose from the rest of the house and baked me like a potato. It was a terrarium and I was the iguana.

The house had a dirt driveway, which complemented the dirt lawn quite nicely. A memory from this house that perfectly epitomizes my childhood—the mediums and the lows—took place one hot August afternoon on that dirt lawn. Having a choice of three and a half stations on a thirteen-inch black-and-white Zenith, no dog, no swimming pool, no basketball hoop, no money, and a dad who hated the outdoors but loved philosophy books was a perfect storm of boredom. I should also mention that this is all, of course, pre-masturbation. That immediately leveled the playing field. It's what they call a game changer. Even if there was nothing to do, you could always beat off. But I was still a few years away from learning the joy of sex with myself, so I engaged in something that now sounds pathetic but at the time seemed like a good idea. I took the plastic, misshapen, swollen, laceless football that I found at the park and used the aforementioned miniature plastic cup I'd received for best defensive player as a kicking tee. I booted the ball aimlessly back and forth from one side of the yard to the other all afternoon. Eventually the cup broke and instead of being repaired was thrown out. A sad and pathetic tale for sure, but on a happy note I'll get to torture my kids with it every time they complain about not being able to find a pair of 3-D glasses that stay on in a bouncy castle.

This house covered my time at Walter Reed Junior High. You might have seen a picture of it behind John McCain during the 2008 Republican convention when they should have shown a picture of Walter Reed Army Medical Center. In keeping with tradition, I gravitated toward the structure of sports. An outstanding memory from this period is the time we had an interschool softball tournament and played a team from Compton. My team won, and during the forced postgame handshake the team from Compton started talking smack. They were saying they would have beaten our asses if we were playing football. I said, "Bring it on. Football is my sport." Before I knew it, a three-hundred-pound black chick, a relative of the first baseman, was on top of me swinging at my head. I had my feet in her chest trying to push her off, but she had a 150-pound advantage so I couldn't. Fortunately, this created enough distance that her wild swings were just grazing my nose. Everyone, including the coaches, was stunned and just gathered around staring. I finally shouted, and this is an exact quote, "Get this bitch the fuck off of me!" They removed the sister and I dusted myself off without any physical harm. It did, however, make for a very long ride home on the same bus with her cousins.

My dad wasn't so much into discipline. When I was a kid, I only got hit by him once. I can't remember what I had done but he gave me a choice: be grounded or get a spanking. I looked at his arms and thought, Have at it, wuss. I'd rather get whacked with your wet-noodle arms than miss a fresh new episode of *Chico and the Man*.

By the way, I've only been hit by my dad once, but I was hit by the parents of two different friends growing up. And I'm cool with that. I think if a kid is being an asshole an adult—whether it be his friends' parents, a teacher, a relative, or even a stranger in a restaurant—the adult should be able to give him a nice smack. One time back when I was still living with my mother, I was with my friend Monty in the back of his mom Roberta's station wagon. We were playing that hand-slapping game, the one that every human being has played but no human being knows the name of. Its PR people need to be fired. We were clowning around and being loud and she told Monty to be quiet. I saw an opportunity to distract Monty and get up in the game so I mocked his mom's high-pitched nasal voice and said, "Yeah, Monty, be quiet." Then the slapping game moved up to the next level. Roberta reached back and smacked me across the face. Take a second to think about the irony of that moment. Imagine you are channeling all your focus and concentration into not getting the backs of your hands whacked by an eight-year-old and then immediately getting smacked in the face by a forty-year-old woman. That would be like carefully stitching something with a thimble so as not to get your finger pricked and then being stabbed in the head with a fireplace poker. She instantly regretted it and said that she'd have to explain it to my mom when she dropped me off. I told her it was cool and that she didn't need to. I figured my mom would probably take her side and I'd get in trouble again after Roberta had already taken the punishment, literally, into her own hands.

The other time, I was in another station wagon with my friend Teddy. I can't remember the context, but as usual I was mouthing off. This time I got slapped in the face by his dad, Grandpa Al Lewis from *The Munsters*. The difference was that Al didn't apologize or regret it. He was a grumpy old fuck.

I bring up my dad and discipline because of an incident that occurred around this time. My friend James was a soft-spoken half-Asian kid who wasn't what you'd call a hooligan, but if he was back in God knows whatever country his mom was from he'd definitely be on the losing end of a lot of canings. Anyway it was a Saturday night, I was sleeping over at James's house, and we decided to head out looking for fun. We knew an older guy, Brett, who worked at the 7-Eleven and probably wouldn't hassle us if we got up on the roof with a trash bag full of water balloons and chucked them at cars driving down Moorpark Street. The 7-Eleven was tailor-made for this activity because it had a flat roof with a three-foot parapet you could hide behind once you'd thrown your balloon. Plus it had a dumpster in the back that made roof access as easy as climbing onto a rolling dumpster and then dragging your belly and elbows up six feet of rocky stucco. (My favorite gay porn name, by the way—Rocky Stucco.) We were hitting cars with our water balloons, laughing and ducking. The night was going according to plan until we hit a Honda driven by Charles Bronson's evil twin. He quickly screeched into the 7-Eleven parking lot, and moments later a hatch in the roof opened and we heard Brett say, "Come down the ladder." We froze and considered jumping off the roof, but then climbed down the ladder into the back of the 7-Eleven to find the most pissed-off guy who's ever driven a subcompact. He was angry and short. He had what psychologists call a Neapolitan complex—the kind of rage people have when you bring home that shitty three-flavored ice cream. This guy was aggressive. He said to me, "You're lucky you're not eighteen. I'd beat the crap out of you." I was fourteen at the time and was already pretty big from lifting weights for football. So *au contraire,* you diminutive fuck, at eighteen I would have kicked your puny ass. But I was fourteen and scared, so I kept my mouth shut while this guy threatened me. He gave me and James a choice: Either *we* called our dads or *he* called the cops.

I went first and woke my dad up, which should go without saying. It's not like I would have called and interrupted a late-night poker game with the fellas. I told him what happened and that there was a maniac threatening me and repeating he wanted my dad to beat me since he couldn't do it himself. My dad was about as pissed as his temperament allowed and said he was coming to pick me up.

Now it was James's turn. He called his house and his Spicoliesque brother, Curt, picked up. James said, "Get Dad." Curt, being half-asleep and still stoned from earlier that night, made some sort of grunt but then passed out, dropping the phone. We tried calling back several times but got a busy signal. It was like something out of a sitcom, and I got stuck with the worst-of-both-worlds scenario. The short man with the shorter fuse decided the deal was off because

James's dad wasn't coming. He called the cops. In the meantime my dad was on his way so I had the cops *and* him to contend with. The officers arrived a few minutes later and gave us the scared-straight routine. They said we were guilty of "throwing a missile." It was that zero-tolerance bullshit where they said that "in the eyes of the law" there was no difference between us throwing water balloons or a bench vise. And by the way, to a fourteen-year-old, when you call it a "missile" you make the idea of throwing one off the roof of a different 7-Eleven next week a lot more intriguing. My pajama-clad dad arrived a few minutes later, put me in the car, and took me home. I don't think we ever talked about it again. I'd like to think he made a decision that being lectured by the cops and threatened by Danny Bonaduce's non-redheaded doppelganger was punishment enough, but the sad and simple truth is that disciplining me would have cut into his Kierkegaard reading time.

So that was my dad's A-frame. I'm sure if there had been something called a D-minus-frame we would have ended up living there instead. But fortunately it would only be a few years before I'd be in high school and a new house.

3

HOME IMPROVEMENT: MY DAD'S SECOND HOUSE

NORTH HOLLYWOOD, CA

YEAR BOUGHT: 1979

PURCHASE PRICE: $99,000

1,800 SQUARE FEET

ONE AND A HALF BATHS

TWO BEDROOMS WITH STEPMOM ADDITION
(NONPERMITTED)

WHEN I was finishing up the ninth grade, my dad moved to a new house. Some of you will remember it as the place we renovated on my TLC show. By comparison to his last house it was a palace. I would consider it the first normal house I lived in, and for the first time ever all seemed right with the world. It had an actual lawn that wasn't brown. The kitchen had a double sink, which was amazing to me. *Two* sinks! I felt like Elly May seeing the cement pond for the first time ever. My dad had gotten remarried to a normal woman named Lynn, and the plan was to start pretending like we were a real family. It was me, Dad, Lynn, my sister (occasionally), and my new older stepsister Hilary.

For the first three years we lived at this house, I slept in the smaller bedroom. (Stepsister Hilary took the semiconverted garage.) My dad and Lynn had the "master" bedroom, which was a spacious nine by nine. For the size of it, my room had a large closet, which brings me to the next story.

At this time, the tenth grade, my friend Chris had a hot girlfriend. One day he said to me that he wanted to bring his girl to my house to make out with her. My dad's house was a short distance away from North Hollywood High if you wanted to ditch class and go make out. I thought about this for a second and asked, "Do you think her top is going to come off?" Chris said yes. I said, "I'd like to see that." He said, "You could. Just hide in the closet." Now, I know it sounds creepy, but this was before the Internet and I was fifteen. So we hatched a plan. I'd go home, hide in my closet, and then at lunchtime Chris and his girl would leave school and come by my place to get to second base. I asked if I could invite anyone else into the closet and he said no. It was worth a shot. My dad and stepmom were at work and I had my lunch pass so I headed home, hopped in the closet, and about five minutes later they came in and started making out. A few moments after that, the sweater came off. And a few more moments after that, my stepmom came banging on the door. "What's going on in there?" Turns out her car was in the shop, she had called in to work, and had been there the whole time. She asked Chris, "Where's Adam?" He played dumb. But my stepmom said, "I saw him walk in." I hung tight in the closet while my stepmom told him this wasn't his house and to get lost. Eventually everyone cleared out. I had no idea how I was going to get out of the closet without her seeing me. And the clock was ticking: I had to get back to school or I might miss something important like a ceramics final. My scholarship to Brown was hanging in the balance. I sat there paralyzed with fear for about ten minutes and then made my move.

The house was L-shaped and I was in the back, at the top of the L. Chris and his gal pal had left, but my stepmother was still lurking somewhere in the house and presumably looking for me. From my position, I had no way of telling if she was standing outside the door to my room or on the other side of the house. Either way, I couldn't get to the front of the house without being spotted. I was left with only one alternative. I dashed out of the closet and hopped into the small bathroom connected to my room. Actually it was a half bath, just a sink and a toilet. I cracked the small window, squeezed myself out, and then began scaling the high rickety wooden fence. Naturally my neighbor was standing there and saw me, covered in sweat, climbing into his yard. For some reason at twelve thirty on a Wednesday he was there with a hose casually watering his lawn. I flopped over the top of the fence and rolled on his grass like Belushi on the lawn of the sorority in *Animal House*. The neighbor matter-of-factly said, "Hi, Adam." I yelled "Hi, Mr. [Whatever His Name Was]!" as I ran past him, just beating the bell that signaled the beginning of fifth period.

. . .

As far as North Hollywood High goes, don't let the word *Hollywood* confuse you. It was mostly working-class whites and Latinos from the Valley, with a dusting of Jews from the hills and blacks from the buses. And don't let the word *school* confuse you, either. There was no schooling going on. The only thing I learned how to do in high school was cover a textbook with a grocery bag. North Hollywood High was part of the L.A. Unified School District, which had no standards at all. To get held back in the L.A. school system you have to defecate on three teachers and try to kill a fourth.

My first year of high school was one of the worst periods in my life. My grades were horrible, and in the first semester I failed biology. To me the only important class was driver's ed. I was fifteen and three quarters, hitting sixteen at the end of May, and school got out in June. It was time to get some wheels. I had it all laid out. I'd take driver's ed the second semester of my tenth-grade year, then over the summer I'd go to Sears, take driver's training, and hit the road. (For clarity, driver's ed was the classroom portion; driver's training was when you got in the car with the barely employable dude sitting in the passenger seat with the second steering wheel.) There were two guys who taught driver's ed—Mr. Smith and Mr. Jeffries. Mr. Smith was a cool guy with a handlebar mustache who coached the football team and loved me. Think Dandy Don Meredith. Mr. Jeffries was a super-uptight, Brillo-headed asshole who was probably a closeted homo and definitely had anger issues. Guess which one I got? Of course it was Mr. Jeffries. But I wasn't sweating it. I didn't need to be in the top of the class, I just needed to pass so I could take driver's training. On the last week of class, out of the blue, Mr. Jeffries demanded a twenty-page report on passive restraints. Not turning this in would mean automatic failure. He just dropped it on us: It was not part of the regular curriculum. My reading and writing ability meant a twenty-page paper on anything was impossible. I couldn't write a twenty-pager on big-tit porn, never mind seat belts. But my hope was that I would just not turn it in and squeak by with a D because I had almost perfect attendance.

Nope. Mr. Jeffries failed me. I hope he's rotting in hell. Seriously, I picture him in an old-school double-steering wheel driver's training car while Satan is in the driver's seat hauling ass and laughing maniacally.

I wound up going to a dusty, depressing strip mall in Van Nuys, paying the ninety bucks I managed to scrape together from all the birthday money I got from the regular, step- and grandparents, and doing one of those six-months-of-training-in-four-days-type programs, where you go for a couple of marathon twelve-hour days and then take the test. I managed to pass that and took driver's training through a private company. I picked the cheapest one in the phone book. It was what you'd think: driving around with a loser in the passenger seat saying, "turn here," "merge there," et cetera. Except my instructor looked like the creepy Armenian guy who would be hitting on Kate Hudson at the singles bar when her friend convinced her that a girls' night out was just what the doctor ordered after Matthew McConaughey left her at the altar. At a certain point he said, "Hold up. Pull in here." It was a 7-Eleven in a bad part of Hollywood. Ten minutes later, he emerged with a sack of jerky and a *Hustler*. Except this *Hustler* was in 3-D. He just sat there in the passenger seat looking at the *Hustler* with cardboard glasses on. At a certain point he said something along the lines of, "Wow, look at that pussy jump right off the page." This was back in the day before people would drop a dime on each other. It was a simpler time. Nowadays the car would have been wired with a nanny cam and a tumescence monitor and this guy would have been fired and had to register as a sex offender.

My guidance counselor was named Mr. Tomi.

I had two memorable encounters with him. The first was when I wanted to take a class he thought was too much for me to handle. I wanted to get into it because all of my friends were taking it, but he said, "I would steer away from that one. It's a pretty tough class."

Mr. Ron Tomi
12th Grade Counselor

He thought I'd be in over my head and he was probably right. It was the ego-crushing equivalent of going to a Home Depot, picking up a cordless drill, and having the guy in the orange smock say, "I think that's a little too much tool for you."

My other incident with Mr. Tomi happened when I got suspended and the school pulled my "emergency contact card." There's no real story to tell surrounding the suspension. I had a pass to go home at lunch and I tried to leave campus without it and the guard stopped me. He said if I left I'd be suspended. But I was hungry so I split anyway, and thus the suspension.

They sent me to Mr. Tomi, and he had to pull the emergency contact card so he could call my folks. This was that card you fill out at the beginning of high school to reach your guardians in the event of an earthquake or compound fracture at football practice. But because I was me, I never brought the thing home. I filled it out myself the Monday morning before class registration. And since I was doing it while I was standing around with my buddies, I decided to get stupid. We treated it like a Mad Lib. Then I faked my dad's signature and handed it in. Little did I know that two years later I'd get suspended and Mr. Tomi would pull it out to call my dad. He took it out of the file cabinet, looked down at it, took a long pause, stared at me, and said, "Did *you* fill this out?" I thought he was just talking about my chicken-scratch handwriting and misspellings. I'd forgotten that I'd fucked around when I was filling it out. Where it asked for "mother's work address," I wrote "Hollywood and Vine—Call Big Earl," like she was a prostitute. For her home address, I wrote "Ronald McDonald Halfway House." When it came to my dad, I wrote that he was employed as a "Secret Agent" and then under phone number, work address, and home address I wrote "Classified."

In my senior year we were having a pie-eating contest in the quad as part of a lunchtime school spirit event. Because of my parents' policy on not having anything in the house that didn't taste like gerbil pellets, when it was announced that we'd be having a pie-eating contest I gladly threw my pan in the ring. Of the three contestants, I was probably the favorite to win. I was a big guy at the time, captain of the football team, and I was hungry for the victory. Literally. I had the pie of the tiger. So they tied everyone's hands behind their backs, blew a whistle, and the contestants to my left and right buried their faces in the pies. But not me. I just stared at it. The entire school was there screaming, "Eat, Eat, EAT!" They were pissed. I don't know if there was gambling going on, but they kept yelling at me to eat the pie. So I taunted them a little by just nibbling at the crust. I wouldn't bury my face in it. I was in the middle, so the guys on either side of me were covered in pie. It was in their hair, their ears, and under their eyelids. At some point they held up a guy's hand who had a face full of blueberry pie and declared him the winner. I then quietly picked up my unmolested pie and started heading home. There was still twenty minutes left in the lunch period, just enough time to run home with the pie, sit down at the table, get a knife and fork, take out a big jug of milk, and blissfully eat the whole damn thing. Mrs. Tani, the little Asian woman who was also a guidance counselor and was running the event, went ballistic. It was as if there had been some sort of Geneva Convention for pie-eating contests and I had violated it. She demanded, "You throw away that pie!" I replied, "There are kids starving all over the world and you want me to throw away this perfectly good pie?" She said, "You toss it, right now." I held the pie up over my head and shouted to the crowd, "Mrs. Tani wants me to throw away this perfectly good pie." The crowd turned on her and started booing. I used this as covering fire to make my escape. As Mrs. Tani reached for the pie tin, I reached for the pie and using my bare hands scooped it up and carried the oozing and crumbling mess home.

A little pie-related tangent connected to my future roommate, "The Weez." It happened later when we were living together, but I tell this story now to show how nuts I was about free food, especially pie. When a girl would break up with The Weez, he would hit her in the face with a pie, Three Stooges–style. Word got around after that first breakup, and his next girlfriend was aware this was his MO and didn't want to suffer the embarrassment after she dumped him. The Weez assured her he was unarmed. It was like in a mob movie when the guy holds his jacket open to prove that he's not bringing a piece into a meeting with the boss. After he was patted down for pie, the girl agreed to go on a walk with him down the street. But like Michael Corleone putting the gun behind the toilet, The Weez had preset a pie on the step bumper of my truck, which was parked on the street. When he got to the back of my truck, he grabbed the pie and creamed her.

I'd always get pissed at him for this. I didn't care about the chick, I just couldn't stand seeing good pie go to waste. I'd say,

"Why don't you just put some shaving cream on a paper plate? Don't waste eight dollars' worth of pie." He would go to the Four 'N Twenty pie shop and get a nice fresh one instead of the cheap two-day-old pie from the bakery thrift store. It was like an assassin using golden bullets. I'd come home and see that pink box in the fridge and get excited, but The Weez would say, "Don't touch it. That's for Melanie." Here's how desperate I was. I would get the pie remnants after the assault and eat them. Like those little fish that go flying up after the hippo shits in the river. I would literally scoop the broken pie off the asphalt and consume it, bits of gravel and all. One time I actually ran into the recently humiliated girl's house with the pie debris I'd snatched up and was eating it as she walked in moments later to clean up, her face covered in cherry filling and tears.

Naturally I went out for the North Hollywood High football team—the Huskies. And I was a gifted athlete. I had a great sense of balance and I was also stronger than every other kid I played with. As a matter of fact, wrestling with Chris got so boring that I would just let him pin me and we would see how long it would take me to throw him off and pin him. Later on when puberty kicked in, the results were very different.

Puberty for boys is essentially steroids. One minute you're spindly with a voice like a girl, and the next thing you know there's a vein in your arm and a chip on your shoulder. Your genes decide how much juice you're going to get from the steroid injection. My problem was my dad was five foot nine and 145 pounds and had calves skinnier than his ankles. Picture the guy Screech would have beat up in high school. So while most of my buddies' syringes were filled with high-grade bull testosterone, mine was filled with Ensure and tap water.

When football season started my tenth-grade year, I got the most depressing news of all: I was riding the bench on the junior-varsity football team. Seven years of being a star in Pop Warner and all of a sudden I was a nobody. A combination of not knowing any of the coaches, having a senior playing in front of me in my position, and a genetic hand that was a pair of threes, a six, and two Uno cards led to me watching the game from the bench for the first time in my football career. Up until that point I was all brawn and no brain. Now that it looked like the brawn was gone, I was devastated. The worst part is that I was still friends with all the guys I used to throw around like rag dolls, and now they were all starting over me. It came to a head one day when my buddy Steve Hughes, who was a baseball player but always knew I was the best at football, asked me what happened. It was depressing because he wasn't razzing me or making fun of me; he honestly wanted to know why I wasn't good anymore. Kind of like the difference between somebody calling you a fat-ass from their car window and a doctor at a party earnestly asking if he can help with your weight problem. It was at that point I knew I could either roll over or I could go to work. So I decided to go to work.

I was about 150 pounds, and the coach said if I kept my weight down I'd be starting next year. Let me explain. I called it the junior-varsity team just for simplicity, but it was really called the B-team and it was meant for tenth graders. But as long as you kept your weight under 165 pounds, you could play as a junior or a senior. When Coach Smith came up to me at the banquet and told me not to eat too much, I told him, "No problem." But I had already made my decision. I was going to have another spoonful of au gratin potatoes and live in the weight room. The following year I would play varsity. I didn't care if I sat on the bench. I figured if I did it this way, by my senior year, I would have a chance to start. The next year was just an extended training montage from *Rocky*. (*Rocky I*, not the gay biracial montage from *Rocky III*.) By the time the next season had begun,

**ADAM CAROLLA
LEFT GUARD**

I'd put on thirty-five pounds of muscle and made my way on to the varsity starting offensive line.

I also did the long snapping. Worst gig in sports. You look through your legs at a skinny white guy who's standing forty-two feet behind you. With your shoulder pads and helmet on, you can barely move your arms and the plan is to rocket back a spiral that hits him in the chest while the biggest player on the opposing team drives you into the ground. They have a rule against that now because you're in such a vulnerable position that it's dangerous. Back then the thinking was if they could jack you up enough and get you to worry more about being driven into the ground than getting the ball to the punter, you'd fuck up the snap. If you complete your task successfully, nobody says a word. But if you snap the ball over the punter's head or bounce one back to him, that's all they're going to discuss the next week. I always thought that if I was in the Mafia and I was going to fix the Super Bowl, I'd pay off the long snapper. He's the lowest-paid guy on the team and if he throws a missile over the punter's head that bounces out the back of the end zone, or one off-target snap on a field-goal attempt, it could dramatically change the outcome of the game.

When the season was over I went right back to the weight room, but first I hit the Denny's for three Grand Slams. By my senior year I was 210 pounds and starting both ways. It seemed I was able to temporarily overcome my bad genetic hand with hard-boiled eggs, bench presses, and ten years of experience. I led the team in tackles, received the trophy for best defensive player, and was the only person on the squad to get first-team all-league honors on offense.

Allow me a quick jag. The everyone's-a-winner bullshit we're knee-deep in right now goes back a little further than you might think. On offense I played guard, and on defense I played inside linebacker. But if you open up the 1982 North Hollywood High yearbook and look at the pictures of the starting defense, you'll not find my fat Brillo-covered head among them. It's ironic because I led the team in tackles and have a trophy in my bar that says BEST DEFENSIVE PLAYER NORTH HOLLYWOOD HUSKIES 1981.

So why no picture with the team's defense? Because they took photos of the starting offense and in an attempt to be fair, wouldn't allow anybody to have two photos. But for time immemorial, when your grandkids' grandkids' great-grandkids are going to the Library of Congress to look at the North Hollywood High yearbook, they'll see Alex Richardson squatting at my position. Is that your definition of fair?

The most memorable game of my senior season was the last one. We stunk. I think we were 1–7 going into the game. We were playing the Monroe Vikings. (They were the actual team that played Spicoli's team in *Fast Times at Ridgemont High*.) They had an all-city running back, and if we could stop him we might have a chance. I convinced the coach to rejigger the defensive scheme to stop the

ALEX RICHARDSON

LINEBACKER

run, and by the middle of the week I was cautiously optimistic about our ability to shut him down. Unfortunately, since it was the end of the season, we had injuries to many of our skill position players and no way to score ourselves. That's when I heard the news. Robert and Lenny had died.

Robert and Lenny were two of the most beloved players from the previous year's team. All of the seniors like myself had played with these guys as juniors the previous year and still hung out with them, since they went to college locally. Robert and Lenny were carpooling in a Pinto station wagon on their way to Cal State Northridge when the accident happened. Their car was pinned between two other cars, leaving them no way to escape when the Pinto burst into flames. Robert and Lenny never got out. The team was devastated, although it was too much for me to comprehend. Wendell Shirley, the slowest 145-pound black man in the league and perhaps the world, announced he was going to take one to the house for Robert and Lenny. At the time I thought, That's a great gesture, but highly unlikely considering your history of having no history with scoring. Robert's funeral was scheduled for Friday

41

morning, the day of the game. Lenny's was planned for Saturday. Everyone on the team wore a black armband made of electrician's tape, and of course in the locker room we dedicated the game to Robert and Lenny's memory.

1980—North Hollywood High football field. The fact that Robert and Lenny were randomly in this picture together mere months before the accident still haunts me.

My new defensive scheme worked to perfection. We held them to only one touchdown and took out their all-star running back. But with only minutes left in the game they remained ahead, 7–0. As I mentioned earlier, our offense was decimated and we couldn't move the ball. And that's when it happened. They punted to Wendell Shirley. Wendell fielded the punt and took it 70 yards to the end zone, just as he had promised. Our sideline went crazy. I snapped the ball for the extra point and just like that, with almost no time left on the clock, the game was tied. Our celebration lasted until the ensuing kickoff, when the Vikings ran a reverse and their kick returner took it 80 yards for a touchdown himself. Obviously he wasn't a fan of Robert or Lenny. The gun sounded, and even though I didn't know it at the time, that was the last football game I would ever play in.

Okay, that was maybe a little bit of a bummer, so here's one last quick story about my high school football career. I was getting my required physical before I could join the team. I was fifteen. I was in the doctor's office and he said, "Get into your underpants, I'll be back in two days." I love how they tell you to get into your underwear and then make you sit there for forty minutes in your tighty-whiteys. At fifteen I could get into my underpants in 7.3 seconds. They should tell you to kick off your shoes and hang out. Their time is important, but I think they can spare the three blinks it would take for me to get into my skivvies.

The worst part is that in those pantsless forty-five minutes, three people will come into that room. A nurse comes in, then the receptionist, then a guy filling the vending machine. Anyway, I was standing there in my underpants for ten minutes, then fifteen minutes, then a half hour with no problem. Then all of a sudden I think, Oh, Jesus, here it comes. In high school before you're finished saying the word *boner* you can get a boner. For no reason. At that age you can't even think about it. Once you've thought about it, it's on. So there I was with a boner knowing that the doctor or some other random person could come into the room at any second. Killing a fifteen-year-old boner takes a wooden stake and a silver bullet. Wishing it away only makes it stronger. And then I came up with an idea that would not only kill my boner but make me look that much better in my underpants if the nurse came in. I got down and started doing push-ups. When is the last time you had a boner while doing push-ups? The blood in your triceps calls down to the blood in your cock, "Hey, quit playing grab-ass and get up here, we've got a Code Five." When the doctor came in, he saw me all sweaty and must have thought I was trying to fuck the linoleum.

Like Jim Thorpe, Bo Jackson, and Deion Sanders, I was also a multisport athlete. I played baseball, right field. On one particularly hot, dry day, my nose began to bleed. It's only happened to me twice in my life. Something about the heat and the dryness. The blood was pouring out of my nose and onto my white Huskies uniform. I didn't know what to do, I wasn't sure how to call a time-out from right field, and it didn't seem severe enough to stop the game. So in between pitches I got hold of a 3 Musketeers wrapper that was blowing by, pulled off a piece, balled it up, and shoved it up my right nostril. It didn't stop the bleeding but it did slow it down, sort of like when you do that cup thing with your hand to give your dog water at the park. Nobody knew what was going on out there except for me, so it was a surprise to everybody at the end of the inning when I got back to the dugout and there was blood all over my jersey. The coach said, "You should go to the locker room and take care of that," but I was up first that inning and there was no way I was going to miss an at-bat. I stood in the batter's box watching the red blood drip onto the white home plate and quickly got two strikes on me. I remember thinking, "Great, now I'm going to strike out and then go to the locker room. I should have just listened to the coach and gone in to see the trainer." The third pitch, however, I drove into the power alley in left field. My high school didn't have a left-field fence so even though the ball flew past the outfielders and kept rolling down the football field I still had to hustle around the bases. I arrived at home plate to a hero's welcome. Not only did I hit a home run, but I did it with blood pouring from my nose. That somehow made it better. As soon as the celebration was over at home plate, I started to make my way to the locker room when I saw the pitcher throw the ball to the third baseman and the umpire yell, "You're out." It's something you rarely see in baseball, but every now and again somebody will claim that you missed the base, throw the ball back to that base, and if the umpire calls you out, you're out. No home run. And it goes in the books as a double because it's the same as you hitting a double and trying to stretch it into a triple and getting thrown out. They almost never call this, and why they decided to do it now with my bloody nose and my home run is beyond me. I'm sure I pushed off the edge of the base like I was taught, but even if I didn't, they still would never call this. My bloody-nose home-run had been downgraded to a bloody-nose double.

The following game we were playing Fairfax High and I hit the ball into exactly the same power alley in left field that I hit with the bloody nose. I was running toward first when my buddy George Espinoza, who was coaching first base, started laughing and said, "Don't miss the bag." I stepped directly into the middle of first base and ended up with a triple. As I was standing on third, I witnessed something I thought I'd never see again. But this time with a twist. They threw the ball to first, and the umpire punched me out. That goes in the books as an out. The home run I could tolerate, because at least that helped my average with a double. My triple just got converted to an out. To this day I still have no idea how something that almost never gets called got called on me in two consecutive games.

As I said, high school was just some place I had to be for a couple of hours before I was able to fuck around with my friends. And typically those good-time buddies were Ray and Chris. Ray has his own chapter later in this book because I have so many stories of petty crime, practical jokes, and painful moments with him to share. But for the time being I'd like to focus on Chris and some more of our early misadventures.

As you can tell by the pie-eating-contest story from earlier, when you grow up like I did, the allure of free food is powerful. When I was fifteen, Chris was working at the mall in Sherman Oaks at a place called Snacks 5th Avenue. That's not a typo, it's a bad pun. It was one of those food kiosks that sold oversized chocolate chip cookies, candy, and giant soft pretzels.

Does anything go from great to terrible when miniaturized more than the pretzel? The gap between the giant, warm, mustard-covered soft pretzel you get at the ballpark and the stale, salty mini-pretzel you get on a plane is a chasm that Evel Knievel couldn't jump in his Skycycle. Most stuff takes a dip when it gets smaller, especially tits. But nothing takes as steep a decline as the pretzel. Except perhaps regular corn on the cob versus that awful miniature corn that shows up in stir-fry. That shit's been on ten million plates but in zero stomachs. Note: Here's how you know a food is bad—if no one has ever purchased it in a store. Think I'm exaggerating? When's the last time you returned from the market with a bushel of miniature corn? I've tried many times to have this blight removed from store shelves and Chinese restaurants, but the midget-scarecrow lobby is too powerful.

Despite Mr. Jeffries's assholery I got my learner's permit, was able to borrow my dad's car—a 1976 VW Rabbit—and drive over to pick Chris up after work. He greeted me holding two extra-large root beers courtesy of Snacks 5th Ave. A block from the mall, Chris started pissing on me. He just whipped it out and started peeing on me while I was driving on a busy Los Angeles street. We could have easily died. It's a miracle I didn't go up on the curb and hit some pedestrians and then a phone pole. But I stayed on the road. I couldn't think to do anything else but take my jumbo root beer and douse him with it. Of course he retaliated in kind, taking his root beer and dumping it on me. So the inside of my dad's car had two full thirty-two-ounce root beers—one of the stickiest substances

ADAM CAROLLA

known to man—and a bladder's worth of Chris's piss in it. The inside of the car smelled like it was pulled from either the worst or the best river in the world. But for once my dad's cheapness paid off. He had gone with the full vinyl interior and opted for the rubber floor mats—because, you know, carpet might have cost an extra twelve dollars. There wasn't a stitch of fabric in the car, so we were able to hose it out like an ice chest. The only difference between that car and a monkey cage was a drain on the floor.

Chris and I did some stupid shit in that car. The very first thing I did when I got my driver's license was pick Chris up in the Rabbit and say, "Come on, buddy. We're gonna catch some air." We went to Chandler Boulevard because it's split in two by train tracks sitting on a six-foot mound. I said to him, and I remember this specifically, "Hang on, Starsky." I was hell-bent to get all four wheels off the ground or I wouldn't be able to show my face in the tenth grade again. The next thing you know, we were airborne. Unfortunately, what I couldn't see until we had all four wheels off the ground was the pickup truck attempting to turn left onto Chandler in front of us. I slammed on the brakes, although when the tires aren't making contact with the earth's surface your braking capability is vastly decreased. We landed, swerved, and narrowly averted catastrophe. The next outing we decided to go on foot, this time to our friend Este's house.

Chris and I had known Este Cholodenko since the seventh grade. In that silly junior-high style of dating, she declared that she liked both me and Chris and was going to think about it and decide which one of us would get to be her boyfriend. Chris and I waited anxiously together by his phone for the moment when Este made her decision. It was like when they announce a new pope: We were eagerly awaiting a smoke signal to let us know who would be her man. Este called and gave me the news. She said, and this is a quote, "I'm going with you . . . all my friends think I'm crazy." It was my first in a lifelong series of what the great Albert Brooks coined as the "complisult," something that starts as a compliment but quickly becomes an insult.

Este was my girlfriend for the majority of seventh grade. At the time she was kinda awkward and dorky. And then, as my luck would have it, she got superhot and dumped my ass but wanted to remain friends, I guess just to torture me. We did stay friends, and a couple of years later in high school she made the mistake of letting me and Chris loose in her kitchen. As you know, the Carollas had only the basic elements of food—tarragon, flour, bouillon cubes, but no lasagna or leftover Chinese—so I would ravage my friends' kitchens when given the opportunity. Este left to run some errands, so we just scurried around eating, jumping into her swimming pool, and rifling through her drawers looking for panties. At a certain point in our scavenging we found a pot of wax, the kind used to remove eyebrows. Chris and I decided that since we had that teenage unibrow thing going (thank God I lost that), we were going to heat up the wax and get rid of the hair at the bridge of our noses. The wax was as solid as a rock. So we put a flame underneath to melt it down and walked away. At a certain point during our dip I said to Chris, "We ought to go check on that." Chris casually brushed it off. I got out of the pool, and when I turned the corner to the kitchen I was greeted by a ball of fire on top of the stove. While we were out at the pool, the wax started smoking and ignited. When that kind of wax burns, it chars and starts sending pieces floating into the air, which then settled all over the kitchen. I used a dish towel to put out the fire and breathed a sigh of relief. I had narrowly avoided disaster. Este's father was a big Israeli guy and a "contractor." I didn't know what he did for a living, but he had a very scary commando Israeli Mafioso look. He was not your Northeastern Domesticated Jew. He was short with thick, hairy forearms. He was like a cross between an Israeli and a pit bull. I called Chris in so we could have a laugh about our close call when we noticed black soot settling on the counter, the curtains, and the hood vent. As fast as we could wipe it off, a new layer would settle in its place. The pube wax had become weaponized and was leaving a black coat of film throughout the kitchen.

I grabbed some Easy-Off oven cleaner to try to wipe down the avocado-colored hood of the stove vent. (God, our color palate was so fucked-up in the seventies.) To my shock and dismay, it took the paint off. What kind of product would work perfectly on the inside of what it is supposed to clean but destroy the exterior? Good work, engineers. Well done. The place was a disaster, wax and smoke everywhere and smeared avocado paint on the oven hood. The kitchen window was wide open, and I was trying to fan the place out with a towel.

Enter Este's dad. He pulled up in his Ranchero and stopped right in front of the open window. I thought, Holy shit, turned to Chris, and said in a tone like someone in *Alien* or *Jaws*, "He's here." I thought the guy was going to kill us. Chris panicked and hid. Then, like something out of a movie, Este's dad stuck his head out of the car window, looked at me, and yelled in his best El Al security voice, "Where is Este?" Thinking they might be the last words I ever uttered on the planet, I stammered out, "Sh . . . sh . . . she's not h-h . . . here." Then, against all logic, he said, "Okay," settled back into his car, and took off. What were the chances he wouldn't walk in? The fact that this guy drove to his house, saw a sixteen-year-old in his kitchen, and decided not to enter was, as his people would say, a mitzvah. I then found Chris cowering in a broom closet and yelled at him for abandoning me.

That night I got a call from Este. She said, "Someone wants to speak to you," and handed the phone to her mom. It was horrible and tense. She simply said, "What went on here?" I had to play dumb. "What are you talking about?" I said. She went insane on me. They had just remodeled the house and they were very particular about the kitchen. She shouted that I needed to replace the entire stove and the curtains, then said, "Put your father on the phone." Luckily, he was out on an elephant hunt after finishing the Paris-to-Dakar rally. Actually, he was home doing his best to blend into the sofa upholstery.

After an hour on the phone with her irate mother, I hung up. The next day, Este called and said she was going to her grandmother's house in a town a little outside of L.A. and that the least I could do was come and keep her company on the ride. I said okay, she came, pulled up my driveway, and honked the horn. I bounded out of the house to find her mom sitting in the passenger seat. Now I was thinking, "Holy hell, I have to drive to Cerritos with this woman who wants to murder me." Needless to say, it was a very long ride, but I was able to smooth it over and didn't have to pay for anything. Not that I could have anyway.

It goes without saying that high school is the time when you start experimenting with alcohol. Everyone loves a good drunk story, so here is my first. I was with a guy named John Tyler. I was sixteen at the time, and he was a couple years older, so the peer pressure had turned to beer pressure. The weekend before, he had gotten some Henry Weinhard's Private Reserve and we were chugging them in his kitchen. But I was unable to keep up. The beers were bubbling in my nose and swelling my stomach. I said, "I don't mind the alcohol. I can hold my booze like any sixteen-year-old. But it's the carbonation." The next weekend our buddy Chet, who worked at the AMPM convenience store around the corner, ripped off one of those big jugs of . . . hold on, I have to take a minute to think about big jugs . . . okay, I'm back. He had ripped off one of those big jugs of Boone's Farm white wine. You know, the big, cheap, glass kind with the handle you put your thumb through. He took it back to Tyler's place. So John said to me, "This doesn't have bubbles in it. Start chugging."

Imagine taking white wine—sweet, cheap white wine—and filling a tumbler with it and downing it as fast as you can. You can do it with that stuff in a way that you can't with vodka or beer. It's almost like Gatorade or apple juice. So I was chugging full sixteen-ounce glasses of white wine. Glug glug glug. "Hit me again," I said with pride. Glug glug glug glug glug. "No problemo." It went down very easily. I would soon find out it came up very easily, too.

We got in the back of a VW station wagon and headed out to a party. John had two sweaters that were exactly the same. They were both V-necks, one red and one blue. I remember this because he gave me the blue one so we could go out to drink in a park, a little pre-game before the party. But before we ever got there, I leaned over to John and said, "I think I'm going to . . . *BLAAARRGGGGGHHH!*" I yakked all over John and simultaneously ruined his night and two of his sweaters.

Later on I was able to crawl up my driveway and sleep on the asphalt until the morning. I remember two things from the following day. First, I had bits of gravel in my cheeks from sleeping on the driveway, which was falling apart. (Yes, the Carollas didn't maintain or repair their driveway. Shocking, I know.) The second thing I remember is that my eyelids were bloodshot from heaving. Not my eyes, my eye*lids*. I had yakked so powerfully that I had blown out my eyelids. The strain had broken all the blood vessels. It would be like if someone said, "Take a shit as hard as you can for twenty minutes."

But now I'm forty-seven and I'm drinking as I write this. That's the message to the kids—have a little something called grit. Get right back on that drunken horse. I'm not one of those pussies who says, "I learned my lesson." I absolutely did not learn my lesson. I vomited many more times in my career. I have thrown up because of booze at least forty times since then. Dr. Drew is always sickened by that statistic, and I have to defend my honor by explaining that at least half of those times were at my own hands, or to be more accurate, fingers. I did it to myself to be able to go to sleep. This does not help my argument.

One of the worst parts of my high school house was not actually due to the structure itself. The new neighborhood was nice, but one of the residents had a wild dog. Literally. They had a dog that was half dingo. His name was Moon and he was so greasy and weird his coat had a bluish tint. This mutt terrorized any moving object on the street—snarling at squirrels, growling at delivery guys, and chasing children on bikes. My dad could barely muster the energy for a conversation, never mind a confrontation, but even *he* called the neighbors out on this one. By their own admission the dog was half wild, but they refused to chain it up or keep it indoors. They were probably scared of it too.

One bright sunny day when I was walking home from the park, I looked up to see Moon approaching me. It was tense, think O.K. Corral. I froze in my tracks and considered slowly backing away. But I decided if I stood my ground and asserted my dominance, he would see me as the alpha in the neighborhood and leave me the fuck alone. Someone had to step up and be a hero. And that person was a fifteen-year-old Adam Carolla. I'd had enough. I took a deep breath, got into the linebacker stance, and shouted "Come on!" at him. I then took an aggressive half step in his direction. He backed off a step but then took three forward. This pattern continued until he closed the twelve-foot distance between us. When he got two feet away he lunged at me. I thought I wasn't going to live to see the eleventh grade. I hadn't yet even discovered the joy of masturbation. Hours of Swedish Erotica flashed before my eyes. I knew then I had something to live for. He chomped down, but thankfully he only managed to get my pant leg. This caused me to do the Keystone Cop stepping-on-a-banana-peel routine, landing squarely on my back.

So I struggled free of Moon's grip and ran back to my house. Inexplicably, Moon just walked away, perhaps to go and floss my Toughskins out of his teeth.

With tears in my eyes, I grabbed the first sharp object I could find: a sprinkler key. I was going to put this literal son of a bitch down. But my dad, who for some reason had ventured outdoors, was standing on the lawn, stopped me, and convinced me to drop the sprinkler key. It was a very Johnny Cash "Don't Take Your Guns to Town" moment.

It was while I was living at my dad's second house that I got into the workforce and started a long string of shitty jobs.

My first attempt at employment was at the Taco Bell on the corner of Colfax and Magnolia, across from my high school. It was not meant to be: I put in the application and was promptly rejected. Seriously. Rejected from Taco Bell. A guy who was probably only three years older than me and barely made it out of high school but had a "manager" pin decided I was just not Taco Bell material. Have you been to a Taco Bell? Are those employees the cream of the crop? I don't know what I did on that application, but it seems to me that if you didn't fill it out with your fist clenching a crayon, you'd be in. But not the Ace man.

You know what it's like being rejected from Taco Bell? Can your self-esteem get any lower than that moment? "Sorry, buddy. We've got retarded and elderly people to hire. Actually, Dennis over there is old *and* retarded, so you're definitely out. Bottom line is we just don't trust you to make Bell Beefers."

Looking back, I wonder if I fucked up the application. Because even now I fuck up paperwork. Can we all get on the same page about what goes above and below the line on applications? I'm forty-seven and I'm still writing my address where my name should be. It's pathetic asking the receptionist for Liquid Paper.

A couple years later I also applied at Hot Dog on a Stick, because they paid above minimum wage. It was about two and a half bucks at the time, but they paid twice that. But this time I was rejected because of *my* hot dog on a stick. I had a penis. Hot Dog on a Stick only hires chicks. Where was Gloria Allred when I needed her?

Still stinging from my Taco Bell rejection, I headed over to the Studio City McDonald's. It's still there, on Ventura. Unfortunately, I filled out the application correctly and ended up getting the job. It was 1980, the summer between sophomore and junior year. People think of the eighties as the go-go eighties, the era of yuppies and Wall Street and "Greed is good." I ushered in the eighties getting $2.22 an hour to work a grill.

My manager's name was Ken. He was a fat black guy who took his job very seriously. And at first I did, too. There's always that moment in a young man's life when he's at his first shitty job and thinking, "Oh, yeah, one day I'm going to be managing this McDonald's." That's as big as your dreams can get at the time. Or at least mine. I remember thinking it when I was getting the speech from Ken about how to really work the grill. Ken would point out one of the older guys and say something like, "You see Trent over there on the grill? He's got six years on that grill. He knows instinctively when the patty needs to be seared. He's that in tune with the meat. And you know what he's pulling down? He's making three sixty-five an hour. Seriously. He's looking at a used TR-7. He hasn't pulled the trigger on it yet . . ." Then I was thinking, "Wow, man. Three years from now, people will be talking about me. When the rookies come in, I'll be the guy behind the grill shopping for a used TR-7." The beautiful thing about being a human is that eventually you wake up. For me, it was about two hours into my first shift. I looked at that guy and thought, "Fuck this. I'm taking a piss in the freezer and getting the fuck out of here."

As I said, Ken was all business. There was a sign behind the grill that read TIME TO LEAN, TIME TO CLEAN. The other absurd thing was that on my first day, they sat me down to watch a training video. That video started with how to handle a hostage takeover situation. It had a reenactment that showed if violent gunmen were to take over your particular McDonald's franchise, don't be a hero. Just do what they say and wait for the police to arrive. Yeah. I'm making less than three bucks an hour. What do they expect, I'm going to hop the counter, shout, "Not on my watch!" and try to take them out with a spork? It's more likely I'd help them clean out the register and jump into the van with them.

The other policy Ken took very seriously was the one about no rubber-soled shoes. They didn't want you wearing Converse high-tops or Vans. You needed leather-soled dress shoes. So you'd end up wearing a shit-brown McDonald's uniform with a paper hat but wing-tip shoes like an old-time gangster. The only pair of dress shoes I had were from my ninth-grade graduation, but this was a year later and my foot had grown a size and a half and they didn't really fit anymore. But since new shoes were out of the question, I crammed my feet into them. As I mopped the floor I was sliding all over the place because it was wet and greasy and my ill-fitting shoes had no traction.

I wasn't allowed to work the register, so I did my time behind the grill. Which is pure misery. You lean over something that feels as hot as the sun for hours, and the sizzling of Grade D meat is your only companion. That is, until a little light goes off when it was time to flip them. A pigeon could do that gig with some birdseed and twenty minutes of training. My downfall was the three-tiered toaster used for the Big Mac's three buns. I'd always end up toasting the wrong side—the top part with the sesame seeds. If you got a Big Mac where the bun was toasted on the top, that was an Ace Carolla signature burger. I still remember the lingo. "Burger's up. Wrap please." "Cheese count on Macs, please?" These terms are forever infused in my memory like the smell of onions has been forever infused into my cuticles.

The only thing worse than working at McDonald's is when your friends *see* you working at McDonald's. They'd be coming home from the beach, stop in for a burger, and I'd be there in my uniform doing a sweep and a mop decked out in the brown gi. They were having a great time, spending their parents' money on shakes and fries, and I was miserable. One summer day Ken yelled, "Give me a sweep and a mop of the outdoor dining area." As if I wasn't depressed enough while sweeping outside in the hotter-than-shit weather, some ass-wipe kids came by. They were in that sweet spot where they had just hit puberty and thought they could take on the world. You know, that age when you're oozing with sarcasm and covered in acne, on the verge of a learner's permit, just felt your first boobie, and are empowered by your other fourteen-year-old jack-off buddies. These rich kids circled the parking lot on their skateboards and started taunting me. "Hey, you missed a spot." I let it slide. Then the next kid was like, "Hey, say hi to the Hamburglar and Mayor McCheese." I begrudgingly took it, but was starting to get fed up. They were like Japanese Zeros doing a raid on Pearl Harbor. They kept getting closer and closer and more and more bold with each insult they launched. So I started timing them, and when I saw the ringleader, the tip of the asshole spear, take one foot pump, then another, on his third push forward I sprang into action. I dropped my mop and lunged toward him. Five steps later, I was on top of him. I grabbed the kid and pinned him to the hood of a car. I didn't hit him; I just said, "Who's in charge now, bitch?" He started screaming for his life, and his other chickenshit friends took off. It makes you think about what a different time that was. He was being a little shit and he knew he had it coming. Today he would have returned with his dad, threatening to sue me, Ken, and the McDonald's corporation.

One of the few perks was that I'd occasionally get some free food. Not because there was some employee freebie program. Every so often the call would go out that someone had to throw away a pile of Filet-O-Fish sandwiches because they sat under the heat lamp for more than two hours. Being me, I could not let this bounty go to waste. I would take the tray of dried-out, overheated filets, walk out to the dumpster, check to see if anyone was looking, and shove as many down my gullet as I possibly could. I knew I was on the clock and I could only be gone as long as it would take to toss them out. I barely even chewed them. There are pelicans who have eaten fish with more elegance and dignity.

I only lasted about three months. On more than one occasion I seriously contemplated staging an accident and putting my face in the deep fryer in the hope of getting out from behind the grill and onto disability.

I had this thought about name tags. I had to wear one at McDonald's. As far as your job and your name placard go, the farther away from your chest the better. If your name is pinned to your vest, that's a shitty job. If your name is on your desk, that's better. The best scenario most of you can hope for is to have your name on the door outside your office. That's good, solid, middle-class, middle-management stuff. If your name is on the directory on the first floor of the building you're in really good shape: You own the tax-preparation service or the dental practice. If you have your name on the outside of the building your office is in, that's great. You not only have your own company, but you have enough departments to warrant your own building. Now, if your name is on a building on the other side of an ocean, you've really arrived.

After my retirement from McDonald's—by the way, my final press conference announcing I was stepping down was quite moving—I ended up at Flask Liquor on Ventura Boulevard. My job was to deliver booze.

This job was the second in my long streak (which continues today) of jobs in which I never got a tip. At the same time I was schlepping hooch for Flask, The Weez worked for a place called Valley Stores, also delivering booze. Except he would deliver it a bottle or two at a time, and when he handed off the twelve bucks' worth of Cutty Sark, the guy would give him an extra five. I delivered liquor by the case to weddings or events at the movie studios. So I'd wheel in the cases on a hand truck and the receptionist or wedding planner would tell me where to put them and that would be that. I probably dropped off $250,000 worth of alcohol and got $0 in tips.

One hot day in July I was out on a delivery run in the liquor store's station wagon up in what we referred to as Hebrew Heights. I was passing The Weez's cousin Michelle's house, so I decided to stop in. She was a good friend of mine and I had some time to kill. I knocked on the door and it just swung open. Like the house was haunted. I heard music coming from inside. So I stepped into the entryway and called her name a couple of times. There was no reply. The house was laid out like the letter C with a little grassy area in the middle. As I was walking through I looked out the window into the courtyard area and saw two completely hot and completely naked chicks sunbathing. I knew them from high school. One of them was The Weez's cousin and the other was Beth, Molly Ringwald's sister, a girl I'd had a crush on for a while. Unfortunately, from my angle all I could see was that they were naked and not much else. So I crept around to the back of the house to get a better view from the master bedroom. I climbed up on Michelle's mom's dresser to get a view from an upper window. Unfortunately, all I saw was half an ass cheek as they walked into the house and slid the door closed behind them. I was cut off: There was no way to the front door and no back door to get to. I was hoping they were going to walk in for a drink and walk back out, but they didn't. I was trapped like a rat with

ADAM CAROLLA

a boner. So all I could do was hide in the closet. I couldn't just walk out of there—that would make me seem like a weird perv who broke in as opposed to a lucky perv who happened to catch them at just the right moment. So from the closet I could hear them talking about needing to take a shower. Fortunately not together: That would have blown my mind and I would have passed out in the closet because all the blood would have left my brain and gone to my wang. Beth said she would take the first shower and got in, but I was still trapped in the closet because Michelle was wandering around God knows where and I could have easily run into her. At a certain point I decided to take my chances and make a break for it. I was supposed to be on a fifteen-minute liquor delivery and I'd been gone almost an hour at that point. I slowly crept out of the closet, snuck down the hall, and peeked around a corner and saw that she was still naked in the kitchen, on the phone, with her back turned to me. I had about eighteen feet of carpet to cover, then a hard left to freedom. I went like a blitzing linebacker shooting the B-gap. I was two steps away from being in the clear when she spun around and spotted me. She dropped the phone and started screaming. So I started screaming, too, and pretended like I didn't know what the hell was going on. I sprinted out of the house, jumped into the car, and sped off. It was all very innocent, but it was such a traumatic experience that to this day I can barely beat off to it.

4

FINALLY, PEOPLE POORER THAN ME:
TIJUANA

TIJUANA, MEXICO

YEAR BUILT: 1889

9 BILLION SQUARE FEET

POPULATION: 1.7 MILLION

875,000 BEDROOMS

ONE BATH

THERE were several nights back in the day when my only shelter was a blanket and my bed was the beach in Mexico. Being young and dumb in Southern California means frequent trips to Tijuana. Me and my idiot friends went down Mexico way at least a dozen times. And the majority of those trips ended with me crashing on the beach with the blanket and pillow from my own bed and waking up surrounded by dogs that walked sideways. That's never a good sign.

You all know Tijuana as a family-friendly crime-free zone perfect for church groups and Scout troops or day trips with the kids. But it wasn't always Legoland South. Are you sitting down? Believe it or not, there was a time when Tijuana and even other parts of Mexico were filled with criminals, corrupt cops, and three-year-olds selling Chiclets on the street. But it's not like there were any trips to Paris or Florence on a young Adam Carolla's calendar, so Tijuana was about as exotic a locale as I could get to. Plus those places had art museums, not seedy strip joints like the Unicorn Bar. And that's what my gang of poor, bored, and fearless seventeen-year-old buddies were looking for. Most people fear Tijuana because it's lawless. That's exactly why we wanted to go. The Unicorn Bar was usually our first stop.

The strippers at the Unicorn danced to a live band. That sounds cool, but the band was made up of three guys whose average age was eighty-seven. The drum "kit" was composed of a lone snare drum first used in the Battle of Pueblo, and one of them was playing a trumpet that looked like it had been backed over by a U-Haul. The place was filled with marines from nearby Camp Pendelton who were looking for one last chance at love before they were dropped onto the mean streets of Grenada, perhaps never to return again.

Of course, the legendary debauchery you always hear about in Tijuana is the donkey show. If you don't know what this is, Google it, preferably while your youngest is on your lap. Let's just say it ends with a very sore woman and a very happy donkey. One night in '83 we looked for the donkey show for more than four hours. We talked to everyone we could. I didn't speak any Spanish but "donkey show" is part of the International Language. By the way, *"¿Donde esta la biblioteca?"* is the only thing I remember from high school Spanish class. Have you ever found yourself in Mexico wondering where the library was? Sewage-treatment facility would place higher on a list of Mexican tourist destinations. Every time I went there all I looked for were strippers, street tacos, and the donkey show.

I never did any homework in high school and follow-through is not something that's really in my family history, but when it came time to look for the donkey show I was like Magellan. We walked the entire damn city but never found it. We did find a taco stand that had a jukebox in it and we pissed everyone off by playing Rick Springfield nonstop for an hour. We just kept feeding quarters in, hitting D3, and rocking out to "Jessie's Girl." The other thing I remember about that night was the temperature. It was cold. I didn't have a jacket and it was freezing, so I borrowed my buddy Carl's bomber jacket. Carl, for some reason, kept spitting on the back of it. So I told him to knock it off. But he did that super-drunk guy-dude-bro thing and said, "It's my jacket." Touché, Carl, touché. So I ended the night in a spit-covered jacket, a couple bucks lighter from tacos and "Jessie's Girl," and without having seen the donkey show.

We usually went to another place called Margarita's Village. It's still there on the corner of Revolution Boulevard. To get in I had to walk down a tight, dark staircase with an impossibly low ceiling and uneven steps. Much like the mythical donkey show, among the many things they don't have in Mexico are building codes. When you get downstairs at Margarita's Village the waiters are dressed in crazy outfits—sea captains, old-time prison getups, and French maids. Plus most are on roller skates. They do a thing called "slammers" where they pour tequila and 7-Up into a shot glass, slam it on the table, pour the foaming concoction down your throat, and then put their forearm across your mouth and vigorously shake your head like a paint can. And if you decide this is all too much and you'd just like to sit there and nurse your Corona Extra, your buddy will excuse himself to use the bathroom and tell the waiter to give you a double. The next thing you know, you'll be assaulted by the world's worst chiropractor. And if you resist, you'll not only get shamed by the whole bar but you'll end up with some serious neck trauma. It's like being waterboarded with tequila by a rodeo clown.

One time after a hard night at Margarita's Village I stumbled toward the bathroom. I'd had a little too much tequila and cerveza and needed to throw up-a. I couldn't make it to the bathroom so I found the next-best place, the icemaker. I just slid open the door and let it fly. I feel bad to this day wondering if some people upstairs got their margaritas chunky-style. Then I stumbled out the back door and passed out in the alley between some boxes. The last thing I saw was a cop standing on the sidewalk up at street level and I had to do that move where you're so drunk you're seeing double and have to close one eye to focus. You know you're fucked-up when two eyes is one too many for you to handle. I was awoken by a nightstick to the ribs. It was the cop. He miraculously didn't want a bribe and just told me to move on.

This was the kind of crap we got into, if we ever even got there. The trips down to Tijuana were always hairy. One time me and a buddy, whom we all called "Snake," drove alone to Tijuana in his stepmom's '77 Mazda, which was sporting four bald tires and no spare. We were halfway there, near San Juan Capistrano, and out went the front driver's-side tire. This was at ten o'clock at night. Remember, this is pre–cell phones and ATMs, and as luck would have it I'd left my Platinum AAA card in the Countach at home. So we grabbed our pillows and blankets and started walking down the freeway until we got to the nearest off-ramp and began looking for a place to sleep. Eventually we found a grass median near a state beach, spread out our blanket, and went to bed. The next day we hiked to a 76 station and for eight dollars purchased another used tire. It took us a day and a half to get to Tijuana. It should have taken three hours.

Snake, a couple other dudes, and I did another trip to Mexico in another piece-of-shit car. This time it was my sister's Dodge Dart. This just goes to show how pathetic I was at the time: I didn't even have a piece of shit of my own. Among the many problems with my sister's car was a bad radiator. It was overheating the whole way down. The water-temp gauge was pegged in the red the entire trip. I knew it was fucked-up, so every sixth off-ramp I'd have to pull over, put a rag over the radiator cap, undo it, let the steam shoot out, dump more water into it, and start driving again. So it took us eight hours to get three quarters of the way there. I declared at that point, me usually being the voice of reason in my group of stoners and drunks, that we had to go back. They were outraged. We'd spent forty bucks on coolant and oil and eight hours of our lives and they wanted to keep going. I said, "*If* we make it to Tijuana in this car, we ain't making it back. So the farther we get from home, the farther we get out of range. We've got to turn around right now, and if we're lucky we'll get home and maybe find another car." Everyone was screaming, "Keep going!" I decided as captain of the ship to turn us around. I drove down the off-ramp, made a left off the freeway, went under the overpass, took another left onto the on-ramp of the freeway in the opposite direction, started to accelerate, and *POW!*

As always, I was right. We threw a rod through the engine block. It was a noise I'd never heard before and hope to never hear again. It went straight through a cast-iron engine block. The scene went from everyone screaming at me that I was a pussy and we needed to keep going to stone silence. Fortunately we just coasted to a stop on the side of the freeway. So like my previous trip with Snake, we started walking. Eventually we found a pay phone and called a friend to pick us up. (For those of you under twenty, a pay phone is like a giant cell phone bolted to the side of a glass closet on the street into which you feed old-time round money.) Our friend Tom had a seminormal family, and they drove two cars down so we could finish the trip with one and they could drive back with the other. Take a moment to imagine me calling my mom and asking for that kind of help. She'd still be laughing to this day. My family didn't have two cars that could make it that far anyway. We ended up packing five big dudes into a two-door Corolla hatchback and continuing the trek.

This Mexico trip took us not only to Tijuana but farther down the Baja peninsula to Ensenada. And like all of our Mexican excursions, this one landed us at a strip club. There's a big difference between strippers south of the border and the ones stateside. Up here we have weird rules about how if there's alcohol served they can only be topless, and some cities require six-foot boundaries between the strippers and the fellas. In Mexico for a buck you can get onstage and attempt and often succeed in performing oral on the stripper without a 250-pound bouncer kicking the shit out of you. If there are any consequences to getting aggressive it will be the stripper herself hitting you in the face with her stiletto heel or smashing a bottle on your head. They're tough down there.

But it doesn't always end up that way. On that trip to Ensenada there was a drunk surfer dude, not a member of our team, who jumped onstage with the stripper and got completely naked and generally made an ass out of himself. He was spreading his butt cheeks, shouting, and pouring beer down his chest. This lasted about twenty minutes before his buddies coaxed him off the stage. In the U.S. he wouldn't have lasted ten seconds before a B.A. Baracus look-alike stomped him to death.

The best part of this story is what happened the next day. Me and the gang were on Rosarita Beach when we overheard this group of dudes in front of us. They were heckling one of their friends. "I can't believe you did that, man. You showed your dick to a roomful of people." It was the surfer dude from the strip bar. He was brushing off the chop-busting, saying, "Nobody knows me down here. It's not like anyone will ever hear about it. It's Mexico, they don't even speak English." This was the opportunity of a lifetime. We ran up to the group like a bunch of starstruck teenage girls and said, "Hey, it's the dude who got naked on stage last night! You were awesome!" His friends nearly died. That's a moment all guys live for. Your jackass friend thinks he's going to get off the hook for his jackassery, and a group of strangers appear at precisely the right moment to back up the story and double down on the humiliation.

Baja was a fun place and became a regular destination even up into early adulthood. Once a year me and a medium-sized group of guys I worked construction with would meet at a Denny's off of Topanga Canyon at five A.M., load up on Grand Slams, and make the pilgrimage to the peninsula. On this particular trip it was three four-wheel-drive pickup trucks and a Chevy Chevette. Each truck was filled with surfboards, motorcycles, sleeping bags, and a bunch of guys who you wouldn't let house-sit for you if Ted Kaczynski was available. In five short hours I would be drunk in the bed of one of the pickup trucks going down a dirt road lighting M-80s from a cigarette and chucking them at the truck behind me. Once we arrived on a good stretch of beach, it would be time to either get naked and go surfing or put on underpants and go dirt-bike riding. My two most cherished possessions at the time were a bottle of mescal tequila and a huge sombrero I'd purchased in town. At some point one of my drunken buddies said, "Isn't that your sombrero over there?" I

1988—Baja, Mexico. Me and my sombrero.

looked over my shoulder and saw my award-winning sombrero sitting flat on the sand twenty-five feet away. I called out its name and started running toward it (think Tom Hanks and the volleyball from *Castaway*). As I approached it, it exploded. One of the Cambridge alumni I'd been traveling with put an M-200 under it and used a cigarette as a delay. It blew a hole through the top that was black and trumpeted out like when Yosemite Sam would lose his cool. I spent the remainder of the trip wearing the sombrero with pride.

The following day began with a long morning of duct-taping M-80s to the sides of bottle rockets that would have been too big for a Sparkletts bottle, twisting the fuses together, and firing them into the ocean. Let me do a quick PSA on why fireworks are so dangerous. You start off cautiously by igniting your first firecracker with one of those extend-o lighters, running, and then diving behind a log. Five minutes later the same guy is holding a beer, lighting an M-80 with the Tiparillo dangling from his mouth, and throwing it at the campfire his buddies are sitting around.

After we'd exhausted most of our fireworks supply, my buddy Chris decided to head out on his Honda 250. An hour later we heard screams coming from around the bend. We rushed over to investigate. Chris was helmetless, gloveless, and shirtless on top of the scariest cluster of cacti you've ever seen. The cactus that grows wild in Baja makes the stuff you see in the gardening section of Home Depot look like a marshmallow wearing a goose-down bathrobe.

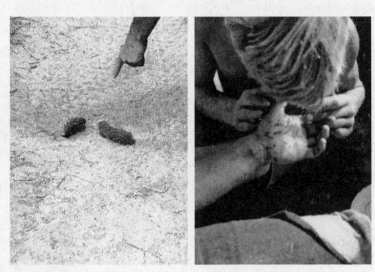

1988—Baja, Mexico. The killer cactus and Chris's shredded hand.

His entire body was riddled with three-inch needles. We had to use pliers to remove them. At first we tried leather gloves, but the spines sticking out of him would pierce them and stick us. This would have killed any of the guys I later sat with at various writers' tables. But not Chris. He was simultaneously super- and subhuman. He would later go on to survive having a wine bottle broken over his head at his girlfriend's house. On another occasion after beating up a guy on the Pacific Coast Highway he survived being run over by a VW bug. Years later paramedics jammed a syringe filled with adrenaline through his rib cage to restart his heart. He still has all his hair and despite never working out looks better than all of us in his underpants. It's all in the genes. But anyway, there were no hospitals in the vicinity and driving two hours only to end up in a Tijuana emergency room didn't sound like a plan. (Tijuana Emergency Room does sound like a hell of a drink though—Cuervo Gold and insulin.) So we bandaged him up and got on with our vacation. The only time it even came up after that was whenever he took a shit. His hands were still bandaged so we'd have to play rock, paper, scissors to decide who got the pleasure of wiping his ass.

1988—Baja, Mexico. John should have gone with rock; he lost and had to use paper, toilet paper.

I forgot to tell you what happened to my sister's car. We pushed the Dart off the freeway and to a side street where hopefully it would get stolen over the weekend. But unfortunately when I returned the following Monday on my motorcycle, it was still there. I found a guy who made Fred Sanford look like the Monopoly man and convinced him to buy the car from me. Imagine what must have been going through my sister's head. This was not her *extra* car, it was her car, her only mode of transportation. I borrowed it on a Friday and came back the following Monday without the car but with forty bucks. I handed her the money along with a unique observation: "It's a good thing *I* was behind the wheel when that rod let go. You could have been stranded on the wrong side of the tracks." She rolled her eyes and went back inside the house. We never spoke of the matter again.

One of our usual Tijuana companions was a goofy guy named Rudy. He was a good dude but a bit of a fuck-up and a blackout drunk. He once woke up chained to a hospital bed. We all decided on one of our trips to TJ that we should each buy a bottle of mescal, the kind with the worm in it, and bring it back with us. As if we couldn't get tequila in North Hollywood. It was me, Snake, Chris, Tom, and Rudy. We're walking back across the border when Rudy dropped his bottle. It smashed all over the cement sidewalk. He was pissed and was practically in tears. And then Chris did one of the most comedically satisfying things I've ever seen. He was laughing his drunk ass off at Rudy and pretending to be him, mocking him. "Der, I'm Rudy, I don't know how to carry a bottle!" and then *SMASH!* Chris dropped his bottle, too. He got pissed and started stomping on the glass.

On our way out we all stood by Rudy's car and decided who was the least fucked-up, aka the designated driver. Nobody was sober. That was a given. We decided that Rudy was the least drunk. So he got behind the wheel and drove us all back to The Weez's cousin Michelle's dorm at San Diego State. We left Rudy at her room, then found our own places to crash in the fetal position and vomit into trash cans. Somewhere in the middle of the night Rudy had an alcohol-induced psychotic episode where he decided that he had to get in the car and go back to Tijuana to, and I quote, "get the rest of the men out." Somehow enough tequila had turned a nineteen-year-old from the Valley into a grizzled Vietnam vet having a flashback. "We've got to get the rest of the men out!" At some point Michelle called me at whichever dorm room I was puking in to tell me that I needed to come and get Rudy. My response was to unplug the phone and pass back out. Rudy proceeded to run up and down the halls of Michelle's dorm banging on doors and shouting about rescuing comrades in Tijuana. The next day we discovered him in the street asleep *under* his car. Again, this was the guy we chose to be our designated driver.

Passing out was a big theme in our drunken Mexican shenanigans. Another time that we got to the crossing at San Diego, we decided to play "Border Patrol." We were running around laughing and shooting each other with fake machine guns. We made it to the other side laughing and out of breath but down a man. Chris was MIA. We waited for what seemed like a long time and then decided to investigate. We headed up the spiral walkway, and halfway across the bridge we spotted Chris sprawled out facedown on the cement. Here's the difference between men and women. If this were a group of girlfriends, one woman would have said, "Someone call an ambulance, I think Cindi's hurt." Not dudes. Snake came over and kicked him. No response. So then he hocked a loogie on him to see if he was faking. Again, no response. So we lifted all two hundred pounds of him, put him over my shoulder, and I carried him to Tom's small Toyota hatchback. People forget how tiny those old Japanese cars were. We were big dudes and that was a fucking clown car. But we jammed in and started driving back. Chris, who had not so much as batted an eyelid in the past forty-five minutes, suddenly sprang to life. It was like someone hit him with a set of jumper cables. He popped up in his seat and shouted, "Captain, we can't feed them boys sticky rice." This was the tagline to an Uncle Ben's commercial that had been on TV seven years earlier. To this day we have no idea why he said that. Given the amount of alcohol consumption and stupidity happening, it's a miracle those weren't his last words. Imagine that on a gravestone.

I lugged him back to the motel in San Diego. We had managed to pool enough money between the five of us to get a room at one of those cheap places, the kind with two single beds that were taller than they were wide. I plopped Chris down on the bed and went to the bathroom to clean up. I was brushing my teeth when I heard a *KABOOMP!* I came out and Tom was lying on the bed casually watching TV where I had just left Chris. He had just rolled him off onto the floor. And that was where Chris stayed until the next morning. Again, another example of stuff guys will do to their passed-out buddies that chicks never would.

Say what you will about Tijuana and the poor but proud (of what, I don't know) folks who live there, but if you're ever tired of being judged—and don't mind possibly having your head end up in a duffel bag—then Tijuana is the place you should open that fro-yo joint you've always been dreaming about.

5

A LITERAL
LATERAL MOVE:
THE GARAGE

NORTH HOLLYWOOD, CA

YEARS RESIDED IN: 1982–1984

324 SQUARE FEET

RENT: $0

NO PLUMBING

NO HEATING

NO AIR-CONDITIONING

was on the verge of high school graduation and it was time to step out on my own. I leapt boldly into my adult life and moved fifteen feet into my dad's garage. My stepsister Hilary, who had originally been living there, split, so I got to move in. Now when I say garage, I mean garage. It still had the big wooden door, which had been tarred shut, complete with the original rusty hinges. It was windowless stucco and had all the comforts of the hot box they locked Cool Hand Luke in. There was no insulation or ventilation. What little air circulation I got was from a noisy metal fan sitting on the floor. It wasn't a nice oscillating fan or anything like that. Think of the fan you'd find in a warehouse in India. That's what I had. It hardly kept me cool and definitely kept me awake. And it became a real liability one day when my buddy Jeff Katz decided it would be hilarious to turn it up to full blast and dump an entire sack of Gold Medal flour into it. My room looked like the inside of Tony Montana's nose after he buried his face in that pile of coke. The surface of the moon has less powder on it. No matter how much I cleaned, I never got all of it. I was still finding flour and weevils years later.

The only thing that made my sweat lodge worse was the fact that there were pools on three sides. The neighbors to the left, right, and rear all had pools. The entire summer I heard people shouting "Marco . . . Polo . . . Fish out of water!" while the only pool I had was the pool of sweat I was sleeping in. The San Fernando Valley isn't quite Phoenix in August but it gets pretty fucking close, only about five degrees off on those bad summer days. That garage could easily hit triple-digit temps, and it was unbearable. On those nights, around two A.M. I'd hop the fence like a Navy SEAL and take a dip. To me this was perfectly normal and natural; I didn't give it two thoughts.

While I had the fan blowing all summer, come winter it was time for the space heater. Being that my room was a garage, the ambient temperature outside was the same as inside. At some point in its life span, my space heater's cord got cut and I jerry-rigged it back together in a very non-OSHA way. But it was good enough. At night as I slept it rested right next to my bed on the rug.

When I say rug, please don't think Persian or nice wall-to-wall. It was a bad burnt-orange eight-by-eight scrap of carpeting that had been pulled from another part of the house when my dad got some awful blue carpet. It was a sign of the times. Carpet like that today would be thrown out. But not in the Valley in the eighties. That was a commodity with value. It could be wrapped around a pole in your carport so you didn't scratch your door; you could line the bed of a pickup truck with it or add a touch of class to a custom van. All you needed was some duct tape and a little chutzpah. (*Chutzpah* is probably a poor word choice. There's not a Jew in the world who would attempt any of what I just described.)

Not actually being tacked down to a floor, the carpet curled up at the edges. One time during the night, one of those curled ends connected with the space heater's sliced cord and ignited. I woke up to the smell of the smoke and put out the fire with my orange polyester blanket, the same one I used on the beach in Mexico. It got charred on the end but stayed in use for a long time after that. The carpet, which was now literally burnt orange, remained in the bedroom as well.

It was my senior year and I was ready to graduate, but only if I passed my Spanish final. So I cheated answer for answer from the Asian girl, Cynthia Nagatani—who sat in front of me—got a D, and was able to graduate. I still feel slighted. I checked every single box on my test exactly the same as Cynthia, and I know she didn't get a D.

Cynthia Nagatani

While I did technically graduate, I never received a diploma because I owed the book room $19.95 for a textbook called *We the People*. Their policy was, you don't get your diploma until we get our money. I didn't have $20, and I also instinctively knew that where I was headed, nobody would ever ask to see a diploma. That usually doesn't come up when you're begging someone for a job digging ditches. So I was like, "Suckers. I just saved a cool twenty bucks." Through the next couple of chapters as I break down the terrible jobs I had later in life, you tell me if you think I ever had cause to produce my diploma.

For graduation I was given an eerie harbinger of things to come. My uncle Gobbi sent me the card on the opposite page.

I also got a gift from my dad's cousin and his wife—Vince and Pat Bruno. It was just what every eighteen-year-old wants: a decorative popcorn tin. It had a cardboard divider to assure that the caramel, cheddar, and regular popcorn didn't comingle. Like a prison yard where they have to keep the Crips away from the Lowriders and the Lowriders away from the Aryan Nation. Going one flavor at a time, I ate every kernel even after it got stale. By the way, these are the same

NOWADAYS TO GET ANYWHERE A GRADUATE HAS TO HAVE <u>TALENT.</u>

YOU HAVE **TALENT!**

A GRADUATE HAS TO HAVE <u>FRIENDS.</u>

YOU HAVE **FRIENDS!**

A GRADUATE HAS TO HAVE AN UNYIELDING DESIRE TO <u>WORK.</u>

people who every year on my birthday would give me a card with slots for dimes. I'd get one dime for each year. So the same year they gave me the popcorn tin, I was worth a buck eighty. Thankfully, I didn't toss the popcorn tin after I devoured its contents, for the following reason: The garage had no plumbing, and I would frequently return from my carpet-cleaning jobs in the wee hours of the morning. If you're doing the carpets at the Sizzler in Whittier you start after closing, which means you finish somewhere around three A.M. Thus I would often be locked out of the main house. Anyway, if you haven't done the fecal math yet, let's just say the popcorn tin served double doo-dee.

When I graduated from high school in 1982, there were no jobs to be found, but that was of no consequence because I was off to Valley Junior College to pick up a few credits and show the coaches how the position of outside linebacker was supposed to be played before I transferred to one of the many "real" colleges that had tried to recruit me. I wasn't ready to let my lifelong dream of playing football go just yet. No matter how bad things were at home or school, I could always count on football as my beacon of hope on a moonless life. That was all about to change. Unfortunately, football players aren't known for their heroics in the classroom, so I found myself on a team with eighty guys, mostly composed of the All-Valley players from my league and other parts of the city, vying for a few precious starting positions. They were bigger than me, stronger than me, and faster than me. And this time my hard-boiled-egg-and-bench-press plan wasn't going to be enough. My back was bad and my chances of starting were worse. After eleven years it was time to stop doing the only thing I ever wanted to do. My next good year wasn't until the middle of '94 when I met Jimmy Kimmel. Until then it was more drudgery and misery.

At this time my idea of a dream job was working at a supermarket. I thought it would be a pretty cool job, especially if you could get into one of the unions. Every once in a while I'd hear about a guy who was in the baggers' union and was making $10.50 an hour and got golden time for nights and weekends. I'd think, "Damn, he got fifteen dollars an hour *for four hours*! Holy shit, man!" But it wasn't meant to be.

I took the only job available and began my career in the fast-paced, lucrative world of carpet cleaning. A buddy was working for a guy named Art Fuss who had a carpet-cleaning company and got me the gig.

Carpet cleaning was back breaking, dirty, and miserable. I didn't shampoo people's imported rugs in their entry halls, I used a steam cleaner on barbecue joints. Imagine what the carpet at a Tony Roma's or a Pizza Hut looks like at the point where it meets the tile that leads into the kitchen. It was barely a carpet anymore. It had a thick coating of dropped food mashed into it. And, as I said, we could only work when these establishments were closed. Which meant showing up at eleven P.M. and cleaning till four A.M. I knew it was a shitty job one day when I was looking forward to emptying the steam cleaner's catch tank. That means you hold a five-gallon bucket under a valve on the side of the machine, twist the valve, and out comes a four-and-a-half-gallon bouillabaisse of grease, barbecue sauce, and roach shit. Then you drag a bucket filled with this putrid soup as it slops on your jeans to the men's room and dump it down the toilet. I know it sounds disgusting and horrible, but it's still easier than being bent over scrubbing that steam-cleaning wand on the almost-black carpet in front of the kitchen. ("Carpet wand" is one of those things that sounds way better than it is, like it's magical.) So I was busting my back pushing around a wand with a guy named Juan. The only perk was the food. Like when we would clean the Hamburger Hamlet in Westwood. Ray would get behind the grill and make his triple-decker burgers while I was up front removing huge wedges of German chocolate cake from their refrigerated glass palace.

(Surreal sidebar: As I write this I'm sitting in the middle of the California desert, shooting a segment for a car show at the Mojave Air and Space Port. It's 106 degrees out, but I'm in a $460,000 2012 Rolls Royce Phantom Coupe-Villa to get a little air-conditioning. I just flipped on the satellite radio and immediately heard a ten-year-old episode of the Howard Stern show with me and Jimmy laughing at a guy named Mr. Methane continuously farting for forty-five seconds on a chick's head. At first I didn't recognize my voice. I just heard a guy ask the farter, "Do you do weddings?" and thought, "That cat is funny . . . oh, that's me.")

We were cleaning the carpet at the Russian Tea Room on the third floor of the Beverly Center and they left us alone with a bar. Bad move. It was me and Chris and a rookie named Dave. He got behind the bar and started pouring full tumblers of whiskey. No lime, no ice cubes, no umbrella. So we ended up shit-faced throwing chairs at each other, spilling sudsy water all over the place. At a certain point I staggered into the kitchen in search of sustenance. What I found was a walk-in refrigerator filled with cream puffs. Delicious cream puffs. I surreptitiously ate as many as possible before the other guys could realize I'd been gone for a while, come looking for me, and find the cream puffs. Chris would tear that walk-in fridge apart. I wiped my face, snuck out, and hoped they were none the wiser.

The following morning I was jarred from my hungover slumber by a call from the boss. Art said, "How'd it go last night?" This was out of character for Art. I sheepishly replied, "Fine, why?" He matter-of-factly asked, "Did you eat anything?" I more sheepishly replied, "Not that I can remember. Why?" Art said, "Because I found a case of cream puffs wedged into the steam cleaner's solution tank."

("Solution tank" also sounds way better than it is, like a charity Al Gore and Richard Branson would found to provide potable water in Sub-Saharan Africa.) Evidently Chris had smuggled out a case of cream puffs but, shit-faced from tumblers of whiskey, he'd forgotten to remove it when we dropped the van off.

Even if we hadn't been desperate for food growing up, we still probably would have gorged as hard as we did when we had those opportunities. When you work crazy-long late-night hours for shit pay, not only are you sleep-deprived but you eat worse, drink more booze, and smoke twice as much. In fact it's because you're sleep-deprived. Nature has built a schedule into us. We're supposed to go to sleep at ten and get up at six, with a full eight hours in between. Each half hour you get away from that schedule, the more fucked-up you feel. Nobody who works the graveyard shift is into organic food, filtered water, and exercise. It's cigarettes and fast food all night, some booze to knock you down to sleep after your shift, and then more greasy, shitty food when you wake up. With that kind of routine, your body gets traumatized and wants to be soothed. The alarm goes off and you're on three hours' sleep so your body says, "Give me a cigarette, some whiskey, and a breakfast burrito, I'm hurting." I would love to see a long-term study on the dietary habits and substance abuse of people who work the graveyard shift. I bet their life span is seventeen years shorter than it is for people who work regular hours. This did, however, give me a great idea. I'm going to invent an alarm clock that, thirty seconds before it goes off, spits out a puff of bacon-and-coffee scent. That will ease the transition for people as they get up. Your brain would register that waft of fresh-roasted Colombian coffee and Canadian bacon and waking up wouldn't be as jarring to your body.

We also had to clean the carpets at the Beverly Wilshire Hotel. One place was called the Pink Turtle, which sounds like a Kama Sutra position. I was delighted a few years ago when I went back there to eat. It is now Wolfgang Puck's restaurant Cut. Even more enjoyable was my return to the bigger ballroom at the Beverly Wilshire—the Grand Trianon. I cleaned the carpets there one night in '83. More than twenty years later I returned as the celebrity auctioneer at a benefit for Bob Saget's charity. I was dumbstruck and slightly giddy. The last time I was there I was cleaning the carpets with Ray, and this time I was shooting the shit with John Stamos.

But back to Art. He was a dick. He wouldn't pay us for driving time. The clock wouldn't start until we got to the job. So we'd be out for seven hours and only get paid for five. Every now and again we'd park the custom van on the wrong side of the street and get a parking ticket. Art would then take the cost of the ticket out of our already pathetic pay. Actually, we'd end up owing him. The ticket would be thirty bucks and we'd only made twenty-four for the night.

Art got his comeuppance, though. On Ray and Chris's last night working for him they took Art out, got him drunk, and beat the crap out of him with his own shoe. They also threw his car keys onto the roof of a commercial building, never to be retrieved.

After one of our carpet-cleaning cohorts, a man of color who called himself Everlast, was convicted of murder for shooting a guy in a gay bar, I realized it was time to move on.

Though I was no longer going to work with them, Ray and Chris were still my pals, and we still had plenty of drinking and fucking around to do. One night toward the end of my time in the garage there was a party down in Orange County at the palatial estate of our buddy Umgad's sister's boyfriend (now her husband). All the usual suspects were going to be there, including Chris, Ray, and Snake. With those guys on hand this party was sure to be a blowout.

The only team ever assembled that was even close to this drunken, testosterone-fueled wrecking crew was when Lee Marvin put together the Dirty Dozen. This party was gonna be trouble. The cops would definitely be called, probably the fire department, and, if there was tequila on hand, the National Guard. In one of my more sensible moments, I said I was going to pass. I called The Weez and told him to gas up his dad's Bronco. We were going to escape the fallout zone and go camping. While we were safely atop Mount Pinos the following story happened.

Chris had an on-again-off-again girlfriend named Carrie. I can't recall if they were on or off at the time, but that didn't matter to Ray. He thought he should be with Chris's girl. Secretly Ray and Carrie had been sneaking around behind Chris's back for months and had grown so brazen that they attempted to hook up at this party that Chris was also at. Ray and Carrie were having a private makeout session. But it didn't remain private for long. Snake walked in on them. This was trouble. If Snake told Chris about it, we would have an epic battle on our hands. Chris and Ray were huge, aggressive dudes. Not only would they beat the shit out of each other, but the

1986—Chris, another friend, Carrie, and Ray at a bar called Midnight Rendezvous.

collateral damage would be catastrophic. It would look like Tokyo after Godzilla and King Kong went at it. For clarity, Chris is a fairly mild-mannered guy, but he's like that scientist who, when angered, turns into the Hulk. Don't make him angry. You wouldn't like him when he's angry.

Snake declared that he was going to tell Chris. Ray knew this would spell almost certain disaster and told him not to. Snake then came up with a novel solution and said, "Let me make out with her and I won't tell." Without asking Carrie, Ray agreed. He'd let Snake make out with the girl he had stolen from Chris in order to prevent Chris from finding out and thus starting World War III. I have to assume Carrie played along because she knew Chris and Ray would tear each other to shreds. Then came the negotiating. Snake proposed that he get a minute of makeout time. Ray countered, then Snake made his rebuttal offer, and eventually these two gentleman settled on twenty seconds.

Snake and Carrie began the makeout session while Ray sat there and watched. Ray later conceded that he got a little turned on. But the damage to their friendship had been done. The seed of resentment had been planted, and through the rest of the party it would be watered with booze.

A little background before the next part of the story: Snake was an animal lover. He was also nuts, especially when drunk. Later on, when he had a dog, he would stack cans of dog food in the fireplace of his small condo and shoot them with a .22 rifle, saying he was "hunting" food for it. Snake also had a yellow-and-gray miniature cockatiel named Remus and a cat named Wilshire because he was found on Wilshire Boulevard. One morning Wilshire was found dead under what Ray deemed suspicious alcohol-related circumstances. Snake denied involvement and would deny it to this day.

Unfortunately, on this night, with everything else happening, Ray decided to call Snake a cat killer. Snake became furious and the fight began. I wasn't there but I heard the tales and saw the scars. Snake wanted to step it up to a death match and kept shouting, *"Get two knives!"* Luckily it didn't get to that point. After many punches were thrown and the scuffling on the ground started, Snake bit Ray in the calf, drawing blood. Ray then tossed him off and threw him into a planter, dislocating his shoulder. In the midst of the chaos, Snake revealed to Chris that Ray had been sneaking around with Carrie. It then turned into a three-way battle royale spanning the entire house. Once the guys had let off some steam, beating each other to a pulp, Chris, in a real bros-before-ho's moment, broke up with Carrie and took Snake to the hospital. The following day when The Weez and I returned from Brokeback Mountain and heard about the carnage, I had the same sad yet satisfying feeling as the handful of people who heeded the governor's warning and blew out before Katrina blew in.

After I got out of carpet cleaning, I landed a job at Hoffman Travel. The Weez was working there and had a job running airline tickets between offices. This was back when you had to go to a travel agent's office or an airport to get plane tickets. Not only did I have a desk that faced the wall, blank except for a clock that mocked me as I slowly died of boredom, I also worked with a bunch of angry yentas. I have to say honestly, they broke me down. Middle-aged female travel agent is just about the only thing above publicist on the evil meter. I was constantly bombarded with verbal assaults from one of the twenty-eight shrews there. Here's an actual exchange that happened.

Shrew: Merv Griffin hasn't gotten his tickets yet! Where did you put them?!
Me: I don't know.
Shrew: I put them on your desk. What did you do with them?

Me: I didn't see them.
Shrew: [dirty look]

A few minutes later, Shrew finds the tickets under the blotter of her desk.

Shrew: Hey, I found Merv Griffin's tickets.

Other shrews react as if she's a hero, and the accusatory bitch-out session with me is completely ignored.

THE END.

This scene was played out several times a day for the entire time I worked there. I couldn't handle it. If I hadn't been fired, I would have quit.

The story of my being fired from this job centers on a street called Valleyheart. Valleyheart runs parallel to one of the major streets out here, Ventura Boulevard. On a Sunday night I was eating whole-wheat pasta with low-sodium organic tomato sauce at my mom and stepdad's house. I brought up the fact that I had a bunch of warrants for traffic violations, hoping they would offer to help out with the $525 I owed and thus prevent me from getting arrested. Instead of getting the money I got a tip: "On your way to work tomorrow morning, don't take Ventura, take Valleyheart. It's a smaller street and there's no cops." I heeded my mom's advice and took Valleyheart, and the following morning I was arrested. Not a week later. Not three days later. Less than twenty-four hours later. The cop who pulled me over said he normally wasn't on that street but he'd been patrolling there because someone had been breaking into a nearby school. Not thirteen hours after the conversation with my mom I was arrested, brought into the North Hollywood Police Department, and fired from my job at Hoffman. It was probably for the best. I would have gone on a killing spree if I had to stay there any longer.

I quickly got back to the business of rotting in my garage. This is the worst position a young male can be in. Rudderless. This is what the military is for: guys who are nineteen and have no idea what the future holds. I was like a leaf in the wind, blowing wherever life took me. At one point my mom knew a guy who knew a guy who was a merchant marine and thought he could get me in. That didn't happen. I actually attended a job seminar and remember looking at pamphlets about becoming an ambulance driver or an underwater welder. Neither happened. I can't tell you how anxiety provoking that position is. I had no reading or writing skills and a family somewhere between apathetic, impotent, and hostile. I had no map, no compass, and no safety net.

One night my phone rang and my buddy John asked if I wanted to work the next day. He said, "All you have to do is show up in Silverlake and pull ivy off the side of a house and drag it up the hill to a dumpster." Before I knew it I was digging ditches and doing other shit work on construction sites. The pay stunk, it was always hot, and the job sites were all the same—twelve Mexicans and three racists named Mike. And they only liked those twelve Mexicans because "they're the good ones." People hear I was a "carpenter" and think it's nice, like I was sitting around with Bob Vila putting wainscoting in a Cape Cod manor. No, I was lugging trash in the blazing sun. It was dirty and mind-numbing. It's the repetition that will kill you. You have to do the same motion over and over and over again for ten hours at a stretch. And if you have a functioning brain like I do, you will go insane.

And you work with assholes. On my first construction job the foreman, Mike, was a Vietnam vet who was strung out on painkillers. He would announce to a group of us in a ditch that he was going to get someone to quit by the end of the day.

Another example of what an ass-wipe he was: On one particular job we were doing something called repointing. Picture a brick facade the size of the big screen in Dallas stadium. You'd have to grind out the mortar an inch deep around every brick and then refill it with new mortar using a tuck trowel, a trowel so thin that it fits between the upper and lower brick so that you can push the mortar in. It's as monotonous and repetitive as a job can get. I was sitting on scaffolding twelve feet in the air tucking away the time with one of the only other English-speaking guys sitting next to me when Mike walked by and shouted up, "No talking."

It was also dangerous. One of my first gigs was at a house in the Hollywood Hills. It was one of those houses where the first floor is on street level but the bedrooms are below, dug into the hill, with a little yard below that. So it had a steep cement staircase outside, in between the house and the place next door, leading to the back door and the yard.

I was working in the kitchen on the first floor. Or, more appropriately, I was working outside of the kitchen on the first floor. I had to cut some stucco outside the kitchen window so John, who'd gotten me the gig, put together some makeshift scaffolding. It was just a pair of two-by-fours sticking out the window with some plywood nailed across it for me to sit on. So my feet were inside the house and the rest of me was outside. Above me was the wall being torn up by my deafening hypoid saw, covering me in stucco dust, and below was ten feet of space ending in the concrete staircase. Unfortunately, John isn't as good a carpenter as me, and his jerry-rigged scaffolding collapsed. I could easily have wound up with a broken hip, elbow, and wrist and a hypoid saw embedded in my skull. But instinct prevailed, and I threw the saw into the house as the scaffolding gave way. I landed hard on my ass but managed to put one palm out in an attempt to break the fall. I limped away with a badly contused hand and an epic charley horse.

But because of who I was, how I was raised, and where I was at that point in my life, I didn't say anything about it. I just went home hoping to recover in time for the next day's work. I was afraid I would get fired if I didn't show up the following morning. That's how bad my self-esteem was at the time. And it was reinforced when I got home and told my dad. He gave me a not-caring grunt. This is how immigrants get exploited. They're desperate for the work and don't have the means to take care of their injuries so they just put up and shut up.

People ask me all the time, "Why did you do all that shit work? You're intelligent, you're capable. Why did you choose to clean carpets and dig ditches?" It was a perfect shitstorm of low self-esteem, an apathetic family, and higher unemployment than even in today's economy. I saw a news report last year that said we had the highest unemployment since 1983 and I thought, Yep, that's why I was digging ditches in '84. So when my preachy pampered lefty friends tell me white people won't do certain jobs, I say this honky begs to differ. I did tons of dirty, dangerous, low-paying shit work alongside Guatemalans, Mexicans, El Salvadorans, blacks, and whites of all different sizes and shapes. The only thing we had in common was poverty. When you say white people won't dig ditches or mow lawns, you're basing that on the educated gay couple with the frosted tips you just finished brunch with. Not me, Chris, and Ray in the early eighties.

THE WORST DAY OF MY LIFE

The garage was also the setting for the worst day of my life. Once again I needed a shit job. I knew someone who knew someone who was able to get me a gig painting commercial office buildings. You know the old saying about commercial painting: It's not *what* you know, it's *who* you know. So I took a job for seven bucks an hour. The day would start at seven A.M. and wrap up at five. Let me say this: Not only is ten hours of painting mind-numbing, but when it's commercial painting in an office building, it's a whole new level. Think of an average office in a high-rise building. There's no baseboard or molding or any detail work to do. It's just rolling beige paint onto an endless wall.

As if that weren't enough to make me jump from the roof of the building being painted, my companion for those ten hours was a dude named Andy. He was a Jehovah's Witness with nine kids, each one named after a different apostle. So the conversation was very Jesus-centric. Andy would invite me to the big Jehovah rally at Dodger Stadium that weekend, and the radio was constantly tuned to the Christian station.

This particular job was painting a lawyer's office on the thirtieth floor of a high-rise building in Century City. Remember the twin towers where they filmed *Die Hard*? That's where I was working. I had an hour commute each way, but in keeping with my pathetic-ness, I had no transportation. So I asked Chris if I could borrow his motorcycle.

I got up at six A.M. and hauled my ass over the hill from North Hollywood to Century City. When I got to the place I saw that it was $18 to park in the underground garage. I didn't want to blow a third of my paycheck to park, and there was no street parking near the building. So I just locked the bike up next to the cement facade off to the side of the parking structure. It seemed safe enough.

I spent the next ten hours listening to guys sing about how much they loved their Lord and Savior, trying to come up with excuses to miss the rally at Dodger Stadium and covering a wall in Navajo White paint. (Which I think is insulting to the Navajo people. That would be like naming a paint color Wesley Snipes Beige.) I left the building zombified, ready for the long commute home.

But when I got outside, the bike wasn't there. There was no sign of it.

Thinking Chris was going to kick the shit out of me for getting his bike stolen, I went to the security guard shack. I told him what was up, that my motorcycle had been stolen, and he said, "No, I had it towed."

Let me say two things. First, this is a total mindfuck. In my life I've had four motorcycles towed. When you get back to where you left it and it's nowhere to be found, your initial impulse is that it's been stolen. When I'm president, my first act will be to mandate that when something is towed, the tow-truck driver must leave a sticker in the spot telling the owner the vehicle has been taken and the location of the impound lot and a little sack of honey roasted peanuts to ease the pain. Second, and I'm addressing this to the people who have stuff towed, FUUUUUUUUCCCCCKKK YOOOOOOUUUUUU!!!!!! If my car is parked on the steps blocking your front door or on top of your special-needs child, that's one thing. But all the people who have cars and bikes towed because they were in the wrong place between certain hours should be crucified on that T coming out of the back of a tow truck.

The security guard gave me some bullshit about it being "an internal-combustion engine that contained fuel and could not be parked within the parameters of . . . blah blah blah." I protested. How could it be a fire danger sitting next to a concrete facade. He just said, "That's the rule." Seething with rage, I asked him where it had gone. His answer was like a punch to the kidneys—Santa Monica. For those unfamiliar with the geography of the L.A. area, Century City is twenty miles south of North Hollywood. Twenty miles south of that is Santa Monica. I was stuck dead center between my home and my means to get home.

I was fucking exhausted after a full day of drudgery, and now faced with this, my spirit was officially broken. I had no friends or family to pick me up and probably couldn't scrape together the dime to give them a ring from a pay phone anyway. Hell, the one guy I knew who did have a mode of transportation was Chris, and that just got hauled to Santa Monica.

So I started walking with my thumb out in the hopes of hitching a ride back to my dad's house. I pose this question. Who's scarier: guys who hitchhike, or guys who pick up hitchhikers?

I was on what is called Little Santa Monica, a street running parallel to Santa Monica Boulevard, at the point where Beverly Hills becomes West Hollywood, when someone pulled over. In keeping with the fact that one more step would put me in Boystown, it was a big gay guy in a white '72 El Dorado with red leather interior. He didn't have a gay flag on his car or anything, but between the interior, the location, and this next fact I can safely assume he was gay. It was only a minute or two before he dropped the line on me: "You wanna get high?" This is gay code, a way of straining out the straights. It works like a charm. The plan is, "I've got a place just around the block, we'll park, smoke some weed, one thing will lead to another . . ." I passed on that, politely explaining how long a day I'd had. Shortly after that, he dropped me off at the entrance of Laurel Canyon about halfway back to my place—still a long uphill journey to go before even being able to *see* the Valley. I can now say I understand what it's like to be a hot chick. I was eighteen and played a little high school ball, so I was attractive to a fella who was attracted to the fellas. If I looked like Danny DeVito, I'm sure I would have ended up hoofing it the entire way.

I stuck my thumb out again, and another car got me to the top of the canyon, at Mulholland Boulevard. Then, luckily, a friend of mine from high school named Stacy happened to drive by, recognized me, and gave me a lift back to my dad's garage.

I borrowed some cash from my dad and stepmom Lynn, and Chris borrowed his mom's car to give me a ride to Santa Monica to get the bike. I then had the joy of dealing with the dapper gent behind the counter at the impound lot. I know I teed off on tow-truck drivers in my last book, but the guys who work at the impound lot make tow-truck drivers look like Prince Harry after a bath.

Getting the bike out of impound cost me $70, ironically exactly what I had made that day. At eleven that night I drove back in the cold from Santa Monica, arriving at my garage by midnight. I had left my house at six A.M. that day. I spent eighteen hours of my life on this ordeal and broke even. Five and half hours later, my alarm went off again for another stimulating day of painting with Andy.

Looking back, I think rather than suffering through the several years of misery you'll soon read about I should have just bitten the bullet, gotten it on with the gay guy, and made him my sugar daddy. But behindsight is 20/20.

6

TIME FOR THIS BIRD TO SPREAD ITS WINGS AND FLOP: THE LAUREL CANYON APARTMENT, PT. 1

NORTH HOLLYWOOD, CA

YEAR RENTED:	1984
RENT:	$380 A MONTH
	600 SQUARE FEET
	ONE BEDROOM
	ONE BATH
	ONE FUTON, TWO DUDES

EVENTUALLY my stepmom decided I needed to grow up and move out of my bedroom/garage. It was her idea of tough love, and my dad went along with it. He isn't big on confrontation. He's just a piece of driftwood calmly going down the stream of life avoiding the rapids and the whirlpools and forever flowing toward the great storm drain in the sky. Plus they needed a place for his '79 Buick Regal.

I ended up in a one-bedroom apartment on Laurel Canyon Boulevard in North Hollywood. This was the infamous apartment where I lived with The Weez. After my parole from North Hollywood High in 1982 and The Weez's time-served release in 1983, we discovered each other. Maybe it was our mutual love of cars or the fact that he always had a bong loaded and ready to go, or maybe it was the VCR and the *Taboo II* VHS cassette. You have to remember that The Weez had actual possessions—a TV set, stereo, et cetera—so therefore in my mind, he was rich. It was probably all of the above and maybe just a little pixie dust that had us looking for our first apartment together.

Our unit was on the second story and faced the west. It was right off of Laurel Canyon, one of the busiest thoroughfares in the world. Summers in the San Fernando Valley saw many days in triple digits. And unfortunately for us the apartment had no central air, no swamp cooler, not even a window-mounted unit. Even hours after the sun had gone down the stucco on the outside of the building would be hot enough to fry an egg on, thus turning the apartment into a kiln. Yet The Weez would quickly fall asleep on the shared futon in our Easy-Bake bedroom while I paced and panted like a Saint Bernard at Burning Man. The only way I could fall asleep was to stand in the shower, douse myself in cold water, dive onto the futon without drying myself off, and fire up the oscillating fan. When The Weez's clock radio would go off at six A.M., my pillow would smell like mildew. But I was fresh as a daisy and looking forward to a day of toiling in the sun with illegal aliens.

As I said, The Weez and I shared a futon. Not in a gay way: It was out of desperation. Let me stress how horrible futons are. A futon is the world's most uncomfortable sofa that folds out into the world's most uncomfortable bed. I'm convinced the word *futon* is Japanese for "bear trap." I happen to know this is a secret ploy to pay us back for Hiroshima.

I have a theory about mattress height and its relationship to a person's level of success. When you hit the optimal distance between the top of your mattress and your floor, then life is good. Here's how it works. If your mattress is lying directly on the floor, you're a loser. If it's on a box spring that's on the floor, you've added seven inches but you're probably still working at a car wash. If you add the five inches for a cheap metal frame, you're in better shape and probably somewhere in the middle class. Conversely, you don't want the mattress to be too high off the ground. That puts you on a makeshift loft in a bachelor apartment or prison bunk. I became obsessed with this idea one day and went around measuring various mattresses. After exhaustive and costly research, I've determined that 30.3 inches is the target we should all strive for. That's the height of a good pillow-top mattress on a nice box spring and frame.

Our one-bedroom had one bathroom whose upkeep was a notch below a Greyhound bus depot in Beirut. We had a tub that was in constant use. Not for baths, but as a vomitubium. That's another sign of where you are in life. When you're vomiting into the tub and sitting on the toilet simultaneously because your bathroom is so small, that's not just a sign you had a bad night or had some bad clams. That means you're having a bad life.

The one nice room in the place was the kitchen, and we had a diner booth in there. It was a burgundy Naugahyde diner booth that fit perfectly into the breakfast nook. I built a table to go with it so it looked like a fifties diner. Except instead of drinking milkshakes and listening to Buddy Holly, we were doing tequila shots and listening to Van Halen. We didn't even have a normal shot glass; we had a jumbo version with two lines on it. The line at the midway mark was labeled HOG. An inch above that was a line that read MAN. I'd usually opt for what I called "the Mog," halfway between Man and Hog. But back to the booth.

A booth is a magical place filled with good friends, warm pie, and warmer memories. Nothing bad has ever happened in a booth. The booth's evil cousin is the chamber—the gas chamber, torture chamber, chambering a round, the chamber pot. Nothing good ever happened in a chamber.

A little backstory on our booth. I managed to get through eleven years of organized football without ever damaging my knees. But when I was playing a pickup football game at age twenty-one, while running for a touchdown in the open field, I heard a pop. My right knee was momentarily dislocated. When I hobbled into the apartment that afternoon, I said to The Weez, "I think I blew my knee out." He said, "That's bad timing because we have to grab this booth that's in the back of the Bla Bla Café on Ventura before somebody else takes it. It won't be there tomorrow morning." I told him I shouldn't be moving furniture, to which The Weez responded, "Don't be a pussy." This is another difference between men and women. If Janet told Chrissy she hurt her knee blowing Jack, Chrissy would say, "Oh, sweetie. Let me get you an ice pack," not call her a fag and tell her, "We're picking up Mr. Furley's player piano tonight."

Smash-cut to me pushing a huge diner booth up a flight of stairs with a blown-out knee. The booth was so big that I had to pull the pins on the hinges and remove the front door of the apartment. But even then it wouldn't quite make it through. This was now midnight, and my knee was throbbing. I told The Weez he was on his own and went to bed. He took it to the alley behind the Jack in the Box and broke it into three pieces with a hammer and reassembled it in the apartment. The next day I was greeted with a shiny red diner booth and a swollen black-and-blue knee. That's where my self-esteem was at. Six months later, I had my meniscus surgically repaired.

What the fuck is up with the human body? As I write this, I have a torn meniscus in the same knee. This time the weapon of choice was a jump rope. I've skipped rope on almost a daily basis for at least the last twenty years. I can do it in my sleep and am so smooth I could do it with a tumbler of Sunny D on my head and not spill a drop. But yet the other night, five minutes into my routine, my meniscus decided it was time to tear again. One meniscus tear from running in a straight line, the other from skipping rope. This is in a life littered with street fights, kickboxing tournaments, catastrophic scaffolding failures, and subsequent falls with nary a complaint from Mr. Meniscus. The only good news is that according to my calculations, the next time my meniscus is due to tear I'll be in an urn.

Our building was managed by a guy named Al. He was a cryptic, weird perv who lived beneath us. He wore horn-rimmed glasses, a windbreaker, had a ton of pomade in his hair, and constantly carried two things. The first was a beer in a worn-out styrofoam koozie. It had the logo for some beer that they haven't made since the seventies, and you could see the indentations where his grip had slowly worn it down like the Colorado River shaping the Grand Canyon. I'm constantly amazed by how long dumb people hang on to ten-cent items. But I digress. The second thing Al always carried was a piece. He had a .38 Special on him at all times, and it was loaded. He said it was for security, but I actually felt less safe around him. We found out about this fact in a weird way. We lived directly above him and made a lot of noise, as you'll read about a few short paragraphs from now. I asked him one day if our constant raucous partying was cutting into his sleep. He said he wore earplugs, but not because of us. Then he asked, "You want to know why?" This is a question that never gets pulled out when the person being asked actually does want to know why. I reluctantly said yes. He lifted his windbreaker, revealed a revolver tucked into his waistband, and said, "In case I have to use this." What's the plan? You wear earplugs so if you have to put a cap in a guy who breaks into your apartment you won't damage your eardrums, but you wouldn't be able to hear the guy breaking into your kitchen in the first place? Al slept like he lived at a gun range.

The only thing Al loved more than his gun was his garden hose. It was his prized possession. It was on one of those rolling spools made of cheap PVC plastic tubing. But he treated it like a Fabergé egg. He kept it inside his apartment to protect it. You know, from all those international hose thieves you read about in the paper. He wouldn't even let me borrow it the one time I asked to hose off my porch. He said he didn't have one. I could see it behind him in his kitchen through the screen door, but he was trying to do that blocking move where he stood in front of it. "No, I don't have a hose." As if I hadn't lived there for three years and seen him use it a thousand times. I pointed it out and he said, "Oh, that hose." He then proceeded to tell me he had been entrusted with the care of the hose by the owner so he couldn't let it out of his sight. But if I wanted to schedule it, he could come up and hose off my porch for me. I love when people get overprotective of their valueless junk. Al acted like I'd asked to take his mother to the Poconos to fuck her over the Labor Day weekend. What did he think was going to happen—I'd throw the hose over my shoulder and make a break for it shouting, "See you, sucker! I'm heading to Mexico to start a new life"?

Al was, as I said, a perv. He would often say about the many ladies we had over, "Why don't you send one of them down to me?" These were nineteen-year-old junior-college students. Did he think we were going to tell our chick friends, "Hey, go downstairs and suck off our sixty-three-year-old apartment manager who lives with his dog Skipper"?

One evening there was a knock on the door. I opened it to find Al standing there holding a giant cardboard box. He stepped into our living room and announced he'd brought some gifts the guy in unit 5 had left behind when he moved out. He opened the box to reveal a murderer's row of dildos, vibrators, strap-ons, and butt plugs. They were all out of their shrink-wrap and were what auto dealers would euphemistically describe as "previously owned." They were used. Al set the box down and headed back to his apartment to rape Skipper. But before he left, he doubled down on the creepitude by telling us he also found a blow-up doll but was keeping that one for himself. Now, I'm not uptight or a germophobe (see previous Tijuana chapter), but even I announced I wasn't going near that box. These had been in strangers' orifices. And this was long before Purell. It was the mid-eighties, which might as well have just been called the mid-AIDSies. Fast-forward twenty-four hours. One of our female friends had donned the strap-on and was chasing me around while Ray bashed me in the head with a dildo the size of a six-foot sub.

Our place was a mess. We had two rabbits and a kitten named Max. One of our girlfriends got the kitten from someone outside a supermarket, and somehow we ended up taking care of it. The Weez was the one who brought home the rabbits. He thought it would be fun to get stoned and watch them run around the apartment. And he was right. There is nothing cuter in the world than a kitten wrestling with an overgrown rabbit. Unlike the human residents of the apartment, the rabbits were well fed. They'd eat whole heads of lettuce. They were "dwarf rabbits," and the guy who sold them to The Weez said they wouldn't get any bigger. They started out the size of an apple, but within a month they had gotten up to watermelon and had outgrown their cage. So we'd let the rabbits just hop around the apartment shitting pellets all over the place. (One of the benefits of having rabbits as pets is that you can clean up their shit with a pool cue.) As they loped around the place, Max the kitten would pounce on them. He'd be biting their ears and getting lost in their big ball of fur. A lot of this interspecies wrestling would happen in the infield of our slot-car track.

Keep that image in your mind for the next story. We had bounced our rent check. Shocking, I know. So I needed to go down to the bank to deposit some money. On the way there, I saw a guy selling speakers out of a van and of course being the wise financier that I was, bought the speakers instead of depositing the money. A moment about vans. A lot of stuff in the seventies and early eighties happened in vans. They used to be cool back then. You'd customize them. There was a guy in my neighborhood growing up who had RADICAL RICH written on the side of his van in rainbow tape. Now vans fall firmly into my more-harm-than-good category. For every piece of furniture that has been moved with a van there are ten hookers, schoolkids, or CNN camera crews who have been abducted in one. But back to the speakers. I brought them home and immediately said, "We've got to test these out." The Weez hijacked his brother's CD player, which was brand-new technology at the time, and we put on Van Halen's "Eruption." In the midst of Eddie's screaming guitar solo I thought I felt some vibration that wasn't coming from the speakers and told, nay, shouted at, The Weez to turn it down. I went to the door. It was the owner of the building, Jim. He was there to confront us about the bounced rent check. He said he could hear the noise blaring from our apartment in his car as he was driving up. Please take a moment to picture yourself as a landlord: You're driving to your building, you're a full block away, and you can hear what is to your fifty-plus-year-old mind an ungodly racket blasting from one of your units. You then knock on the door to ask about a bounced rent check and a collection of stoners opens it to reveal a kitten fighting two rabbits in the middle of a slot-car track on a carpet covered in shit pellets and a capsized bong.

We eventually had to get rid of the rabbits, so The Weez killed them. Not with a cleaver—he just thought it would be a good idea to release them into the wild. So he brought them up into the hills where he grew up and set them free. Except that those hills are full of coyotes. You can't have a cat or even a small dog in that area because a coyote will jump into your yard and eat it. The Weez went past those houses way into the brushy hills and said, "Be free." I'm sure the rabbits were pounced on by coyotes before he even got to his car. How did he think they were going to survive? They went from a mall pet shop to our living room to the wild. The only way they made it through the first night was if the coyotes thought it was a trap. I like to imagine two coyotes having this conversation. "Check it out. There's two declawed morbidly obese rabbits some stoner Jew just dropped off. Let's go get 'em. We'll eat like kings." Then the other coyote says, "Hang on, Burt, this is way too good to be true. Nobody could be that stupid. Those things have got to be filled with gunpowder."

One of the classier touches of the apartment was the Centipede arcade game. The Weez's father had done a transmission job (his dad being one of the eight Jews on the planet who does automotive work) and had received the game as trade. It ended up in our kitchen. Initially The Weez set it up to work for free until I yelled at him that we were losing money on the deal. People would come into our place to nail their girlfriends, smoke our weed, use our phone, and eat what little food we had, so I wanted a couple of quarters in return. Once every six months we'd remember we had $41 in quarters sitting in the machine. And despite the fact that we were practically broke, we decided it was "free money" and thus "party money." It was immediately spent on a dime bag of weed (paid for in quarters). We'd then take the rest to the Sherman Oaks Galleria, the mall where they filmed *Fast Times at Ridgemont High*, and ironically wasted the quarters playing arcade games. If we had anything left, we'd walk across the mall to the theater, catch a movie, and end the day with a slice of pizza.

The point is that we were working adults; we weren't in junior high. We had slot cars and bongs and rabbits and arcade games but no health insurance. We were idiots. To illustrate this point, please enjoy this list of things we did that normal adults don't do.

- Long before the *Seinfeld* "master of your domain" episode, The Weez, some of our other bonehead friends, and I had a contest to see who could go the longest without masturbating. The winner was to receive a sweatshirt that read COLD JERKY on it, but it was really more about pride. The current record was twenty-one days. Unfortunately for The Weez, he thought it was nineteen. So that day he was loaded for bear and ready to have at himself. When I informed him that the record stood at twenty-one, the normally mild-mannered 127-pounder lunged at me, grabbed me by the lapels, pushed me against the wall and yelled, *"DON'T FUCK WITH ME!"*

- Grabbing the casing above the door leading into the kitchen like a chin-up bar with my fingertips, I attempted to thread my legs through the opening in my arms, got my feet tangled up, and landed directly on my head.

- To protect the innocent, who now have children and careers, I'll keep this generic. One of the guys I was hanging with at the time brought a sack of bootleg Quaaludes back to the apartment. Another buddy inhaled fourteen of them, washing them down with tequila. This guy had recently nearly OD'd. So the buyer of the 'ludes freaked out, grabbed the bag, and ran for the bathroom to flush them. I jumped in front of the door to block him. So he took the next logical step, ran out to the side yard, and buried them.

• Then there was the time The Weez ignited a fart and I actually lit a cigarette off the flame that shot out of his ass. By the end of this book you'll hear a few more stories about lighting farts. I wish I didn't love it as much as I do. Years later when I was telling this story to Dr. Drew, I lit some farts in the studio. Drew is a classy and, dare I say, uptight guy. But he went from disgusted to fascinated to doubled-over laughing. There's no one on the planet who wouldn't laugh at that. James Lipton would bust up if The Weez lit a fart at Sir Laurence Olivier's funeral.

The apartment was a flophouse for assorted losers, addicts, and the unemployable. I used to meet people on the street and let them crash with us. I spent a lot of time in our garage, which opened to the alley behind the apartment building. I'd do quite a bit of wrenching down there; it was my own little Zen garden. I met a dude in the alley once who claimed to be a quick-draw six-shooter champion. Remember, this is pre-Google so I had to take him at his word. He was a complete alcoholic and one day showed up with both forearms in casts. He said he'd been kicked by a horse.

Another time The Weez came home to find a guy asleep on our couch. He was a fortysomething haggard alcoholic cement contractor who was missing his two front teeth. I had met him in the alley and he threw himself on the mercy of my court because his old lady had just kicked him out. His name was Mike. He was fully dressed and covered up to his thighs in dried concrete as if he'd waded through a cement river. I said to The Weez, "Look. He's a cool guy, it's okay." At that very moment, in his sleep, Mike sat up and hocked a loogie into the air. He must have thought he was at his house or in the drunk tank, but he hacked up something onto our curtain without missing one Z.

There are a couple of other Mike stories that don't necessarily involve the apartment, but since I'm on the topic, here we go. In '85 when I was doing an addition on my grandmother's house, he and his brother came over to help with the concrete. After putting in a full day's work, my grandmother brought out dinner and we ate at the patio table. She even brought out a bottle of white wine. Mike shot down a large glass of wine like he was giving his liver a Gatorade dump and then held the empty glass up, grunted, and gestured at Grandma for a refill. Mike's brother, a typewriter repairman (he's probably living large right now), would argue with him in front of my grandparents, shouting profanities. After a couple glasses of wine, Mike's brother had to relieve himself. So he politely asked to be excused, but instead of going into the house he walked twenty feet away and started taking a leak in the ivy. All of us could see him. Even Mike, the indoor loogie hocker, was outraged. "Hey douchebag. What the fuck is wrong with you?" he shouted. "You're pissing in front of Grandma!" Mike's brother responded, "What? I turned my back!"

Another time after a day pouring a concrete slab, Mike and I pulled up to the Golden Chopstick for a little pork fried rice. Mike drove a Ranchero with caved-in driver's-side door, which meant he had to climb through the window to get out. It was like a retarded version of the Dukes of Hazzard. Strike that, a *more* retarded version of the Dukes of Hazzard. Just as he crawled out of his piece of shit, Mike noticed a good-looking chick waiting outside, presumably for her boyfriend to arrive. Mike looked her up and down and said to me, "You wanna go get some?" I stared back at him with a look that said, "You drive a Ranchero with a concave door, you're toothless and covered in concrete. Why would she go anywhere near us?" Mike reiterated, "C'mon, man, let's go get some of that fine pussy." Rather than say what I was thinking and insult the man, I simply said, "Let's just eat." Mike replied, "What, you don't want to get laid? Don't you like pussy?" He said this matter-of-factly, as if it had been offered up. He acted like she had come over and offered to service both of us in the bathroom of the restaurant and I had turned her down. I'm sure the only reason he didn't call me a fag was because he was too much of a gentleman to use that term.

This was the type of guy I'd meet in the alley and allow into my abode. I attracted them for some reason. I was the porch light to their alcoholic moth.

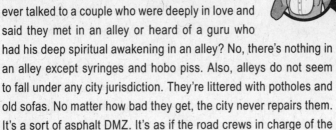

When I'm in charge there won't be any more alleys. They're officially more harm than good. Have you ever talked to a couple who were deeply in love and said they met in an alley or heard of a guru who had his deep spiritual awakening in an alley? No, there's nothing in an alley except syringes and hobo piss. Also, alleys do not seem to fall under any city jurisdiction. They're littered with potholes and old sofas. No matter how bad they get, the city never repairs them. It's a sort of asphalt DMZ. It's as if the road crews in charge of the alleys are based in Mozambique.

But as I said, I was always in my garage off the alley wrenching on something. It was my sanctuary. One morning after a night of partying we were heading out to Good Neighbor, a great breakfast place, to tamp down our hangovers with some banana pancakes. When we got to the alley, everything had been tagged. I didn't care about the alley itself, but they had tagged the garage door. *My* garage door. This was my personal Pearl Harbor. I had been attacked on my home turf. The tag simply said "Eggbert." Snake, interestingly enough said, "I bet Toad knows who this is." Toad was another guy we knew. Fortunately, that was as far into the nickname animal kingdom as we had to go. Toad was the guy who knew shit. So we piled into Snake's car to find Toad. We hadn't even traveled two blocks before a car passed us going in the opposite direction and somebody yelled, "That was Toad!" So we banged a U-turn and started following him and his buddies. He turned onto Ventura Boulevard and we pulled up alongside of him at the first red light and told them to pull over, we needed to talk. He said nothing and kept driving. So we followed. Unfortunately, there was an LAPD cruiser that was behind both of us for what seemed like a hundred miles. Eventually the cop turned off, Snake turned up the heat, and Mr. Toad's Wild Ride began. He and his crew started evading us, thinking we were chasing them. We eventually pulled up next to them and Snake, who's a smart guy but a little bit nuts, rolled down the window and yelled, "You either pull over now or I will find you and do something horrible to you and you won't know when." They agreed, pulled over, and we explained that we weren't after them but wanted the goods on Eggbert. We demanded he cough up the information. At first he was coy but eventually started singing like a canary. He dropped a dime on his buddy Eggbert. The guy's name was Greg Bertrand, thus Eggbert. I knew his older brother and knew where he lived, so we went to his house. Some of my buddies wanted to just kick in the door and then kick in his face, but I convinced everyone to play it cool. I was the Jimmy Carter of the group. I knocked on the door and his parents answered. I said, "I need to talk to you about your son." They asked what the problem was and we told them he had tagged our place. His mom was not surprised. She even mentioned that they were missing some spray-paint cans. Eggbert was just stepping out of the shower when his mom called for him. He entered the living room wearing only a towel. She pounced on him, "Were you out doing graffiti last night?" A shocked and dumbfounded Eggbert blurted out, "Yes." This poor son of a bitch was out tagging all night without any witnesses and by ten the next morning an angry group of tag-ees was at his house. My favorite part was that his dad couldn't get over the Eggbert handle. He asked, "Eggbert? What the hell kind of stupid nickname is that?" I explained to him and his parents that our drunken manager Al carried a sidearm and that Eggbert would be better off dealing with us than him. Greg ended up having to repaint the entire alley.

A little PSA on tagging. When you see graffiti, you assume it's done by black or Mexican gangbangers from the inner city. Well, this kid was blond and from the suburbs. So next time you see the side of a building or a billboard tagged up, pause for a moment, and then still assume they're black or Mexican. Who are we kidding?

In another of our long series of boneheaded financial decisions, The Weez and I decided to kick in $750 each, well over our rent at the time, to cobble together fifteen hundred to buy a limo he had found. It was a twenty-two-foot-long 1964 Cadillac Series 75, the kind you'd see Elvis or the Beatles in. We picked it up by the airport on a Sunday night, and shortly thereafter the road trips commenced. We'd pile

1985—Across the street from the apartment. Note my truck in the foreground, plus the shirtless Weez and underpants-clad Ray.

into the limo and go visit our friends who had actually made it out of the Valley and gone to college.

One of our usual destinations was Palm Springs for spring break. We'd just hop from motel to motel getting drunk by the pools. There was a place called the Ocatillo Lodge—it's still there, though it's gone from looking like someplace Lucy and Ricky would visit to someplace Ricky and Ricky would visit. Palm Springs is now a gay mecca. Back then it was the kind of place where the following story could happen.

I was sitting in some random person's room. I have no idea who, we used to just get shit-faced and bounce from room to room. The phone rang, so I picked it up. This was long before caller ID, so when a phone rang you'd just answer it. I don't know why, it's not like I'd pick it up and it would be my dad. I said, "Hello?" and there was a guy on the other end. He said, angrily, "Where's Stacy?" I said, "I don't know who Stacy is, I'm just sitting in this room." The guy said bluntly, "Bullshit." I reiterated that I had no idea who Stacy was. He replied, "You put her on the phone or I'm gonna come over there and kick your ass." I said, "Come on down," and hung up. I had no idea who this guy was or if he was built like Brock Lesnar. Ten minutes later there was a knock on the door, and I opened it to reveal two dudes. They were just average white guys from the Valley and announced they were there to kick my ass. So we stepped out into the walkway in front of the room. The first guy threw a bad punch at me, missed, and I hit him in the face. He went down. The second guy then took a swing and I dodged and punched him in the face. He went down too. I casually said, "You should get some ice on that," and they got up and walked away. I got in a fight with two dudes over a girl I never met.

We'd also taken the limo to visit our friend who went to college in Santa Barbara. One time on the way home we had the limo full. There were twelve people packed in there, and Chris was driving.

We were coming up to a red light, and Chris told everyone in the back of the limo, "No brakes!" Everyone started freaking out and screaming. We blew through the red light, fortunately didn't get T-boned, and drove right onto a freeway entrance. The brakes were always an issue with the limo. It was roadworthy, we rebuilt the engine and suspension, but it was so heavy that we'd burn through the brakes pretty quickly.

There were many other road trips that you'll soon read about, but they didn't involve the limo. So let's get back to the apartment.

One night Chris and The Weez came home, each with a bottle of tequila in his belly and a skank on his arm. Chris was particularly out of control. Since I didn't have a room of my own to escape to, I took The Weez aside and tried to enlist him to control Chris. But he had other plans. The fact that he had used the tequila to wash down some mushrooms was preventing him from being able to "maintain." Moreover, he was about to hook up with a fat chick. Now, I know the large ladies need loving too, I've got no beef with them, no pun intended. But I knew The Weez would regret it the next day. So I gave him one of my many "You're high. Let me save you from yourself"–style lectures. It seemed to work, but then I turned for a moment and when I looked back I found him making out with his BBW. So I said fuck it and decided to bail out and head over to Ray's for the night.

The next morning I returned and instituted a new apartment policy. After surveying the Sodom and Gomorrah–like landscape composed of piles of hungover people, broken beer bottles, and cigarette butts, I declared "Clean or Leave." I couldn't take the floozies and flunkies littering our place anymore. I'd have to work construction in the morning and the gang would be in the living room making a bunch of noise and I'd come out in my bathrobe and yell, "Hey!

Keep it down. Some people have to work in the morning." They'd yell, "Shut up, Walt!" and rip another bong load.

The Weez eventually moved out because it had gotten too crazy. And this was The Weez. That's like John Belushi going, "I can't handle this anymore." Unlike the gentiles, who, when they leave home don't return, The Weez was able to go back to his parents' house. But he took his futon and the limo with him.

7
WITH FRIENDS LIKE RAY . . . :
RAY'S APARTMENT

NORTH HOLLYWOOD VIA GERMANY

YEAR BUILT:	1963
RENT:	LOW
	TWO BICEPS
	ZERO BATHROOM ETIQUETTE

LIKE most people from depressed chaotic families, I tried to spend as much time away from my houses as possible. One of my homes away from home was the apartment of my buddy Ray Oldhafer. I met Ray at Colfax Elementary in the fifth grade. I didn't play football with him, unlike my other friends growing up, because he was a huge German man-boy and was too big to play in the same league as me. He was ripped. Ray was a year older, four inches taller, and fifty pounds heavier than everyone else in our class. He was not husky; he was built like an action hero. It's rare to see fourteen-year-olds with veins in their arms and calves like a Roman soldier. Ray was the bench-press champion at our junior high. One time I walked into the weight room to find a spindly geek on the ground with a barbell over his neck pinning him to the floor. I asked him what happened. He told me that Ray had commanded him to lie down so he could put the weights across his throat. That's how scary Ray was. He didn't even have to physically beat a nerd into submission, he could just ask and said nerd would humiliate himself.

Don't get me wrong; Ray is one of the sweetest guys you'll ever meet. He just grew up in an equally, yet differently, fucked-up family as mine. He's a sensitive guy despite his size and tendency to hurt and humiliate. He's like a big St. Bernard that knocks over tables and toddlers. It means no harm; it just doesn't know that it's big and dumb. He would ask me when we were kids, "Why is your lawn so high?" or "Why is your room so small?" or "Why doesn't your mom shave her armpits?" He wasn't trying to be mean or bust my balls, he genuinely wanted to know what was wrong with my family.

Ray was and continues to be the least subtle person I know. When I was a kid I used to sneak into movie theaters, sometimes with Ray, sometimes without. If I wasn't with Ray we'd go to the back, wait for someone to exit, and slither in through the open door. If we were with Ray, we had a different technique. Ray would walk up to the front door of the theater and bang on the glass until someone going to the bathroom noticed. Ray would wave them over and yell at them to open the door.

And Ray had an ingenious technique for getting personal information out of people. He would look them straight in the eye and ask. Like the time he asked my mom if it was true that she met my stepdad at a primal-scream encounter group, which she had. Ray turned right around and informed me of this fact. Another time when we were teens I was telling Ray how cheap my dad was and Ray immediately told him. He didn't think twice about it. It was a fact and therefore needed to be shared. God forbid you ever get a pimple or put on five pounds if you're friends with Ray. You will be notified without delay or sensitivity. He wouldn't say, "Are those new jeans? They look a little snug." It would be "You're getting fat," followed by him grabbing your love handle and pinching it until it bruised. That's Ray in a nutshell. He's intensely conscious of his own feelings but is blissfully unaware of when he backs over other people's.

That's not to say that Ray didn't sometimes intentionally create awkward situations for his own amusement. Ray's mom had a friend named Kathy. She was a heavyset woman—about five four, 240. The first time I met her, she'd come into Ray's mom's apartment and started yelling at her son, who was visiting. I said to Ray, "Who was that woman? She could play guard for the Rams." As soon as she walked back into the room, Ray said, "Kathy. This is my friend Adam. He says you could play guard for the Rams." Ray is like the world's worst parrot.

Another time Kathy made the grave error of sitting down in Ray's mom's apartment and trying to talk on the phone. Ray was about sixteen at the time. While one ear was occupied with the phone receiver, her other ear was wide open for attack. Ray came up behind her and put his dick in her ear. I wish I could tell you why, but there was no good reason.

Speaking of dicks, Ray once asked his mother who had a bigger dick: his dad or her new boyfriend, Jim. Her reply was very telling and shows where Ray got some of his gift for creating awkwardness. Without hesitation she replied, "Jim has more girth."

I loved Ray's mom, and one of my earlier Ray memories involved an awkward exchange with her. I used to stay over at Ray's when I could because unlike my mom—who, if she did manage to get some food in the fridge wouldn't know what to do with it—Ray's mom actually cooked what scraps found their way into the Oldhafer estate.

One night I was having a sleepover at Ray's when he produced a magazine called *Frisky*. It was easily twenty years old when we were looking at it. It was a crazy 1950s nudie mag full of topless chicks in huge panties with huge beehive hairdos and huge cans with huge saucerlike nipples. We didn't have any Internet back then, so it was any porn in a storm. Ray had to go upstairs and babysit the neighbor kids, so I told him I'd hang back with the *Frisky*. I was sleeping on the floor, of course. Ray's mom came in and with her thick German accent said, "Get up, I'll get you a mattress." I had quickly slipped the *Frisky* under the blanket, so I said, "No, I'm okay. I'm comfortable, I don't need a mattress." She said, "Get up." I repeated, "I like it on the floor, I'm used to it. I sleep in a closet at my house." She wasn't buying it and eventually started tugging at the blanket. I was holding the *Frisky* and the blanket at the same time while having this retarded tug of war. I bunched up the blanket and the *Frisky* and stood up. She said, "Give me the blanket." I managed to keep the *Frisky* under wraps. I'm not sure how. That secret has been lost to history.

Later on, Ray came back from babysitting and I told him what had just gone down. "Whew. You would not believe what just happened. I really dodged a bullet. I was looking at the *Frisky* and she came in to make the bed and caught me. But she never saw it. I kept it out of sight." The following morning, we were all eating breakfast and he said, "Hey, Mom, guess who had a *Frisky* magazine under the blanket last night?"

· · ·

Ray was a troublemaker and I used to get into all kinds of shit with him. Another time I was staying over at his apartment and his mom walked out with two bags of garbage and told us to take them out. The dumpster in that apartment complex was located in a odd position. There was a long skinny driveway and then an immediate 90-degree turn. And there was no lighting. Ray walked out with his bag and I talked to his mom for a beat and walked out a minute later with the other one. Ray thought I was right behind him and didn't realize I had hung back. As I was walking down the dark driveway, I heard the sound of garbage flying and a woman screaming, "OH SHIT! OH SHIT!" Ray thought it would be funny to hide behind the dumpster in the dark and then jump out to scare the crap out of me. My delay was longer than he thought and he ended up traumatizing some poor sweet little old lady named Debbie from the building. All 225 pounds of him. Ray doesn't do anything half-assed, either—he goes all in. He didn't just step out and say, "Boo." He leapt out and screamed like a knife-wielding maniac.

When I was thirteen I was babysitting my neighbor and invited Ray over to hang out. Ray was the only guy I knew who ate more than me. We looted that pantry like a Best Buy during a race riot. Five minutes later, we were roasting marshmallows over the stove when mine caught fire. It was fully engulfed in flames and burning with napalm-esque ferocity. Realizing it could no longer be consumed, I didn't want to miss an opportunity for a little horseplay. So I held the flaming marshmallow up by its skewer and announced I was "The Great Adam, world-renowned fire eater." I then proceeded to arch back and open my mouth as wide as I could and mime swallowing the flame, being careful not to come too close to my delicate face. Just as I was pulling it away from my open mouth, Ray shoved my elbow and the flaming marshmallow became one with my cheek.

Ray really shined on Halloween. He once wore Jolson-esque

shoe-polish blackface and an Afro wig for a costume in eighth grade. And speaking of Ray, Halloween, and blackface, one year I decided to dress up as Mr. T. I was over at Snake's place getting my head shaved for Mr. T's signature hairstyle. Snake had the clippers out for himself, too, because he was going as a Mohawk Indian. Ray walked in not knowing what was going on. He didn't have a costume planned, but he saw the clippers and said, "Put me down for a Hare Krishna."

He had long, straight hair at the time, too. In the end he looked so authentic that people at the Halloween party thought he actually had become a Hare Krishna. This was 1984, before Michael Jordan hit the scene and bald became cool. Bald was weird back then. When

1984—The apartment. Ray as the only Hare Krishna who would beat you with his tambourine.

Ray came home, his mother broke down in tears. My haircut actually garnered a response from my normally indifferent dad, too. I came back with the Mr. T and he muttered, "Good luck getting a job now."

1984—Me and my buzz cut at our friend Liz's house.

I'd like to present you with some of Ray's greatest hits, just to give you a better sense of who I was dealing with. Some are from our youth, others from when we were adults. The sad part is you won't be able to tell which are which.

- Ray has broken two guys' arms: Chris's brother Ricky's and Dr. Bruce's (the guy who often filled in for Dr. Drew). Not intentionally—it was just roughhousing gone wrong. One of them was nine and the other was forty-seven.

- When Ray was later working on Kimmel's show, Jimmy had a human-interest guest—Kyle Maynard, a quadruple amputee wrestler who was there to talk about overcoming adversity. He boasted that he had such extraordinary upper-body strength that no one could pull what was left of his arms apart once he locked them in place. Cut to Ray on top of a guy in a wheelchair trying to tear his arms apart.

121

- Also while working on Jimmy's show, he was formally warned by ABC human resources that he could no longer play something called The Breathing Game. This consisted of Ray getting you in a bear hug/headlock and putting his giant hand over your mouth while pinching your nose closed. The "game" part was whether you could get out of his grip before you passed out.

- Ray was at a liquor store with Snake, Carl, and a couple of other guys trying to buy a bottle of whiskey. The squatty Armenian guy behind the register would not sell it to them. Snake threw down twenty-two bucks for the eighteen-dollar bottle and said, "That should cover it with tax." The guy was pissed and about to get more pissed. Ray then said "Nice nail," commenting on his long pinky nail. The clerk then took out his Day-Glo leather key chain and hit Snake with it. Snake retaliated by hitting the guy with an actual chain. The Armenian gentleman then reached behind the counter. Ray assumed he was going for a gun and started to leave. As he was walking out he felt the sting of an aluminum bat on his shoulder. Ray retaliated by punching out the window of the store. What makes this especially impressive/scary was that this was a floor-to-ceiling pane of three-eighth-inch-thick tempered glass. Ray ended up with a shard in his hand and had to remove it with channel locks.

- Every year the big event at North Hollywood High was an unsanctioned broomball game between two girls' groups from our school—the Puffs and the Shana Clares. Broomball is hockey, but instead of pucks and sticks you use a volleyball and taped-up brooms. They'd rent out the local ice-skating rink after closing on a Saturday and the whole school would show up, most of them drinking B they'd BYO'd. Ray and Chris decided this would be the perfect place and time to do some stupid shit. I was always game to go along with their ideas, but when they told me the plan, I decided this was one mission I would not choose to accept. But I was there to witness it. The game was in full swing and the chicks were going at it hard on the ice. I heard brakes locking and tires screeching behind the rink. The two rear fire doors burst open. Ray and Chris, wearing nothing but tennis shoes and paper grocery bags on their heads and junk, hopped the wall and began to run across the ice. Sticking to his plan, Ray went all the way to the far goal and back, running the gauntlet of girls who were armored with pads and armed with broomsticks. These chicks were already whipped up from the game and went after him. He gave a forearm shiver to the titties of each and every girl who blocked his way and attempted to grab the paper bag covering his ball bag. That's how nuts Ray is—one slip and he would have been completely nude sliding across the ice in front of the entire school.

It was at parties where Ray was really in full effect. If there was a cake, his fist was going into it; if there was a shampoo bottle, his dick was going into it; and if there was a pool, *you* were going into it. Eventually people started throwing themselves into the pool on their own volition. That way they could at least take out their wallet first and not have their shirt ripped. One of our friends, Jack Donitz, saw Ray enter a party and decided to cut to the chase. He slipped off his loafers, took out his wallet, and tossed himself, fully dressed, into the pool. When he resurfaced he found his shoe floating next to his head with his wallet sitting inside. Before he could grab it and return it safely to the edge of the pool Ray did a cannonball on it. You can't say he wasn't creative. He also once shot Jack's spear gun through his hamper and into his wall. Eventually we knew that if Ray was around, it meant trouble, and we developed a code. We used to have what we called DTR parties. DTR stood for "Don't tell Ray." The only time I'd ever see Ray upset is when he'd ask what we were doing that weekend and we'd tell him we were going to a party, he'd say, "Pick me up at nine," and we'd have to explain it was a DTR party. So in our world you could RSVP and BYOB for a DTRP.

. . .

For reasons that Freud would have a field day with that but remain unclear to me, Ray and a lot of the other guys I grew up with really enjoyed poop and pee. There are dogs who have urinated on less upholstery and apes who have flung less shit than Ray.

Our high school was built in the thirties and the locker room had separate lockers in the rear known as "the cage." It was made of old prison-type grate and went floor to ceiling, twenty-five feet high. It had a door but it was broken, and the only way to get out once you were in was for someone on the outside to go get a pair of needle-nose pliers. This was bad news if you were the poor schmuck Ray and Chris trapped in there. The locker rows were double-sided and about seven feet tall. There was only about five feet of space in between each row, so once Ray and Chris got their victim trapped in the cage, Chris would get atop the lockers and rain golden terror from above. The victim had nowhere to run and nowhere to hide. You couldn't even climb the cage because the holes in the grate were too small to accommodate fingers. That's not to say this treatment was only reserved for strangers and nerds: I suffered my time in the cage, too. And this behavior wasn't limited to just the locker room.

When we were in high school we had a friend named Alex. Why he hung out with us, I have no idea. Alex was a normal Jewish kid from what we called Hebrew Heights who later went to Berkeley and has since gone on to become a lawyer. But somehow back then he hooked up with two lowland gorillas from the Valley in the form of me and Ray. We used to mooch off him because unlike us he had a normal, intact family system who had two nickels to rub together. We used to convince him to spend some of those nickels on us. One of Ray's finer moments was when Alex took us out to Fatburger and treated him to a double King with cheese, large fries, and a shake. Ray repaid him in gold. While Alex was driving, Ray took out his dick and started pissing on him. This was unprompted by an argument, alcohol, drugs, or even a dare. And it wasn't a crazy weekend road trip either. This was your average Tuesday after school. That's what Alex got for spending his money on food for Ray. And talk about dangerous. We weren't in the parking lot. He was driving. You can't text while driving because it's too distracting. Imagine a large German guy pissing on you while you're behind the wheel. The best part was that Ray got indignant and refused to leave when Alex pulled over and told him to get out. He flat-out refused, shouting "What for?" I was in the backseat the whole time laughing like a maniac. And the angrier Alex got, the harder I laughed.

Ray also took a leak on Snake's leg. This time we weren't in a car; he did it under the table while we were eating at a breakfast place called Du-par's. Urine by its very nature is the same temperature as your body. So when a guy opens up on you under a table, you don't feel it until he's done. So after Ray had emptied his bladder onto Snake's Levi's, he got pissed and threw a glass of water at Ray. Ray retaliated by throwing an ashtray at Snake's head. This erupted into a full-fledged fight, and needless to say we received a lifetime ban from the Studio City Du-par's.

At a certain point Ray graduated from number one to number two. I think I know where it all began. One day when we were sixteen, Ray, Chris, and I cut fourth period. Ray needed to take a shit, so he headed into the bathroom and invited us. I knew that no good could come from me going in there, so I stayed behind. Chris did too. Momentarily. Once Ray was safely on the shitter, Chris went in. Out in the hallway I heard Chris kick open the stall door and yell, "Freeze, baby!" which was the catch phrase he'd shout before the piss hit the fan. I then heard Ray yell "No!" shortly followed by "My eye!" Chris was pissing all over poor Ray, who had his shorts around his ankles. This left Ray with no recourse but to reach down between his legs into the toilet, grab his breakfast from earlier that day, and whip it at Chris. Then I heard what sounded like a body hitting the floor, which was Chris trying to get out of the bathroom and slipping on the piss-covered tile. Fortunately, I never entered the fray. But that was the day the Geneva Convention was broken. It was the shit heard round the world.

Yet like America before Pearl Harbor, I could stay isolated for only so long before the carnage found its way to my shores. I remember vividly when I was pulled into World War Deuce. It was about eleven in the morning, third period. We had a hundred-year-old codger named Mr. Spathe for English. He was on the verge of death and didn't give a shit—unlike my other teachers, who were middle-aged and didn't give a shit. So halfway through class Ray just announced, "We're going to the bathroom." Spathe barely looked up. Me, Ray, and Chris left class. They headed to the bathroom and I was standing alone in the hallway. I wasn't about to follow them in. There had been far too many poop and pee skirmishes in that bathroom for me to put myself in harm's way. A few minutes later, they came out with devilish grins and Ray was holding something behind his back the way you would when you're going to surprise a coworker with a cupcake on their birthday. Ray walked out into the hallway and said, "Ace, come here. I want to show you something." I was nervous because Ray was acting nice so I held my ground. But before I knew it Ray made his move. I had a split second when I saw something was about to happen and tried to duck and slip past him, but it was too little, too late. I felt something go "WHAP" right in my ear.

The story gets a little fuzzy here, but I'm sure you've figured out the bottom line—one of them shit into a paper towel. To this day neither Chris nor Ray will take credit for the stool. Remember, this was before DNA testing; nowadays we could get to the heart of this mystery like CSI—Crap Scene Investigation. Either way, someone's number two was put in a paper towel and then in Ray's hand and then my ear.

My first impulse was to kill Ray. Unfortunately, we had exactly the same foot speed, he had a five-step head start, and I was at an emotional and a drag-coefficient disadvantage. We had a retarded

Road Runner and Wile E. Coyote chase scene through the halls and out into the quad with Ray chanting, "Shithead! Shithead! Shithead!" the whole time. People were now looking out their classroom windows, and I realized I wasn't going to be able to catch him so I cut bait and decided to run to my locker and then dash home. I threw on my maroon jacket, pulled it up over my head, and snapped it closed like Kenny from *South Park*. Only my eyes were showing as I ran toward home in shame. But I had one last barrier, the security guard. He was a big brother with a Jheri curl. But I shoulder faked left and pumped right, jumped over the fence, sprinted home, and took a shower that was slightly longer than Karen Silkwood's would have been if she had been raped on the way home from the plant.

In retrospect, I probably should have seen it coming. When we were in seventh grade, Ray borrowed my L.A. Rams beanie. He had it for a few weeks, and when I asked for it back, he handed it to me like a lunch bag. When I opened it, I saw that he had crapped in it. And it wasn't like this was some weird phase he went through when we were kids. After high school when I was living in my dad's garage, Ray deposited a large dook inside the entrance to my room. Unfortunately, my father discovered it before I did. Ten years later at our high school reunion, we were side by side at the urinals. Ray turned 90 degrees and started peeing on me. We were wearing suits and this wasn't the end of the night; I still had to go out and see people I hadn't seen in years who already thought I was a loser before I smelled like a hobo who pissed himself on a bus bench. I asked, "What the fuck?" Ray simply said, "Old times." I had to give it to him. It was a nice wiz down memory lane.

You have to remember, we didn't have cable or the Internet back in the day. We had to make our own entertainment. When we were seventeen, Ray and I noticed a billboard above a store called Aahs!! on Ventura Boulevard in Studio City. It looked like a freeway sign and read:

For family fun go to:
1. Knott's Berry Farm
2. Disneyland
3. The beach

We knew this was something we had to fuck with. And in an uncharacteristic burst of ambition, we decided that simply getting a can of spray paint just wouldn't do. There are three important things to understand about this particular stunt.

First, our usual nonsense was free. This one cost us money. We bought some white vinyl and cut out letters in a matching font to apply to the sign. We borrowed the money from our Hebrew Heights friends and roped them into coming with us. It was me, Ray, Rudy, Jack (his shoes were still wet), a kid named Robbie, another named Steve, and the aforementioned Alex. Boy, did we ruin that kid. That was his real bar mitzvah. That day he became a man by committing petty crime with a bunch of assholes from the Valley.

Second, this was dangerous on a couple of levels. It was three A.M. when we climbed on top of a dumpster to reach a ladder that would get us onto the roof of Aahs!!. We were then able to climb another ladder up to the billboard. But the real danger was that Ventura is the busiest street in the San Fernando Valley. It's crawling with cops. You couldn't stand on Ventura for two minutes without a cruiser going by. Yet there we were, shouting at each other about hanging the letters straight, the whole time being illuminated by the light on the billboard. If the Man had pulled up we would have had two options—be cuffed and put into a squad car, or do the honorable thing and dive to our deaths.

The last thing to keep in mind is that there was no YouTube back then. We weren't filming this in the hopes of becoming viral video stars. But thank God one of us had the foresight to come back the next day and take a picture. We just wanted it for ourselves. It's not like I ever thought I'd become famous and be able to put it in a book. But here it is . . . for family fun.

One hot summer night I let Ray put me in a dryer at a coin-op laundry. They lock from the outside, so you can't get out once you're in. Especially if Ray is the gatekeeper. So I just tumbled dry with hot air blowing up my ass. I was three seconds into it when I thought to myself, God, does this suck. I don't know what the hell I was expecting, as if it supposed to be Space Mountain or something. I was in North Hollywood inside a metal cylinder with three-inch-high fins every foot, rolling me around like an old tube sock.

At a certain point I gave Ray the "I'm serious" call. "I'm serious" is the safe word of buddies fucking with each other. Ray eventually let me out. It wasn't like we were eleven or even sixteen: This was when we were in our early twenties. This is what happens when you don't go to college. We couldn't afford vacations, but stuffing your buddy in a dryer only costs a quarter.

Ray and I also took a road trip to Vegas with Chris. While I'm sure there were as many drunken shenanigans as our broke asses could afford, this story isn't about what happened when we got to Vegas, it's about the journey to and from. Chris and I hopped into his '84 Nissan mini-pickup and went to grab Ray. He came out of his apartment, saw me in the front seat, and said, "Get in the bed." There wasn't enough room on the vinyl front bench seat for all three dudes, so one of us needed to get in the back of the pickup. For clarity, this was a bare metal pickup truck bed. No bed liner, no camper shell. I told Ray that I wasn't going to get in the back. We argued for a little bit and I finally said, "Look, I'm a fair-minded guy. One of us will sit in the truck bed on the way there and the other will on the way back." I knew there was no way that one of us was going to get stuck in the bed for both the outbound and return trip. Ray replied, "Get in the back." This worked out well for me. It was the middle of August but it was also eight P.M. when we left. So while the ride to Vegas for me would be warm, the ride home on Sunday at high noon would be horrible for Ray. By my calculations, he'd die somewhere between Death Valley and Baker, California. So I jumped into the back and we left. For the four-hour trek I bounced around the bed, alone with my thoughts—remember I had no cell phone, no iPod, not even a sliding window so I could talk to the guys in the truck. Just me sitting on the driveshaft of a dangerous vehicle in the dark of the desert night being driven by a lunatic in the form of Chris. It never dipped below 85 degrees. Again, my only comfort was knowing that my 85 degrees would be relative luxury compared to the triple digits and blazing sun Ray would be dealing with. He'd be long dead by the time we got to the world's largest thermometer.

I spent the weekend in Vegas getting drunk and laughing every time I thought about Ray. At a certain point it occurred to me that Chris's truck was black, so it was going to go from 160 degrees to 183. I was perversely satisfied knowing Ray was going to fry like bacon in the back of that pickup. Come Sunday morning, we were getting ready to go and I told Ray it was time for his death ride. He said something I never expected: "No, I'm gonna fly." I was dumbstruck. You should know by now that there's no way any of us could have afforded a plane ticket. Ray proceeded to tell me he had run into a middle-aged guy we knew from the neighborhood who had some money, had taken pity on Ray, and bought him a plane ticket.

Some of my most dangerous and most exhilarating moments with Ray took place at the Mulholland Club. This is a high-end tennis club in the hills above L.A., in the aforementioned Hebrew Heights. Obviously we weren't members, but on hot summer nights after an evening of partying, the only thing standing between us and a platinum pass was an eight-foot wall and a little something called grit.

The Mulholland Club had an Olympic-sized pool, a hot tub, and sometimes they'd even leave food out. There'd be leftover party trays from the bar mitzvah earlier in the day and we'd eat leftover cold cuts and/or throw them at each other. We were idiots. We had broken and entered and then spent the night hurling beer bottles and insults while skinny-dipping and trying to get chicks to take off their tops and make out with each other in the hot tub. We could have easily been arrested. We could have even more easily been injured, as you'll soon read.

The club was at the top of a big hill. We would park our cars at the bottom, climb up the steep rocky embankment, hop the fence, and be on the grounds of the club. Typically Ray would do this barefoot. I don't know why, but Ray refuses to wear shoes. At home, riding on the back of my motorcycle, or on construction sites with nails, splinters, and broken glass all around, it doesn't matter. One night at the Mulholland Club, Ray got pissed off because he caught Chris making out with his girlfriend. He was heartbroken. The soles of his feet may be callused and tough, but his soul is sensitive. So he ran away. He dashed out of the pool area barefoot and ran down the

131

rocky slope we had to scale to get in, onto the asphalt parking lot, cutting the shit out of his feet the whole time.

Just getting into the club wasn't the end of the journey. There was a pool and we needed to jump into it . . . naked. But a diving board is not nearly dangerous or idiotic enough. We had to get onto the roof. In order not to end up operating a wheelchair with a crazy straw, you had to get a running start, jump off the three-story roof, and clear the fourteen feet of cement to splash down in the pool.

A quick safety tip for the kids out there. If you're planning on jumping off a roof into a body of water that's surrounded by concrete, make sure you either land in the water completely or miss it altogether and catch nothing but pavement. I know it doesn't make sense, but half pool and half concrete will fuck you up more than full concrete.

Getting off the roof wasn't the dangerous part. The only way to get onto the roof was to build a ladder. Not *bring* a ladder: *build* a ladder. If we walked up a flight of stairs to the upper patio, the roof was then in striking distance. From that base camp we would stack up two outdoor metal dining tables and top them off with a patio chair. I can't begin to tell you how hairy this was. The tables were round and their three legs were bent and uneven. And remember this was under cover of darkness and we were usually drunk and always nude. Once we were on top of this rickety monstrosity, we'd have to stretch out and grab a piece of rigid conduit protruding from the stucco with a light attached. One of us would use that to pull himself up onto the roof. After that guy dragged his balls against the shitty sponged-on seventies stucco, he could reach down and do the fireman's grip to pull the other jackasses up. More than once it was my balls being dragged across the stucco.

The first time we did it, we were all up on the gravel-topped roof, naked, and I remember that I, like always, was the voice of reason. I gave an impassioned speech about how dangerous this was and how we all needed to be careful, that there was a lot of concrete between the edge of the building and the beginning of the pool and that someone could easily end up spending the rest of their life being picked up by a special van. As I was saying this, a naked Snake flew past me, shouting, and jumped into the pool. He made it in safely and the other jack-offs quickly followed suit. (Except Rudy, who stood there with his legs quivering for a half hour until our taunts and his realization that getting down the makeshift patio-table ladder would be even more dangerous.)

A little addendum to this part of the story. Twenty years later, we were attending a wedding at the Mulholland Club for our friend Michelle. It was a very nice affair—a band, servers in bow ties, grandparents—the whole schlemiel. At a certain point, somebody asked where Ray was. The next thing we knew, his naked ass was sailing by the floor-to-ceiling glass window of the ballroom and landing in the pool. Someone attending the wedding who wasn't part of our crew heard the old stories and paid him $50 to get naked and jump off the roof. The poor sap probably thought Ray wouldn't do it. I suspect he would have done it for free.

Another time we left the club and started walking down the street. Ray was looking in people's windows. Not in a Peeping Tom way, just glancing as he walked by. On this night, he saw a couple getting it on. They were doing it doggy-style with the curtains wide open. And like any guy his age, he got excited and went in for a closer look. The rest of us were hanging back and a moment later we heard Ray shout at the top of his lungs, "IT'S TWO DUDES! IT'S TWO DUDES!" They came out and they were pissed. And these guys weren't your light-in-the-loafers variety of gay, either. They were big, rough-trade gays who could have probably kicked our ass. So we hauled ass. The irony that moments earlier the four dudes shouting, "THEY'RE FAGS!" were wrestling naked in a Jacuzzi together never dawned on us.

But the Ray story of all Ray stories starts at the Mulholland Club and ends at a Jack in the Box. If you're squeamish, under eighteen, have a heart condition, are pregnant, or may become pregnant, you may want to skip this next story. As I've said, this was the eighties and we were broke. We didn't have Xbox or iPads so we had to make our own fun. Also bear in mind as you read this story that it took place sixteen years before *Jackass* premiered on MTV. We weren't copycat Johnny Knoxvilles and Steve-O's. We were the Wright brothers of stupid stunts.

On one of his many dips in the Jacuzzi at the Mulholland Club, Ray felt the warm flow of the jet against his arse and had an epiphany. He discovered through the miracle of science that if he put his butthole up to it, he could fill his colon with water, hold it in, and release it later. And when I say release, I mean unleash at breakneck speed. Ray could propel the ass water over 125 psi. It would look like the stream that comes out of the back of a Jet Ski. He could shoot a rooster tail of shit water that would make the fountain at the Bellagio look an old-fashioned park bubbler.

The first time Ray did this he didn't aim at us. And thank God, because on that initial shot you're clearing yourself out. You'll find a burrito from 1971 in there. But after five high-speed injection enemas you could drink what comes out. Ray probably had the cleanest colon in the state. For the inaugural launch, Ray went off somewhere distant and safe. It was like the Nevada nuclear-testing ground: He should have set up a fake town and mannequins. But that didn't last long. Eventually he realized the power of the weapon he was packing, got bored, and shot it at a girl's head. After that, no one was safe. Our friend Tom found himself drunk, tangled in a collapsed chaise longue with a rolled ankle. As he struggled to get out, Ray filled up. Tom gave the international distress signal of dumbo buddies fucking with each other—"I'm serious"—but Ray shot his ass cannon right on Tom's head.

Ray, with my encouragement, became drunk with power and decided he needed to share this gift with the rest of the world, or at least the Valley. But how? The Carolla house and the Oldhafer apartment sure as hell didn't have Jacuzzis. But my mom did have a hose. We figured we could go to the hose bib on the front lawn, fill Ray up, and have him squirt on unsuspecting North Hollywooders.

It was a Saturday night. We pulled up to my mom's house and grabbed the hose. I'm not sure where she was. Could you imagine being a parent and coming home to find that scene? You pull up the driveway and your son is on the front lawn watching a guy put a garden hose up his ass. I still wonder if my mom was watering the lawn the next day and caught a whiff of Ray's colon.

Now that Ray was fully loaded with hose water, we hopped into a borrowed Toyota Celica hatchback. I had to drive. Ray's got some range. There aren't a lot of guys who will put a hose up their ass but can't drive stick. The clock was ticking. He could go off at any time, like one of those blue dye packs banks put in moneybags. I drove like I was transporting a woman in labor to the hospital. We pulled into the drive-thru and ordered an apple pie and fries. It had to be cheap because we had no money and quick because Mount St. Ray could blow at any moment. We drove around to the pick-up window and I reclined the seat. Ray stuffed his ass out the window and . . .

Nothing. I don't know if it was the emotional pressure or if he had waited too long, but Ray couldn't let the levee break. The guy at the window was confused. When someone is going to moon they usually just do a quick flash, laugh, and then speed away, not let the ass linger while the guy in the driver's seat shouts, "Go, go, *go!*"

I specifically remember how the guy slowly closed the window. The second it latched shut, Ray erupted like Old Fecal. The poor pimpled teenage Jack in the Box employee just sat there with a look on his face like had seen a UFO. I like to imagine him telling the story to his coworkers and loved ones the next day. "So a guy mooned you?" "No, water started flying." "So he tried to piss on you?" "No, the water was shooting from his ass." "Why don't you take the afternoon off, and no more Robitussin."

But the ass-water floodgates had opened. I'll admit that I tried it, but I couldn't quite accomplish the feat. Another friend did manage to pull it off, except instead of the safe out-of-doors this guy took the act inside my grandparents' house. My grandparents were, thankfully, out of town. I, on the other hand, was lying on their floor when this guy shot an ass-geyser at my head. He filled up with the hose, walked into the den, and unleashed the torrent all over me. This was a home, the room where my grandfather watched *Hollywood Squares*.

There's a certain irony to all of these shit-water shenanigans starting at the Mulholland Club, which was named for the man who brought water to Los Angeles. I'm sure if he knew what we were doing with it he would never stop vomiting.

Ray will figure into other stories later in this book, but you can see why he warranted his own chapter. As I said, I love Ray. Despite all of our fights, Ray and I continue to be friends, I'm often his employer, and strangely enough he still sees my dad in therapy. Yes, my dad is Ray's therapist. After seventeen years of hard work, Ray has upgraded himself from a psychopath to a functional sociopath. And I appreciate Ray. There's a beauty to his brutal honesty. I've often said everyone needs a Ray in their posse. There's no way to get a big head if you do. Ray will tell you, without a second of hesitation or forethought, that you look stupid in those cowboy boots, you're too old and too fat for those True Religion jeans, the ponytail makes you look like a fag, and that this chapter sucked.

8

GOOD-BYE, FUTON, HELLO, BUNK BEDS:
THE LAUREL CANYON
APARTMENT, PT. 2

WITH The Weez out of the apartment, Chris, who had been flopping there periodically, decided to become permanently entrenched. In exchange for The Weez's futon he brought an even more pathetic option—his kid brother's bunk bed.

A little bit after that, our buddy Umgad moved in. Umgad is a great guy, but that place was too fucking small to have a third roommate. When you're on top of each other like that, small arguments appear much bigger and you want to murder each other. Fortunately, the building owner got wind of a third person crashing there and put his foot down. Even more fortunately, the letter he wrote was saved.

ADAM CAROLLA

April 24, 1986

Adam,

Once again you are violating the terms of your rental agreement. There are more than two people living in your apartment. If this isn't corrected immediately my lawyer will handle evicting you from the premises. I'll give you one week—till 4-31-86 to correct this. I don't want to evict you but you have left me no alternative. *This can't happen again.* Call me if you want to discuss this, but there can't be any extensions.

Jim

Here's the real story behind the letter, and this has never been revealed until this book: I told Jim to write it. Sorry, Umgad. A mass-published book may not have been the best way to break this to you. But I thought being evicted would feel better coming from the landlord rather than your friends. In my defense, I just asked

Jim to write the letter. I didn't think it was going to be as harsh as it came out.

Now that I've gotten that off my chest let me regale you with another road trip story.

I rode my motorcycle to Isla Vista near Santa Barbara to visit our buddy Carl who was going to UCSB. For those who don't know the geography, it's probably a hundred-mile ride, my longest road trip on that bike. About five minutes after I entered the freeway, it started raining. And I mean monsoon-level rain. The trip was like riding a motorcycle through a five-hundred-thousand-foot-long car wash. And I didn't have any rain gear, just a denim jacket, jeans, and a helmet. I didn't even have gloves. After just a few miles I was soaked through. I was freezing and hypothermic like a guy who fell overboard on a crab boat. So I did the only thing I could think of to warm up. I pissed myself. I just let it flow. You're grossed out right now, but I've got to tell you it was sweet relief for about two minutes. Until it froze. I'd had a generally uncomfortable life up to that point, but this was the jewel in the discomfort crown. I don't know why I thought it was a good idea to ride up to Santa Barbara with the storm clouds gathering. I got to Carl's at ten that night soaked to the bone with rain, piss, and tears. I sat in his bathtub and ran hot water over myself. My hands were purple and had the impression of my bike's grips frozen into them.

It was probably worse for Snake. He went with me on his bike, which was having electrical problems. For the whole trip, sparks were flying out of wires connected to his bike's battery. I'd continually see him reach down and adjust a wire and have some more sparks shoot out. His hand would fly back in pain and I'd hear him yelp. Again, all of this was happening at seventy miles an hour in a torrential downpour at night.

We rode motorcycles because you could fill up the tank for a buck eighty-nine, cut through L.A. traffic, and on the weekend carve up a canyon. All good reasons to purchase a motorcycle. Being seen, and especially being heard, were not part of the equation. That's because we weren't insecure narcissistic poseur douchebags. You fucksticks that pull the baffles out of your Harley exhaust so that people in surrounding neighborhoods, countries, and the un-born can celebrate the arrival of your preening ass and the Harley Softail it's perched on rank just beneath pedophile clown and Nazi prison guard on the cosmic cocksucker list. How many times have you been awoken from a nap because one of these peacocks had to throw out a couple of revs as they were driving past your apart-ment? How many times have you had the shit scared out of you while walking back to your car after a satisfying dinner because one of these guys flew past you with the hammer down? It's called noise pollution, and the chickenshit cops that are busily handing out tickets for no front license plates or illegal window tints should for once focus on something we give a fuck about. My fantasy is to follow one of these guys home some night and hide in the pan-try until he's finished beating off to a cardboard cut-out of himself and fallen asleep. Then I would sneak into his bedroom—past the Lucite box housing the cheap vinyl boxing glove that may or may not have been signed by Muhammad Ali, past the *Harley Davidson and the Marlboro Man* poster—stand at the foot of his bed, and fire off one of those air horns they use to start boat regattas. When he popped up I'd yell, "How's it feel, bitch?"

And just because The Weez had moved out didn't mean the drugs stopped, either. Every now and again someone would get their hands on some mushrooms. They're excellent, but they're hard to regulate.

Sometimes you'll get really high. Other times you won't but the guy next to you will and you'll have to watch him freak out. I know from experience. Back when I was still living in the garage, The Weez was responsible for getting me high on mushrooms the first time. We were at a party and we did 'shrooms together, but his kicked in a while before mine did. I wasn't getting my buzz so I decided to split. When I tried to leave, he freaked out because he didn't want me to ride my motorcycle. He was afraid the mushrooms would start working while I was riding. He grabbed my leg and wouldn't let me get on the bike. I shook him off, told him he was too high, and left. The Weez called my house and couldn't find me and continued to freak until the next morning. He didn't realize I had gone to another friend's apartment where the mushrooms proceeded to take hold and I sat and tripped out for the night.

The thing I like about mushrooms is that when you're on them you're like a newborn baby. You get to stand outside of our culture and observe it like you're an alien who just came down and is trying to figure it out. One time when I was nineteen I 'shroomed out and was watching TV, which really is the true measure of a society and what it's about at that particular time. I saw a commercial for Lee Press-On Nails. My head was abuzz. "So the female of the species sticks long pieces of red plastic to the ends of her fingers to make them look like bloody claws? This makes her more attractive to the male of the species? Why does this world have a multimillion-dollar company that manufactures plastic red things you stick to the end of women's fingers, and why does that give us a boner?" The next commercial was for a monster truck rally, which really fucked with my head. I was watching giant trucks crushing little cars while the partisan crowd cheered, thinking, We're all insane. If you had the constant questioning and wonderment that goes on while you're high on mushrooms in your everyday sober life, you'd go bonkers. Your brain would eat itself. Without mushrooms you just move on and think, I wish this press-on nail commercial would end so I could get back to a very special episode of *Blossom*.

The other thing that happens with mushrooms is, you're having the grooviest time in the world one second, and then are freaked out the next. The same time with the Lee Press-On Nails commercial, I had one of those moments. My buddy who was going to Boulder State came back with a pillowcase full of mushrooms thinking he was going to sell them. The problem was that he liked to get high on his own supply. Like when I would eat the candy bars I was supposed to be selling for Pop Warner. So me, him, and The Weez ate them. And it was awesome. Until Ray showed up. He was high on coke. That's a bad combination. If everyone is doing mushrooms, fine, but you can't mix in people on other drugs. Ray grabbed The Weez and started tossing him around like a rag doll. I was screaming, "Don't hurt him, don't hurt him!" Then the night took an even steeper plummet into Bummerville.

This is the worst thing that can happen to you when you're on mushrooms. Ray's coked-up girlfriend, Monica, locked me in the bathroom to confront me. She was superhigh and licking her lips and had that cokey head twitch. "Listen, I know Ray is your best friend and he's my boyfriend and you're protective of him but I love him and we need to all get along and why don't you like me because I need to know that you like me because there's always this weird energy in the room when we're together and I know you feel that I'm taking Ray away from you but I'm not and if you could only understand what I'm saying then I think . . ." I was protesting, "There's no weird energy, I love everyone." Meanwhile Ray started banging on the door, shouting, "What's going on in there?" I shouted back, "Nothing!" and started to leave but she stopped me and said, "We're not done talking." It was miserable. I need to invent a windbreaker with a huge mushroom logo sewn on the back that you only wear when you're tripping so people don't come up and freak you out.

I don't want to glorify drugs or use it as an excuse: We did plenty of really stupid shit stone-cold sober. I was with the guys walking out of the Sherman Oaks Galleria after a long day of arcade games and cheap pizza. There was a Mohawk-sporting punk kid, probably seventeen years old, with his Sex Pistol–wannabe buddies tormenting people as they left the mall. He was hanging around the parking structure telling people to fuck off, spitting on cars, and generally being a dick. He hadn't threatened us, but we decided to be good citizens. So me, Snake, and Chris told him and his guys to get lost. Usually we're an intimidating team, but this kid wasn't having it. He pulled out a weapon. It was like nunchucks, but the chain was three feet long and the handles weren't wooden, they were solid steel. It was like something you'd see in the Thunderdome. He started spinning it over his head and taunting us, "You want some?" Because it was the eighties, I was wearing a leather bomber jacket. I took it off and approached him holding it out like a bullfighter with a cape. As I inched closer and closer to him, with each step the five inches of chrome steel was inching closer and closer to my skull. All of a sudden out of the corner of my eye I saw something blow past me. It was Snake. He tackled the punk on the hood of a car and started beating him. I jumped in and so did Chris, and we all beat the bejesus out of the little shit. He eventually broke free and ran away, but we had managed to get the weapon.

When we got back to the apartment I asked Snake, "How did you tackle that guy without getting hit?" Snake said, "I might have." He then pulled up his shirt and revealed a chain mark running diagonally the whole length of his back, shoulder to hip. He'd been nailed but hadn't complained about it.

The point is, like my earlier run-in with the skateboarders at McDonald's, if you're a snot-nosed teen and you're out in public fucking with people, not only should society not punish those who kick your ass, it should award them the Congressional Medal of Honor.

Dicking around at the mall and getting into fights were just some of my pastimes as I continued to wallow. I had no health, dental, or car insurance. I was driving a pickup truck worth $600 that I had bought because my construction supervisor offered to pay an extra buck an hour if I could haul stuff. I knew there had to be something better than this. One evening I was in the garage off the alley behind the apartment wrenching on a 240Z I'd been putting back together a paycheck at a time for the last three years and, as always, listening to the radio. I remember it was a Sunday night because that's when KLOS would air a show called Rockline where they interviewed famous bands. I also remember it was a Sunday night because that was always the time I felt most depressed and vulnerable. Somehow having a moment to contemplate the miserable, low-paying week that lay ahead was more painful than living it. The band they interviewed that particular Sunday night was Boston. I'd always enjoyed Boston, but I never really listened to their lyrics. Tom Scholz, the lead guitarist, was talking about one of their hits called "Peace of Mind." In the interview he went on to say that he was working as an engineer at Polaroid, but that his dream was to play rock 'n' roll. "Peace of Mind" is about following your muse.

I understand about indecision, but I don't care if I get behind

People living in competition, all I want is to have my peace of mind

It struck a chord with me and made me realize that I had to try to do something creative with my life, although the engineering gig at Polaroid was sounding pretty good at that point. People were telling me to get my contractor's license and go into business for myself, but I knew that would spell the beginning of the end for me creatively, and since it involved studying and a number-two pencil, I was out. So I sat down and tried to take an honest inventory of my skill set. I came to the conclusion that I was basically good at two things: working with my hands and being funny. I knew the working-with-my-hands part sucked, so I thought maybe I'd pursue the being-funny part. I decided to give myself until I was thirty to make a living doing something creative. The reason I say "something creative"—and not being a star or being a comic on TV—is that I would have been content to just write slogans for a greeting-card company. As long as I was on salary and had health insurance. Being in front of the camera or behind-the-mike millionaire stuff seemed way too lofty a goal at that time.

While I was a long way away from being a celebrity myself, I did know one. When I was twenty, I attended the premiere of *Pretty in Pink* with The Weez. Molly Ringwald grew up down the street from me in North Hollywood. I never had a thing for Molly, but I was nuts about her sister Beth (whom you may recall from the earlier nude-sunbathing story). Molly and Beth came from a showbiz family. Her father, Bob, was blind but was a great jazz pianist. I had a funny moment with him one day. We were making small talk and I told him that I liked jazz and comedy. He said, "I love jazz and comedy too." Then, a breath later, "Dixieland and Gallagher." He'd managed to find the one form of jazz I wasn't into and a comedian I didn't think was funny.

The after party of the premiere was at a place called the Palace, which was the club James Woods's character ran in *Against All Odds*. We drove my 240Z now with a souped-up engine but no mufflers. The drinks were free and The Weez was my designated driver, so I drank like Betty Ford on a cruise. Somewhere between my thirteenth and seventeenth greyhound I realized The Weez was gone. He met a chick and didn't bother telling me he was off to try and get laid. The next thing I knew, the place was empty and the house lights were turned on. I staggered toward the front door. It was raining outside, harder than I'd ever remembered in L.A. I pulled my jacket over my head and started to truck up the hill to the bank where the Z was, but when I arrived at the parking lot I could hardly believe my blurry eyes. There were only two cars in the rain-filled parking lot: mine and the car parked next to it, an LAPD cruiser. I stood there in the pouring rain, frozen in my drunken tracks, wondering what to do. It was dark and the cop-car windows were fogged up so I couldn't tell if there was anyone in it. Imagine a large empty parking lot with your car in the middle of it and an LAPD cruiser parked right alongside it and you're at least three times the legal limit. I finally decided I'd crawl into my car to get out of the rain but I wouldn't start it because that's when I'd get the DUI. I sat alone in my Z, my mind racing: "If I turn this key, is that cop going to turn on his siren? I wonder who The Weez is porking? That Ducky-boy was so gay; I bet that clown will never have a successful sitcom." Eventually I just held my breath and started the car. I slowly backed out of the parking spot. Between the booze, the rain, and a broken defroster I was literally just feeling my way to the street. I managed to get onto the flooded 101 freeway and inched home. I threw up in the bathtub and was so loaded I didn't even attempt to beat off. In the state of California it would have been considered rape. I never found out why that cop car was in the parking lot that night, or how hefty the chick The Weez mounted was. All I knew was I had a tub to clean and a hamper to soil.

THE WORST JOB I EVER HAD

In 1986 I got the worst job I ever had, doing earthquake rehab for the county of Los Angeles. A lot of people get freaked out about earthquakes, but I've been through a few of them and I know about construction so it doesn't frighten me as much. You can actually have a little fun after an earthquake. Head out to the Valley and see all the Mexicans camped out on the lawns of their apartment buildings because they're too nervous to go back in. In Mexico, everything is built of masonry and crumbles during earthquakes. Their buildings are made of cinder block and non-reinforced concrete. Not a lot of two-by-fours and plywood going on down there. Up here we build them better, so they stay up. But some of the older buildings in town needed a little work to get up to code.

I had to do rehab work in some of the worst places I'd ever seen or smelled. Quite possibly the worst was on Wilshire and Normandy. We had to install those square steel plates you've seen on the outside of buildings. They're called shear anchors, and essentially they keep the floors from pancaking in an earthquake. The reason these buildings were so vulnerable is that they're made of brick. In an earthquake the first thing to collapse on a house is typically the chimney. This building was basically a giant chimney. Think of brick as matzo and plywood and two-by-fours as taffy.

It was a five-story building with forty government-subsidized units, all singles. Not one-bedrooms: one room with a tiny bathroom and a Murphy bed. There's a certain math you can do with government-subsidized housing. The more money Uncle Sam is kicking in for you to live there, the worse your place smells. If they're helping a little, your place has a faint, musty gym-sock smell. But if you're basically living for free, then it smells like a rhino took a shit in there. There should be a law against places that small having wall-to-wall carpeting, because it just absorbs the stink. Plus everyone who lives there is old, so they constantly have the heat cranked. When you open the door to one of those units you're hit with a wave of old-man funk.

One tenant had a bucket of shit in his apartment. He had literally saved his poop in a pail. And here's how I know. I was down in the tiny backyard area of the building. It was eight feet deep and ran the width of the building, just enough to string a clothesline. I had my table saw out and was milling wood for baseboards. It was loud and I had my back turned, so I didn't notice when the other guys from the crew grabbed the shit bucket and put it behind me on the ground. Construction sites have a lot of merry pranksters. They were devious because they camouflaged it with some wood and other scraps so I wouldn't notice. They then climbed up to the roof and took the bolts for the shear anchors and dropped them down the five stories into the crap bucket. Because of the sound of the table saw, I couldn't hear the splat of the bolts falling into the dook, but I could smell it. Every three minutes for an hour I'd have to stop milling wood and turn around because I thought someone had shit or farted next to me.

This wasn't out of the question; there was a lot of gas to go around on the site. One of the guys I worked with was named Frazier. He did two horrible things. First, because he was a New Zealander, he introduced me to Vegemite. This is a horrible, horrible creation. One of these days I'm going to put together a bracket system and have countries and ethnicities go head-to-head to find out which has the worst regional dish. The final four would be Vegemite versus poi in one conference and haggis versus gefilte fish in the other. Vegemite is awful, but the other Frazier incident was worse. In this same brick building where we were doing earthquake rehab, there was a woman named Millie. Millie had lived in the building for seven decades and was turning one hundred years old. So all the residents plus the construction guys who had become part of their village of the damned gathered outside the building to take a group picture for Millie's birthday. Frazier was standing on one side of Millie with his arm around her and I was on the other. This is what we heard: "Okay. Everyone smile. One . . . two . . . ugh, fucking Frazier!" Right as the picture was about to be taken, Frazier let go one of his infamous huge farts, probably sponsored by Vegemite, and everyone cleared out. We were all so used to his gas that we knew instantly it was his brand. It went from "Say cheese" to "Cut cheese" instantly. Poor Millie never got her one-hundredth-birthday picture because of Frazier's gasohole.

One of the creepier units I had to enter was inhabited by the guy who had collected thousands of images of missing kids. He had cut the pictures out of the backs of milk cartons and had them stacked floor to ceiling. Again, no hyperbole. Thousands. He would buy two half-gallon cartons of milk each week and cut out the panels from the backs. It was about fifteen years' worth of missing kids.

There was another gentleman in the building named Shakey Jake. He was a black guy, about sixty-five years old, 120 pounds wearing nothing but a wife beater, black socks pulled up to his knees, and a huge droopy pair of boxer shorts. Remember in *Goodfellas* when Pesci's character goes and wakes up Samuel L. Jackson's character, Stacks, and he's in his boxers? Picture that, but with about twenty more years on him. The guys from the crew sent me in to talk to him because I was the only one he'd listen to. Shakey Jake said he was tired of people trying to get into his apartment, tearing out plaster and putting up shear walling. One of the things we had to do to these poor sons of bitches was block out the only window they had. We'd put in rebar and fill it in with concrete blocks. You could see why someone would be pissed. Shakey Jake was fed up and pulled out a double-barrel shotgun. So they called me in as earthquake-rehab worker/hostage negotiator. Jake had the hammer pulled back, ready to blow away anyone who came into his place. Eventually I convinced him to let me into the unit and I sat on the edge of his Murphy bed and we had a heart-to-heart. I said, "You don't want to hurt anyone." He said, "I'm tired of all this." I said, "I'm tired too, Jake." I convinced him to lower the gun, which he did, but he couldn't figure out how to put the hammer back. So there was a lingering threat that the shotgun was going to go off at any moment. I told him to at least point it toward the ground. I had to keep my ears covered just in case. He eventually figured out how to get the hammer back into the safety position, and we were able to proceed to make his miserable apartment even more windowless, dust covered, and bleak.

In order to do a lot of this work, we had to get into the tiny crawlspace under the building with a flashlight and blueprint to find which wall we needed to dig the footing underneath so that we could create a cripple wall. The space was obviously too tight for a shovel. Solution? A coffee can. People constantly talk about their shitty jobs. No matter what you hate about your occupation, it's still better than getting under a nearly condemned building with dead rats and dead cats to dig a footing with a coffee can. It was like being in a casket if you replaced the silk lining with rusty pipes and raccoon shit. Most people's idea of a shitty job is when their boss is an asshole and the vending machine is on the fritz. This was torture.

I ran into a guy I knew from my earthquake-rehab days a few years ago when I went to my kids' pre-pre-pre-preschool to do some bake-sale auction-type thing. (Because how could they possibly subsist only on the massive amount of money I pay them?) He looked exactly the same. I said, "Your name's Chipper, right?" He said yes. He knew who I was, but from being on TV and radio, not from back in the day. I said, "We worked earthquake rehab in downtown L.A. together." He didn't remember me being there but said, "I remember that job. I did it in between courses in college during the summer." I said, "You know how I remember who you are? I gave you your first tool bag." This rang a bell and he said, "Yeah, I still have it." For those who don't know, when you work in construction you have a tool belt with some pockets hanging off of it, usually three—left, right, and back—and they're called bags. Chipper still had the bag I'd given him. Technically it was a single electrician's pouch, which is slightly different from a carpenter's pouch. ("Carpenter's pouch" sounds like a small town in Virginia. "Head on down to Carpenter's

Pouch, stop at the general store, and ask for Zeke.") And that was also my first bag; someone had given it to me.

After a little reminiscing he said, "You weren't friends with Jeff, the racist guy, were you?" I said, "I knew Jeff. He was a nice guy. I didn't know he was a racist." I should clarify at this point in the story that Chipper is a black guy. So I asked him why he thought Jeff was a racist, and he said they had a couple of issues on the site and that Jeff had it in for him. Apparently Jeff came right out and even said, "You don't belong here." I asked Chipper if he knew Jeff's backstory. All he knew was that Jeff was a racist and was obsessed with becoming a fireman. So I told him what I knew. Jeff was a big, strapping white dude from Topanga Canyon whose lifelong dream was to fight fires. When he wasn't on the construction site he took the fire-science classes at the local junior college, volunteered at the Topanga fire station, worked out by lifting fifty-pound hose packs, and was a lifeguard at Topanga Beach. He worked construction for the same reason as me and every other guy on the site. It was kind of a holding place for life—a purgatory job. You weren't going to get anywhere with it, but it helped you pay the bills until whatever you were waiting for happened. So Jeff had this placeholder job for eight years while preparing to be a fireman. Why? Because of affirmative action. He went in for the fireman job and there was an eight-year waiting list.

Here's where it gets uncomfortable. I asked Chipper, "How did you get the job?" He said, "I just showed up, the boss liked me and hired me." I said "No offense, Chipper, but you didn't even have bags when you showed up at the site. And when I gave you mine, you threaded a dress belt through it."

This was earthquake rehab for the city, a government job, so there was affirmative action. We needed a certain number of black guys, a certain number of chicks, a certain number of Hispanics, et cetera. It was an EEOC thing. They didn't advertise it as affirmative action, but that's what it was. This was dangerous. We weren't installing closets in a condo, this was earthquake rehab. We had to hang off the sides of buildings and cut steel. Yet we ended up with Chipper, the world's least experienced carpenter, who probably could have lost an arm building an Ikea end table.

Chipper never knew why Jeff hated him so much: He stood for everything that was in the way of Jeff and his dreams. This was the biggest payday of our lives, nineteen bucks an hour for carpenters, twenty-one if you were a laborer. (Which was completely backward. On a non-government job, in the real world, the carpenters got thirteen an hour and the laborers, guys who just hauled shit, got seven. Don't get me started on government jobs. This shows you just how fucked-up the government is and why you shouldn't want to give them any more money than you already do.) Jeff finally got this bump-up and had to work next to a guy who'd never picked up a hammer and only got the gig because of his skin color. He was just as poor and disadvantaged and came from as broken a home as any of the black guys who got a leg up because of affirmative action. That's the only thing they should consider—socioeconomic status. That's the ultimate race, poor people. Chipper is now a lawyer and probably doing quite well for himself but spent twenty years plus walking around thinking Jeff was a racist and not knowing he got on the job site because of affirmative action. I don't know what ever happened to Jeff. I've considered tossing a Molotov cocktail into a house in Topanga, hoping he'll show up.

I can totally relate to Jeff. When I was nineteen and living in my dad's garage, I took a stab at getting a gig as a fireman. It was perfect for me: I was in good shape and I liked foosball and chili. So I put in an application. But I never heard back, gave up, and lived the life you're reading about. That is, until at age twenty-seven, when I got a call completely out of the blue. My application had gone through and they had a date for me to come in and take the written test. Eight years of my life had come and gone before my name popped up on the list. I went in for the exam. I didn't have a lot of confidence since not only was it an exam, it wasn't even multiple choice. But this thing had been eight years in the making and I had to give it a shot. As I stood in line to register, I was still amazed at how long the process took. I leaned in to the woman in front of me who was the size and color of a Starbucks mocha and asked, "When did you put in your application?" She said, "Tuesday."

This is my beef with affirmative action, not just that it screwed Jeff over or that it screwed me over, it screwed over some poor sucker whose house is burning in L.A. right now. This chick got to the head of the line without any qualifications because of her sex and race. If Barbie's dream condo caught fire, she'd be hard-pressed to throw Ken over her shoulder, much less an actual person.

I hope I've conveyed just how nuts life on Laurel Canyon was. If not, here's one last beat. One of my roommates had a job in the industrial part of downtown in a printing factory. He worked the graveyard shift, so often he'd just be coming home as I was waking up. One morning I walked into the kitchen to find him and a white-trash coworker in there smoking crack. They had turned a piece of gas hose into a crack pipe. They offered it to me. I took a drag, then broke with crackhead tradition and went to work. But, pun intended, that was rock bottom. Our flophouse had officially turned into a crackhouse.

When we moved out, we pulled the couch from its spot in front of the TV set and caught a glimpse of the carpet's original color. A bright island of blue in a sea of black filth. I was the poor schmuck who had to go back and try to get our cleaning deposit from Jim. He told me that in his twenty-six years of owning buildings, he had never seen anything worse. Yet for some reason he saw fit to ask if we wanted to move across the street into a house that he owned. We did.

9

A NEW PAD WITH A PADDED SEAT: THE NORTH HOLLYWOOD RENTAL HOUSE

NORTH HOLLYWOOD, CA

YEAR RENTED: 1987

RENT: $900 A MONTH

825 SQUARE FEET

TWO HALF-BEDROOMS
*(I KNOW YOU'VE HEARD OF A
HALF-BATH, BUT THIS PLACE
HAD HALF-BEDROOMS)*

WE knew it was time to move out of the apartment. Apartments are for guys in their late teens and early twenties to vomit, do drugs, fart, fight, and flop in. We needed to grow up and get into a house to vomit, do drugs, fart, fight, and flop in. Our landlord Jim had just the ticket—a ranch-style house directly across the street from our last apartment. It was me, Chris, and John, the guy who had previously broken my construction cherry. John was smart with a volatile temper, an interesting guy who was quite different from most of the meatheads I hung out with, but shared the one universal quality we all had in common: an inability to succeed.

One of the classier features of this home was the padded toilet seat. It was high-mileage puffy brown vinyl-covered foam and made that weird sigh when you sat down on it, then stuck to your ass when you got up. I'm not a germophobe or anything like that, but it is weird to think about all the ass time this seat had seen before we moved in. This is a horrible invention. What's the plan? You want to create a toilet seat so comfortable that you can fall asleep while you're taking a shit? You're going to show up late for work or end up like Elvis. Isn't the goal to keep it moving? It's a toilet, not a Barcalounger. It sucked when you were sitting on it, but it also made the simple act of pissing a chore. Because of how puffy it was, you couldn't get it past 90 degrees because the foam would butt up against the tank. So you'd have to push on it with your knee and compress it like a Nerf football in a dog's mouth. But once you removed your knee, the clock was ticking. If you just had three beers, you could make it before the drawbridge dropped. But in the time it took to evacuate a six-pack, the compressed foam would retake its original shape, and the seat would come slamming down like a piss guillotine.

This says so much about who me and my roommates were. That foam-rubber fomite (Google it) was in the apartment for God knows how long before we moved in. We never bothered to pool the nine bucks for a new seat. It was still there when we moved out.

It was a shitty little house that had a shitty little garage that had been turned into a shitty little bedroom. This room didn't have water or a toilet and was powered by a hundred-foot extension cord that ran from the main house. It was very reminiscent of the garage bedroom at my dad's house. Having been down that road, I opted for an actual bedroom, small as it might have been. My bedroom was a six-by-seven closet that had one of those plastic accordion doors with the little latch. It had that weird flesh-colored fake-wood texture and never really closed. Plus you can't get in a fight with a roommate or girlfriend and slam it. It was like living in a train compartment.

1987—North Hollywood rental house. No picture can truly convey how small that dump was.

John ended up taking the garage. One day he was napping in this "bedroom" in the middle of the day. Ray came over and decided to crank up some tunes in the living room. This was a good eighty feet away from where John was napping. But Ray really pumped up the volume. I even said to him at one point that he should turn it down because John was asleep in the back. Ray just laughed and turned it up even louder. I said to him again that he should turn it down. From behind me I heard, and felt, an explosion of glass. John had awoken from his slumber and hurled a steel-toed combat boot at the large glass sliding door that faced the backyard and garage. It went right through the window. I literally could have been killed.

I later put a piece of plywood over the window (which you can see in the picture at the beginning of this chapter). I told John he needed to order a new piece of glass for the door. It really needed to be replaced, since the only other way to the backyard and garage was the other sliding door, which didn't function. First, it had horrible action—you'd need to get a good grip and pull with your full weight and both feet firmly planted for it to even budge. Second, we had a large hanging speaker blocking the door. It was huge. Every time you walked into the house you'd hit your head on the damn thing.

John's plan was to take the aluminum door downtown because he knew a glass guy. He could have the pane installed for cheap down there, bring it back, and we would pop the sliding door back in. He said he was going to take the frame downtown, but in the week plus he let it sit in the back of his truck it got stolen, presumably for scrap. That was the last time we ever saw it. The plywood stayed on the opening for the entire time I lived there.

This is less a tangent and more a life tip. We put that plywood up and there it stayed for eternity. There is a window for fixing windows and everything else in your life. If you don't take care of it right away, it becomes part of the scenery. Next thing you know, you've got a dirt lawn full of washing machines and furniture.

So Chris and I ended up replacing the glass ourselves. This adds to the debt that John still owes me. Another time I came home and saw that all the dishes in the sink were broken. I stared at them, trying to come up with a theory on how this could have happened. I was thinking maybe they were in the sink when it was full of water and then the water drained so they collapsed and broke under their own weight. I also wondered if maybe someone was changing the bulb above the sink and accidentally stepped on them. What really happened was that John got pissed off that someone had left their dirty dishes in the sink and had smashed them with a hammer. And it wasn't like there had been recurring fights over leaving dishes in the sink. He just did it, because fuck it, they weren't his dishes and he didn't like the way they were staring at him. Among John's other greatest hits: He threw a softball through the front window (this time a smaller piece of plywood was put in its place). He severed the hundred-foot electrical cord that fed the back room right at the end so it couldn't be mended. And most disgusting of all, he would keep a glass bottle in the fridge. It formerly contained apple juice but now was occupied by tap water and his removable false tooth. (Which didn't stop me from taking a hit off it every once in a while.)

At this time I was continuing to barely make ends meet doing construction jobs. I did a tenant-improvement job at a box factory in Gardena that was thoroughly soul crushing. They made decorative Estée Lauder gift boxes for soap and perfume. While I toiled away I watched the sturdy Guatemalan women working there, knowing they would never receive one of these $280 boxes of bath salts. It's one thing when you see downtrodden women making coat hangers, but when they're sweating to create something they'll never even get as a gift, it's really sad.

I needed to shake things up and try to make some more money, or at least take a step toward my plan of acting like a regular person with a regular schedule. It was time to stop using my brawn and start using my brain. So I sold my truck and bought another motorcycle and headed back to Valley College. There I was five years later, about to give it the old junior-college try again. I went to check out the radio station at the school, knowing I had some aptitude for talking. But I was told that I had to take a Voice and Diction class among a bunch of other required curriculum. I just wanted to get in front of a mike and yak, like I do now. But I had to take real classes and I wasn't a real student. I quickly found myself on academic probation and shortly after that dropped out, sold the bike, bought another truck, and came crawling back to lady construction.

Believe it or not, at this time I had a long-term girlfriend. It was an unlikely match. When we met I was living in that shitty one-bedroom with The Weez and could barely make rent. Stephanie had a Beverly Hills apartment that her rich dad paid for. He was an attorney named Gordon and the whitest man alive. He wore a gold-nugget watch and had big coiffed silver hair. He had a huge house in Arcadia and couldn't figure out why his precious daughter was dating a schlub from North Hollywood. It was straight out of an eighties movie. I thought he was going to escort me into his study holding a brandy snifter, pull out a checkbook, and say, "How much for you to never see my daughter again?" Don't get me wrong, Stephanie wasn't bitchy or stuck-up or anything, but she was a sorority chick from USC who didn't have to work.

I guess I should give you a little flashback on how I got together with her. One of the more important road trips we took in the limo was up to UC Santa Barbara for Halloween. The city used to block off the roads and have a huge bash. There would be drunk people in costumes stumbling up and down the streets. They don't do it anymore because it got too crazy. But back in my day it was still on, and that was where I needed to be. That particular year I had

DIAMOND BALL 1987

borrowed an actual sailor outfit from a friend who was in the navy. I must admit I looked good. Halloween is the single man's holiday. All the chicks are dressed as French maids and Playboy Bunnies and the dudes are dressed as cops. You can just go up to them and pull that "Sorry ma'am, I'm going to have to arrest you for arson. You're just too damn hot for this party." With this in mind, I decided to ditch The Weez, whose costume was Guy Who's Too High on Mushrooms, and start trolling for some chicks.

I stumbled around Isla Vista carrying a twelve-pack of cheap beer. I was walking down an alley and I heard a band playing. I popped my head up over the fence and saw a large crowd with a hot chick front and center. We made eye contact, I held up my twelve-pack, and gave her a "You want a cold one?" look. She returned a look that said yes.

As you know from my unicycle story, I have great balance. So I scurried up the back side of a six-foot dog-eared redwood fence, which was not easy. I was wearing oversized pointy, patent-leather shoes. I stood atop the upper two-by-four that held the fence together. It was precarious. It was wobbly, the shoes were too big for me, I was holding a twelve-pack, and there was a hot chick watching me the whole time. In fact more than just her: I was right behind the band, six feet up. I jumped down, landed, then did another hop to get my feet under me and almost crashed into the drum kit. It was that move done by a gymnast who hasn't quite stuck the landing. Fortunately, I stopped myself before crashing into Ringo. It could have been disastrous but it ended up looking cool. Stephanie and I swapped information and some spit, then agreed to meet up in L.A.

But back to '86. My complete loserdom at this point was starting to wear her down. I was officially a college dropout and was just starting a gig installing custom closets. (You'll hear much more on this job later in the chapter.) Then I did something that definitely added to the tension. One of my first cracks at getting on TV was when they brought *The Dating Game* back in '86. I decided I'd go try out. I wasn't actually looking to hook up; I saw it more as a career move than anything. We've all seen the footage of Tom Selleck and John Ritter going on that show before they were famous. So I figured lightning might strike three times and I could maybe get a break out of it. With this in mind, I decided not to tell Stephanie.

The day of the audition came and I sat in a room with twenty-five guys as they went through the rounds. "Bachelor number one, if you could be an ice cream, what flavor would you be?" That kind of crap. Eventually the producers went into the back to convene for a while, then returned and said, "Great job, everyone. We have your information, we'll be contacting you. I do need a couple of you to stay behind. Bob Johnson, I don't think I have a home number for you. Larry Smith, need your work number. Adam Carolla, I need your address. So you three stay behind." As a joke I announced to the whole room, "She's just being nice. You guys all lost, she's just keeping us behind because you didn't make the cut." A minute later when the producer shut the door she said to me, "You asshole, they did all lose." I was just cracking wise. I assumed because I was functionally illiterate that I really did screw up something on the application. I'm not much of a liar, so I tend to assume other people aren't lying either. I made the cut and went home and told Stephanie. She freaked out. I told her it was Hollywood and I was just trying to get ahead. But she wasn't buying.

I'm not sure how much of a factor the *Dating Game* incident played, but Stephanie dumped me soon thereafter. It might have also been a fight we got into one day when she was in the middle of a little afternoon delight when someone began buzzing her apartment's doorbell/intercom. Rather than ignore it or step up the pace to finish the job, she just stopped. I was not thrilled and let her know it.

As far as the dumping, I remember the day vividly. Music is a great way to capture a memory. A song playing on the radio during a joyful time or the worst moment of your life will capture the memory and lock it in. As I was driving away from the scene of the breakup I turned the radio on and Dionne Warwick and Barry Gibb's "Heartbreaker" came on. I fell into a heap of tears as Dionne and Barry asked the question I had for Stephanie: "Why do you have to be a heartbreaker?" Here I was, a former jock and current construction worker, bawling his eyes out in a pickup truck with Dionne Warwick and a Bee Gee.

It was less about Stephanie and more about where I was in my life. When things are going well, breakups aren't nearly as devastating, like getting a parking ticket when you're rich. Life requires balance. For most guys that covers career, hobbies, religion or spirituality, family, and an intimate relationship. When all the other facets of your life are in a drainage ditch, then all the eggs get put in the relationship basket. And when that basket is fucking another guy in Hermosa Beach, it's catastrophic.

I guess unconsciously I had some hope of reconciliation because I pulled a move that I would recommend to all you future dumpees out there. I left something at her place, so I had to go back and get it. And I hid it so she wouldn't just find it and throw it out. It had to sit for a while so I could go back and pick it up when things cooled down and maybe get another shot. My object of choice: a softball mitt. Six months after the breakup, I went to her house to get it. It did not turn out as intended. First off, her sister answered the door. Stephanie wasn't even home. But it only got worse. I demanded she let me in so I could find the mitt. I went in looking for it (and to do some reconnaissance on Stephanie's post-Carolla life). I rummaged around and eventually went to look under the bed. I lifted the dust ruffle and what I found was not my softball mitt but rather a spent condom. It was devastating. She had moved on and was getting it on. She later claimed she was in Palm Springs and had a friend stay at her place, but it didn't matter. The damage was done. I was in a funk for a good year.

The Weez tried to help me shake it off and took me out barhopping. But the ladies can smell the stink of failure on you. We were at a club and I walked over to a table with a slightly below-average-looking girl and her friend. I was ready to bed down a five-and-a-half just to get my groove back. I said, "Mind if I sit down?" She responded with two emotionally crippling words: "What for?" Without saying anything I turned around, walked back to The Weez across the room, and said, "Let's get out of here."

So I was single and working for ABC—Always Better Closets. We were based in a warehouse across from Burbank Airport. I'd go out to houses in a van and install custom closets with born-again gangbangers. The born-again gangbanger is a particularly scary breed of cat. You know these guys have stomped their fair share of dudes and have the prison teardrop tattoo, but they also have the Virgin of Guadalupe tattoo and would break out into sessions of speaking in tongues and asking for traveling mercies. They wouldn't listen to anything but Christian rock. Just like my previous stint with Andy the Jehovah's Witness painter, I was stuck listening to Jesus music all day.

The weird thing about Christian rock is that some of it sounds good. If you don't know what you're hearing, you'll be tapping your foot and bobbing your head, thinking the guy is singing about some chick he's banging. "Wow, he really loves this broad. He's totally going to . . . praise her? Wait a second." Then you listen a little closer and you realize it's about Jesus. I also think Christian rock is one of those situations like children's books. Just like that author who wanted to write the Great American Novel but could only manage to shit out ten pages of rhyming *cat* with *hat* and *hop* with *pop,* Christian rockers I'm sure would love to be real rock stars but aren't good enough. You can tell because when they are good enough, they stop being Christian stars. Kings of Leon started out singing the praises of Jesus and Mary but quickly realized they had actual talent and started singing the praises of booze and groupies.

You can only hear so much Stryper before you want to be crucified yourself. So one day I said to my closet-installing amigos, "Can we just listen to some normal music? We can just switch it to the classic-rock station and hear some Beatles or something. Not all music is evil. It's not all Ronnie James Dio screaming about the devil—we could get some Doobie Brothers 'Jesus Is Just Alright.' " So we switched it to the classic-rock station and they all gathered around me and the radio while we were installing a closet in some custom home in Malibu. (That's another thing that sucks about installing custom closets. You're always going into rich people's houses and seeing shoe collections that cost more than you made in the past four years.) When we flipped the station, it was right in the middle of Bob Seger's "Main Street." So I said, "See, it's Bob Seger. It's a nice little softly strummed ditty about—" Before I could finish, one of them chimed in, "a prostitute." I was like, *Huh?* Then I listened to the lyrics about her body softly swaying to the smoky beat down on Main Street and thought, Shit. One of the guys said, "He falls in love with a prostitute. We went over this one in church specifically." I took a good five-Mississippi and gave them a hearty "Yeah, but still," and we switched it back to the Christian rock.

It was quite a crew. In addition to the born-again bangers whose names I can't recall, there was a white guy named Big John and a Filipino nicknamed Pogi. I don't think I have a ton of Filipino fans, so I'll translate. One day I asked him what that name meant and he said "handsome." I remember at the time thinking, That makes for a somewhat cute nickname when you're talking to English speakers, but when you're talking to people in your native language, doesn't that make you a gigantic asshole? That would be like me walking around and calling myself "Gorgeous Carolla." Later Pogi was cutting a piece of red oak, a very hard wood, on a table saw. The wood got caught in the blade, kicked back, and smashed him in the mouth. I wonder what his nickname is now?

One of the born-again Latino guys whose name I can remember is Frank. Frank was that scary ex–gang member who doesn't really talk. When he did speak, it was slow and low. He looked like an extra from *The Shield* or that Sean Penn movie *Colors*. I don't know if it's being dumb or too tough to express yourself with anything but fists and knives, but these type of guys hardly talk. Frank's voice was barely audible, but every now and again the spirit would overcome him and he'd start speaking in tongues. Then you could hear him. He'd be in the van with his eyes rolling back in his skull shouting "Shandala shandala."

Frank stands out from the crowd for me because of one particular incident. We were doing a job in a very small Valley house that had an even smaller hall bathroom. While I walked around the house with the owner, a high-strung gay guy, Frank went into the bathroom. When we got into the hall next to the bathroom, Frank was walking out of the can and mumbled, "I wouldn't go in there." The frenetic gay owner was busily talking to me about matching the molding around the bathroom window and stormed, oblivious, into a Chernobyl cloud of Frank's fecal funk. He had done some serious gangbanging on that toilet. I had to follow the owner in like the second guy to get off the Higgins craft on D-Day.

THE WORST MISTAKE OF MY LIFE (SO FAR)

My most memorable closet-installation story was not with Frank or any of the other guys. I was on a solo mission in the Valley. The boss, Tom, gave me an address and told me to take the panel truck out there to install a closet and put a towel hook assembly in the master bathroom.

I arrived at the house, knocked on the door, and was greeted by a Hispanic woman holding a white infant. It was the maid or nanny. She didn't speak any English, but I managed to talk my way into the house. This, by the way, is a great tip for thieves. Anyone could walk into any house in L.A. in the middle of the day and rob the joint if they're greeted by the non-English-speaking nanny and have some tool bags and confidence.

I went into the master bedroom and saw that they had not cleaned the closet out. Everything was still hung up. We always asked people to clean out the closet before we got in there to install our custom system. But once in a blue moon the customer would forget, and we'd have to get everything out of there first. This was a pain in the ass, so I angrily piled their shit on the bed, then pried out the existing shelf and pole and replaced it with the custom unit.

At this point on any other job I would have just left an invoice and gone back to the shop. That was standard operating procedure. But for some reason on this job the boss told me before I left that I needed to get a check from the owner. Assuming they'd left a check with Consuela (you can't call me a racist unless you can prove that *wasn't* her name), I asked her for the payment. She said, "Que?" I handed her the invoice and said, "Dinero." She said, "Yo no se." Getting frustrated, I said as slowly and sing-songy as I could, "El check-o." She shrugged her shoulders. I held the invoice up to her face and pointed to the total on the bottom. She studied the invoice for a second, then nodded her head, and walked into the kitchen. I thought, Finally, I can blow this taco stand with enough time to swing by a real taco stand before the boss misses me. She returned a moment later with something in her hand, and this time it was her turn to shove something in my face. She held up a piece of mail and pointed to the address.

I looked at the address number and then looked down at my invoice thinking, "Yep, that's right, 11231 . . . so far, so good." Unfortunately, that was followed by the street name.

Hartsook. I was at the wrong house.

The house you've read about where I lived with my dad in the garage was on Hartsook. The next street up is Otsego, which was the cross street of our Laurel Canyon apartment. When the boss handed me the address of the job, I said, "Oh, that's where I live." Somehow I had gotten where I *lived* mixed up with the place I was *living* at the time.

You might be wondering at this point how it was possible to install a closet system that was customized for one house into a completely different house. First, they were only one street apart and most of the homes in that area are ranch-style houses built at the same time, so the closets were roughly the same specs. Plus, the way ABC used to do it allowed for a little give. We wouldn't cut the closet pole at the shop; we'd cut it on site, thus giving us plenty of room for in-the-field adjustments.

As I looked at the letter the nanny handed me against the invoice, I had that split second in between 100 percent certain I was right and feeling like the biggest idiot on the planet. I looked up at the nanny with eyes that read confusion, fear, and panic. Our language barrier had suddenly disappeared. She took off like an express train. First stop—kid. Second stop—phone. I ran like the village coward being chased by a hyena. First stop—truck. Second stop—closet.

I set the screw gun to reverse as I ran into the bedroom and did a lightning round of backing out screws and packing up the shelves, partitions, and poles. I then slithered out of the house. Cosmically, this was somewhere between not leaving a note after you backed into a guy's bumper and the Grinch's raping of Whoville. I still had to install the unit in the right house and thus had to take it with me. I often think about what if I'd just left without having to collect the money as I did in almost every other installation. The couple would return and the woman would say, "Oh, Bob. You shouldn't have, it's not even our anniversary." And if he had half a brain cell he'd say, "When you're in love, every day is your anniversary." Instead the owners came home to the entire contents of their closet piled high on the bed, a horizontal stripe of the old paint where the shelf had been removed, and a very confused Mexican woman. To this day I have no idea what she told her bosses.

Our house had a rotating cast of degenerate roommates coming and going and friends of friends that I wasn't friends with crashing on the sofa. There's a reason it's called a flophouse and not a flopapartment. Something about having a yard to park beat-up vans in becomes enticing to these no-job nomads. It's international waters for retarded pirates. So it became clear that it was time for me to set sail for the vacated room in a woman named Joyce Schulman's house in the aforementioned Hebrew Heights.

10

A ROOM WITH A JEW:
JOYCE SCHULMAN'S HOLLYWOOD HILLS HOME

STUDIO CITY, CA

YEAR RENTED: 1988

RENT: $350 A MONTH

SQUARE FEET: WHO CARES.
IN A FEW MONTHS I'D BE MOVING IN WITH A STRIPPER.

I found myself in a rented room in the house of a woman named Joyce Schulman. This is where I was in my life. I had achieved escape velocity and broken the orbit of my deadbeat roommates, but here I was, a twenty-five-year-old construction worker crashing in the extra bedroom that had recently been vacated by one of my normal friends who was off to college, the daughter of a fiftyish Jewish divorcee turned widow. And believe it or not, Ray had rented the room before me.

The house was just like Joyce, a relic of the seventies. Her pantsuits and Rhoda hairstyle fit perfectly with the cottage-cheese ceiling, burnt-orange countertops, and avocado-green fixtures in the kitchen. It was purchased in the sixties, remodeled in the mid-seventies, and never touched again. Also like Joyce. Ray, in his usual bound-by-nothing attitude, asked her when was the last time she had sex. She said it had been twenty-seven years. For my next roommate, it would be a completely different story.

Chris was the one who discovered Star Garden. It was a weird, divey, *Flashdance*-style strip joint on Lankershim Boulevard. The rest of the gang and I soon followed, and it became a regular watering hole. This was where I met my next girlfriend.

My buddy Phillip the Juggler was living out here trying to make it in Hollywood and was about to get married. This next story will chronicle how I met my stripper girlfriend and what a mammoth douchebag Phillip's best man turned out to be. He was a hotshot surgeon from Miami who blew into town to throw Phillip his bachelor party. It started off at an upscale Mexican eatery on the Sunset Strip. Twelve boring guys including Phillip's accountant sitting around eating nachos and soft tacos. When the bill arrived, everyone reached for their wallet but the best man from Miami grabbed the check. I remember thanking him profusely because back then I would have blown a guy for a free burrito, and that was à la carte. He said don't mention it, and it was off to the next location. This time it was Ventura Boulevard in Studio City (across the street from the Bla Bla Café where the diner booth once resided) at a place called Queen Mary, where we drank daiquiris and watched transvestites put on a burlesque show. After about an hour of this cockfoolery I said, "I know the bouncer at a place that has real boobies. We should head over there." Once again everyone reached for their wallets, but the Worst Man said he was picking it up. Once again I thanked him profusely. As fate would have it, one of my favorite gals was working that night. Her real name was Lindsey, stage name *Cat*lin—thus the phrase "I'm going for a Cat scan" was born. Long story short, all of Phillip's boring friends cleared out before closing and I was left behind without a ride, truck still parked at the Queen Mary. She ended up giving me a ride to my truck but not without a three-hour stop at Twains for a piece of a pie and lively conversation.

Before I move on with Lindsey, let me tie up the loose tampon string known as Phillip's best man, Carlos, and why he turned out to be a colossal pussy. When I ran into him at Phillip's wedding a week later, I made sure to make a point of thanking him once again for the free tamales and tipping the guys who had their tamales tucked between their legs. He said no problem. He was one of those guys who, when he came into town, would rent a Porsche instead of a Pontiac like everyone else. That night at the reception, while I was dancing and attempting to get drunk, I was interrupted by a tap on my shoulder. It was Phillip's accountant from the bachelor party. He said, "I'm collecting money for Carlos for the bachelor party." I just laughed and continued what would later be known as the Cabbage Patch. He tapped me on the shoulder again and said, "It's sixty-five bucks apiece." I said, "Are you kidding?" He replied, "No, I'm serious. I'm collecting money to pay for the bachelor party." I said, "Why are *you* doing this? Why isn't he doing it himself?" He said, "Carlos thought I should do it, since I'm Phillip's accountant." I know they've not completed construction yet on the Douchebag Hall of Fame, but when the first bronze bust is ceremoniously placed under its Lucite case, I want it to be of this ass-wipe.

After multiple visits to Star Garden, a romance blossomed. Soon I moved into Lindsey's apartment in the bowels of Hollywood. It was in the basement of an old twenties-style five-story building on Franklin, down the road from the Hollywood Bowl. It was four hundred square feet with one bathroom and no bedroom. It was essentially a closet.

This was 1989, at that time Hollywood was rundown, crime-ridden, and dicey. So I had to protect my wheels. I had an '84 Nissan pickup truck (previously used for that ill-fated trip to Vegas with Ray and Chris). Sadly, it was the most valuable thing I owned.

It had a vinyl bench seat and no headrests. If you hit a pothole, you'd whack your head on the window behind you. In a world full of

DOT regulations that I usually bitch about, this is one I could have used. If I was rear-ended, my head would have gone through the back window at literally breakneck speed. And it was uninsured. Because of the neighborhood, I knew my truck would be stolen immediately, so I went to the Hollywood Pep Boys, bought a toggle switch, a few feet of wire, and a can of brown spray paint. I went under the truck and cut the wire that went to the fuel pump. Then I hooked up my wires, dragged it to the front of the truck, opened up a hole, popped in the toggle switch, and put it underneath the bench seat. My plan was to be able to hit the toggle and cut off the fuel supply. The beauty of this plan is that the truck would start up but would only run for about a block and a half, as there was no fuel being pumped. For you gearheads out there, the truck was not injected and the few blocks it ran was off of what was left in the float bowl of the carb.

Here's why I'm a genius. This system meant the thief would try to steal it, but only get a block away before the truck "died." He would just assume he had the horrible luck of running out of gas and scamper off to his next victim. And it worked. Three times. All three times my truck got stolen, I walked around and found it within a block or two. Before I'd start looking I'd have to pick a direction. "I wonder if they went north this time." I'd also have to remember if I hit the toggle a block before I got home to burn some of the fuel in the float bowl, giving the thief even less range.

Even if they couldn't steal the truck itself, I still had to worry about the stereo. But I had a MacGyver-esque solution for that, too. It had a brown dashboard, so I took a can of brown spray paint, put a little piece of tape over the digital readout of my Sony stereo, and then spray-painted it. Guys wrapping T-shirts around their hands and punching out windows to steal stereos are not music lovers. They're just looking for something to trade for a hit of crack. So what's the junkie gonna do with a stereo that's been spray-painted? Clean it off meticulously so he can sell it? No, he's gonna move on to the next car. All three times the truck got stolen, the stereo stayed in the dash. It's like firing a snot rocket onto your own waffle so you can leave it at the table while you hit the bathroom and return without it being eaten. (By the way, this is a true technique I saw Ray implement with his brother in 1981.)

I did have to start the truck with a flathead screwdriver after one of those assholes popped out my ignition. I just kept the screwdriver on the seat, and it became my key. And because I used to keep the door unlocked so said junkies wouldn't bust out my window, I didn't need to worry about the key to the door. This led to a funny moment. One time I got pulled over by the LAPD. A cop had seen the popped ignition and the screwdriver and thought I stole the truck. Little did he know I was just too poor and pathetic to get it fixed. Joke's on you, buddy.

Our place was too small and the neighborhood was too shady. Lindsey and I needed to get the hell out of there. We retreated to my old stomping ground: From our apartment you could see the North Hollywood High football field. It was a one-bed/one-bath with a small loft that gave it a high ceiling and the illusion of space even if there was barely any.

We were officially living together, but it was far from domestic bliss. In fact, there was even some domestic violence. One time I was out playing softball with the fellas. When I finally returned home, she was pissed off. I was supposed to come back after the game but instead went out and got loaded. She started haranguing me, but I didn't want to deal with her noise so I went to the bedroom to lie down. As I passed out in my softball uniform, she angrily said, "Get up." I stood up, and as soon as my still-cleated feet were under me, she punched me square in the face, knocking me back down on the bed. She was a chick, I used to box, and I was drunk so I didn't really feel it. But I remember having this thought as she stomped out of the room: "Good, I win." That may seem like an odd thing to have in your head at a moment like that, but the argument was over—and since she had escalated it to that point, now she was the one who needed to say sorry. I'd wake up the next morning to an apology, some French toast, and maybe a blow job.

It wasn't all bad. Lindsey was supportive of my goal of getting into show business. I had taken an honest stab at comedy and had hit the ceiling at the Groundlings (the infamous improv training program/troupe that produced Phil Hartman, Pee-wee Herman, and Will Ferrell among others), but she came to me one day with an ad from the *Drama-Logue* about the formation of a new improv troupe that would become the Acme Theatre. I detailed my time with Acme in my last book, so I won't include it here. If you need a refresher I suggest you go out and buy several hundred copies—preferably in hardcover.

While Lindsey was a fan of my improv, I can't say the same for my grandfather. One night we had him and my grandmother over for dinner at our place. Being a writer, my grandfather said he wasn't that big a fan of Acme and didn't appreciate improv in general. Of course, Grandma had to dogpile on this as well. During minute fifteen of their critique of improv and my choice to do it, Lindsey, who'd had a couple glasses of wine, told them to shut up. To me, my grandparents' complaining was just standard operating procedure, and I didn't really notice it. To Lindsey it was shocking. This happens often: Outsiders witness my family's boundless lack of enthusiasm for my efforts, are baffled by it, and occasionally, if they've had enough to drink, will tell them to shut the hell up.

A similar situation happened years later the first time I brought my wife to visit my father's house. She walked around the place and eventually noticed that while there were many pictures of my family, mostly stepfamily, there were literally no pictures of me. Not as a child, not as an adult, nothing. She was disgusted.

While I toiled at improv with Acme, hoping it would lead to something, I made ends meet with more construction. I was working for myself, building cabinets, fences, and anything else people wanted me to do for fifteen bucks an hour. (Thank God none of my clients directed gay porn because I probably would have just said, "Eh, fifteen an hour.") One job, like so many others that had come before it, involved putting in some drywall. Let me just do a quick PSA against drywalling while stoned. It's already boring work, and the clock really slows down when you're high. You start at seven A.M. and by 8:15 it feels like you've been there all day. It's the longest day of your life. And you don't even do the job right. One time I ended up covering the rough electrical—switches, outlets, junction boxes—and the electrician had to poke holes in the drywall with a coat hanger to find all of his work. It was the poor man's version of a metal detector. That was the last time I got stoned on the job.

I also took some other truly odd jobs. One of the many low points that come to mind is the time I auditioned for Party Pals. I swung by my friend Paul Rugg's apartment; he was out of work and also a member of Acme. He said, "I have an audition. Want to come along?" I said, "What's it for?" He said, "It's for one of those companies where you dress up like Batman or a Ninja Turtle and make balloon animals at kids' parties." I said I'd go but just to watch and make fun of him. Twenty minutes later, we pulled up at a strip mall in Encino to the world headquarters of Party Pals. Sadly, there were about twenty people there, all hoping to beat the odds and have the chance to don the stinky turtle outfit and spend the day getting kicked in the shins by kids for sixty bucks a party. One minute we were all standing around a waiting room, and the next thing I knew some lady with a clipboard said, "Let's do an improv called 'the machine.' " This is a very basic physical improvisational exercise in which one person starts a repetitive physical movement, like a moving part of a machine, and then the next person connects to that person with their own repetitive moving part. I thought, "This is gonna be good. I can't wait to see Paul make an ass of himself." Naturally, the woman with the clipboard looked directly at me and said, "Why don't you start?" A combination of low self-esteem, extensive improv training, and adrenaline made me immediately snap into action. I stood there silently in front of nineteen people and made a goofy train locomotion movement with my arms while simultaneously bending and straightening my knees. After doing it for what felt like a lifetime, I looked at her and said, "Should I be making a noise?" She, in her most condescending voice, said, "It'd be nice." My little plan had backfired. Eventually the rest of the desperate actors were forced into this pathetic dance until it abruptly ended with a thud. One of the more ambitious gals had gotten down on her hands and knees under a folding table, and as she began her mechanical movement, she mashed her head into the sharp steel support rail that ran under the table. And that actress's name is Jennifer Aniston. Actually, the only thing I remember about her is that she was crying and literally had a dent in her head. Paul went on to become a proud member of the Party Pal family, and I was also offered a position. I declined and went back into the profession of Jesus. The only difference was that I didn't gouge the elderly. But on my way to carpentry jobs I did enjoy driving by kids' parties over at Beeman Park to laugh at Paul sweating in his Ninja Turtle costume.

I also had a short stint as a comedy traffic-school instructor. It may sound like it's a million miles away from a hit TV show or a syndicated radio program, but if you can do seven hours of comedy in front of a hostile group at a Holiday Inn on a Sunday morning, you can do just about anything.

But before I could teach a class, I had to go to three rounds of traffic-school training—Saturday and Sunday for eight hours straight, plus a Wednesday and Thursday half-day class. I wanted to kill myself, as would anybody who sat through twenty-four hours of traffic school in four days. I believe I should get credited with that. I should have those hours in the bank so that the next time I get pulled over and have to do traffic school, it just gets deducted from my tally.

The thing I remember them stressing over and over again in the training was to tell the people I was a professional comedian and not to be scared to embellish my credits a little bit. These violators could have gone to Sears and paid $18.95 for traffic school, but they chose to spend the extra four dollars to come to "Lettuce Amuse You"—seriously, that's how the name was spelled—and they're gonna want their money's worth. I remember thinking, When I show up to the Y in El Segundo at seven forty-five in the morning, I wonder how the story about just winning *Star Search* or getting off the road with the Rolling Stones is gonna go over? Saying your comedy career is going great to a roomful of traffic-school students is about as believable as telling the guy behind the glass at a pawn shop that you just got a big promotion.

But if you were forced into traffic school, I was the instructor you wanted. I would let people show up late despite the fact that they were required to fulfill a certain amount of time in the class. People would sometimes walk in an hour or more late and instantly launch into their apologies and excuses. I just said, "It's fine, sit down." Once I figured out there were no DMV undercover narcs in the class, I just let people do whatever the hell they wanted. I'd be doing crowd work, asking people questions about themselves and riffing on them. Occasionally we'd go outside for some Frisbee. I wasn't about to force people to read a pamphlet about passive restraints. I was just in it for a few bucks.

In 1989 I decided that I needed a change of venue. I told Lindsey to hold down the fort while I headed north to San Francisco. The plan was to get in at a local comedy club and really hone my stand-up act. I quit Acme after just starting it a few months earlier, packed up my truck, and headed for the extra bedroom my high school friend Zeb had in a house he was renting in Oakland. The club I attempted to make my workout room was called Rooster T. Feathers. By name alone, you can tell this was the comedic low point of my life. I was ready to drive off the Golden Gate Bridge, but I couldn't afford the toll.

This is a good opportunity to talk about Zeb. I learned two very important lessons from him. He was one of my best friends and the only guy with whom I'd had a creative kinship. Ray, The Weez, Chris, and all the other people I hung around with had no interest in my ideas and observations. They just wanted to know why I wouldn't shut up. Zeb hasn't been mentioned previously because his

1989—San Francisco. Me and Zeb in the gayest photo I've ever taken.

head actually contained a brain. He was a lover, not a fart lighter. He didn't participate in our criminal enterprises. Zeb was a long, gangly redhead with thick glasses and a cowlick. He was a wildly interesting and creative guy. He wrote a six-hundred-page book on Russian cosmonauts by the time he was fourteen. In high school he started an underground school newspaper that was very successful with the student body. Most people thought he would end up publishing a really cool magazine and personally do all the photojournalism. Starting at age fifteen he worked at the KFC in North Hollywood and was, at $2.22 an hour, able to save up enough for a used VW Bug and a camera. Plus he was also the only kid I knew with a *Playboy* subscription. This was my idea of having your shit together. Other than that, we were equals in the loser competition. It would have been hard to tell which of us was more destitute and pathetic. But even though he was poor and his dad had abandoned the family, he was able to get a scholarship to UCLA and later transfer to Berkeley. Unfortunately, when he got to Berkeley he found himself a couple credits short of graduating and didn't manage to finish.

Years later after I had some success, my first call was to Zeb. My character, Mr. Birchum, was gaining traction on KROQ, I was signed by William Morris, and things were starting to work out for me. Meanwhile, he was languishing in a rented house in Oakland with a temp job and four roommates. Knowing what a clever guy he was, I told him that he should head back to L.A. and let me introduce him to my new Hollywood connections. No dice. He was trying to mop up the remaining units he needed to graduate Berkeley. Then as *Loveline* and *The Man Show* took off, I tried again. This should have been a dream come true for him. His best buddy from high school was living in a house in the hills and had two shows on TV. While I was on Comedy Central, he was still in Oakland bouncing from one shitty job to the next. I said he should come down and write some jokes for *The Man Show,* but he always gave me some line about a book he was working on and had to finish and said he had to clean his room—literally—before he could even do that. Finally, after a few years of prodding he agreed to come out for a week so that I could set up some meetings. But when he got here all he wanted to do was borrow my second car and chase down some chick he met online who wasn't interested in him. At the end of the week he returned to the same crappy job and the same crappy house filled with the same crappy roommates.

Sadly for Zeb, he was on the losing end of a cosmic see-saw. The more success I'd see, the less he saw. Seven years into my struggle to drag him toward success, I had another of our unsatisfying phone calls. After once again bringing up his never-to-be-completed book, something like *The Gentlemen's Guide to Picking Up Brazilian Chicks,* he also mentioned losing his temp job and declaring bankruptcy over a $3,300 MasterCard bill. Enough was enough. I said, "Cut the bullshit, you're never going to finish that book. Just drop it and move on. You're a thirty-seven-year-old man declaring bankruptcy over a credit-card bill. Your plan isn't working. Listen to me and let me help you." His response was, "You think you can get preachy with me just because you were lucky enough to meet Jimmy Kimmel." And that was it. I thought, Fuck it, I give up. I told him I made my own luck, and that was the last I've heard from him. I've never spoken to him since.

And that is lesson one from the book of Zeb. Internalization versus Externalization. He could not internalize how he was standing in his own way and made everything someone else's problem. I remember him once telling me about a great idea for a domain name but then bitching about a business partner who "screwed him" on the deal. They agreed to split the cost of the domain, $1,200, but she backed out. He got pissed at me when I asked why at age thirty-five he didn't have $1,200. We came from equally fucked-up families where success was not considered an option. Yet I managed to break that cycle by changing my mind-set. But for him it was too overwhelming. He just couldn't get his crap together. His pride got the better of him, he couldn't accept a helping hand from me, and now he's doing God knows what.

The other lesson is that you have to be able to walk away. Six months after we shunned each other, I showed up for our twentieth high school reunion anticipating an uncomfortable public confrontation. Although he was one of the most popular students from the graduating class of 1982, Zeb was conspicuously absent. People, knowing how close we were, kept asking me where Zeb was. I just shrugged my shoulders and said I didn't know anything. At some point one of the Finnegan twins who used to worship at the altar of Zeb ran up to me and said, "Did you hear the news?" Zeb had gotten a big promotion and couldn't travel. I didn't have the heart to tell him the truth. He was ashamed to show his face at the reunion because everyone thought he was going to be Richard Branson and he just turned out to be a Richard.

Two weeks after my tragic attempt at comedy in the Bay Area I returned to my apartment, tail between my legs. Fortunately my girlfriend, construction job, and improv troupe were all waiting and welcomed me back. At least for a while . . .

That year my old buddy Carl was getting married and the wedding was in Hawaii. All the dudes were going: The Weez, Ray, Chris, et cetera. So I told Lindsey it was "just the boys." She was unhappy but rolled with it. That was until The Weez's cousin Michelle and one of her friends who were also flying out saw Lindsey and mentioned that the ladies were going, too. That was the straw that broke the stripper's back.

I went to Hawaii for the wedding. In a scene that seems unimaginable today, we flew in a big empty plane smoking cigarettes the whole time. The wedding was nice, and at one point The Weez and Chris secretly put LSD in Ray's drink. It was as nice and mellow as Ray has ever been.

1989—Plane to Hawaii. Just noticed I'm reading a *People* with JFK, Jr., on the cover. That's a bad omen.

I returned to find that Lindsey had moved out. In an even stranger twist, she had moved in with my grandparents. They were away for five weeks doing one of those Europe-on-ten-dollars-a-day-style tours. She needed a place to stay, and in keeping with tradition, my family was nicer to someone outside the family than to their own blood. Adding insult to injury, I would drive by their house and see the motorcycle owned by her new boyfriend parked in the driveway.

Not only was I out a girlfriend, I was now out a roommate. And I couldn't swing the rent myself. I soon welcomed a succession of dudes renting the loft for $200 a month. As pathetic as I was, the parade of losers I shared my place with were worse. One guy moved in and all he had was a single cardboard box, the kind you use to carry your possessions after you clean out your desk when you've been fired from a job. It had no lid and contained a couple of T-shirts, a pair of folded jeans, and a can of Dinty Moore beef stew. Bob A. was one of these guys. He lived with me for a little over two months

185

until his VW van was fixed and he could thus return north to his homeland of Canada. The night before he moved out, I promised to drive him to pick up the van the next morning and thought we'd have a little farewell party. We pooled our money. It was just enough for a $13 hibachi, some coals,and a chub-pack of chicken. As we sat in front of the hibachi I looked at Bob and thought, I just spent my last nineteen bucks on this cookout, rent's due next week, and I don't have a roommate to replace you. Bad times.

11

THE SANTA MONICA REDEMPTION:
THE FOURTEENTH STREET APARTMENT

SANTA MONICA, CA

YEAR RENTED:	1991
RENT:	$765 (RENT CONTROLLED)
	800 SQUARE FEET
	TWO BEDROOMS
	ONE BATH
	ONE ROOMMATE WITH ONE ANGRY CAT

I managed to convince Lindsey to give me another shot, and we made a fresh start in a new apartment in Santa Monica. It was a two-bedroom, one-bath in an eight-unit rent-controlled building on Fourteenth Street. It was nice to be out of the heat of the Valley.

We quickly found there was a reason we broke up the first time around and I, for the second time in my life, lost Lindsey and was out a roommate.

Looking for roommates when you're entering your freshman year of college is one thing, but when you're entering your late twenties it's just sad. The key was to find someone who, like me, was able to thread the needle between being successful and a homeless junkie. After all, you have to not only live with this person but have heated, accusatory arguments over such hot-button issues as "Who's been getting into my generic shredded wheat?" and "Why are we splitting the utility bill when you have a space heater?" A friend from Acme named Lisa ended up moving in and brought with her a very angry cat named Cicely. She would rub up against my leg, but when I would reach down to pet her she would swat at me. (The cat, not Lisa.)

It was during this period that one night I was returning from the supermarket. As I walked up the stairs to the second floor heading toward my door, I heard a woman bellowing from the street. The apartment had a long, high hedgerow that blocked my view. So I ran down the stairs. I remember the flip-flops I was wearing at the time making their namesake sound as I descended. When I got to the street I saw a hot blonde in her mid-twenties pointing and shouting that someone had stolen her purse. I looked to my right and saw a black guy sprinting away, purse in hand. I took off running after him, knowing full well that even if I weren't in sandals I wasn't going to catch him. I wasn't a fast runner when I played ball in high school, and it had been several years since. And let's not forget that black people are naturally faster runners because of their anatomy. (I failed biology class but I did learn some science from Jimmy the Greek.)

Now, you might be wondering why I bothered. It wasn't just because the chick was hot; it was because I had no regard for my own life. For better or worse, whether we want to admit it or not, as a society we assign a value to life based on a combination of income, education, immediate family, looks, et cetera. At that point the Kelly Beige Book had me valued somewhere between a potted plant and an empty vending machine.

The snatcher's buddy was a little ahead of him driving an RX7 that kept swerving in with the door open so he could jump in and drive away. But I was too close in hot pursuit and the getaway driver decided to get away by himself and took off. The thief saw this, dropped the purse, and picked up some speed. I stopped running, figuring I had the purse and could return it to its attractive owner.

She arrived moments later, out of breath, and saw that the thief had dropped the bag, leaving its contents strewn about the sidewalk and street. With nary a thank-you she began looking around and gathering her belongings, but couldn't find her wallet. She completely ignored my heroics and began complaining. "Oh, man. He got my wallet." I said, "Maybe it's here somewhere." "No, he got it. I knew it. Goddammit. I just went to the ATM." She was now yelling at me. A minute later she found her wallet in the gutter, just off the curb. She declared, "I found it! I found it!" and the whole event became her victory, as if she had actually done something. This is such a hot-chick move. A fatty would have been blowing me. But she mentioned she lived in the next building over, and I thought maybe this would pay off later. Quickly a crowd gathered around the hot chick and her recovered purse. When the cops arrived and asked what happened, Pat Tillman Jr. chimed in with "Somebody took her purse, so we all started chasing him and he dropped it." I thought, "Who the fuck are *we*? I didn't see your ass chasing anybody." The cops got the story without ever taking a statement from me, the guy who actually did the chasing. Someone then offered the blonde a cup of herbal tea, she left, and I slinked away to pick up the groceries I'd left outside my place and beat off.

I spent a good two weeks hoping for a note on my mailbox that started, "Dear handsome hero . . ." and ended with a phone number written in lipstick. No such luck. As I've said, there are horrible people in the world, but hot blonde chicks are the worst. There's no way that she didn't know the apartment complex from which I ran to her rescue. She lived in a neighboring building and was coming home from school when the incident happened. She was standing right there when I came down. Even accounting for the trauma of having your purse snatched, it should've only been a day or two before she shook it off and came calling. There were zero attempts to make contact. Not even a Post-it above the mailboxes of my building. I know I sound bitter, and I recognize that I'm not one of the guys heading up the stairs on 9/11, but I did run out onto a dark street to chase a guy who could've had a gun. I'd say that if not some nookie, that should at least merit a T.G.I. Friday's gift card.

This next story doesn't involve me and didn't take place in one of my various dwellings, but it did go down a couple blocks from my apartment and centers around one of my oldest and most colorful friends, Dave. After being discharged from the navy for beating a superior officer with a shoe, he settled in sleepy Santa Monica to begin his life as an electrician. Dave was a good soul who on occasion would drink too much and run afoul of the law, his neighbors, delivery guys, and anyone in his general vicinity. Don't think "criminal," think "pirate" as I describe Dave. He had multiple warrants for parking violations, a restraining order from a woman who lived in an adjacent building, and once had the cops called on him for playing his music too loud. The twist is that the punk rock was coming through his headphones while he was wearing them when he was passed out. Yet in 1988 he was named Citizen of the Year in the ultra-progressive/liberal hamlet of Santa Monica. It should also be noted that Dave was built like a jukebox dipped in creatine. So how did this not-so-lovable lug end up winning the hearts of the Santa Monica City Council members? One night after polishing off what Dave dubbed a Big Lush (a 7-Eleven Big Gulp topped off with a pint of dark Meyer's rum), he decided a large pizza would be just what the drunkard ordered. But he had two problems: He was in no shape to drive, and his address had been blacklisted by the local Domino's franchise. He had been placed on the "no pie list." God knows what you have to do to make it onto that list; perhaps it involved his shoe. I never got a clear answer. But the only way Dave could get a Domino's pizza was to give an address three blocks away, wait for the unsuspecting driver to show up, and intercept him before he rang the doorbell. So Dave hung up the phone with Domino's, staggered out of the back of his apartment building, and headed up the alley to the drop zone. It was dark, cold, and late, but Dave walked with purpose, making sure he got there before the pizza did. Then he saw something in the distance. It looked like somebody was being pulled into the bushes off the alley. Dave went to investigate. When he arrived, he was shocked to see a young woman being raped by an ex-convict who had just been paroled after serving a twenty-year term for, you guessed it . . . check fraud. He jumped on the guy, and with the strength of ten drunken bears held him in a headlock until the police arrived.

Four months later, it was official. The man who used to run up huge pay-per-view porn tabs and steal all my Tylenol PM when he was working at my house was now Santa Monica Citizen of the Year. The cherry on top of the bizarre sundae was that at the ceremony, the medal was bestowed upon him by Kent McCord. Who's Kent

McCord? He played Officer Reed on the cop show *Adam-12*. Hey, baby, this is Hollywood.

It was the winter of 1991 and my friend Paul's wife (Paul being the Acme buddy I'd auditioned for Party Pals with) worked for the Catholic Big Brothers. She arranged for our group to do an improv show at their church around Christmas. I'm an atheist, but I'm not an asshole. I have no beef with entertaining some poor Catholic kids around Christmastime.

She later roped me into doing some personal Catholic Big Brothering. It was an odd fit. I wasn't Catholic, I had no real big-brother qualities, and there was no pay. As a matter of fact, it *cost* money, since you'd be the one footing the bill for the fast food and the *Apple Dumpling Gang* VHS rental. Despite this, I went in for an interview.

It was their job to suss out the creeps, so one of the first questions was, "How many times a day do you think about sex?" I don't think they were actually interested in the number, it was more of a test to see if you'd start sweating profusely and dive through the plate-glass window of the building. I paused for a second and said "three." I figured if I said zero they'd know I was lying. If I told the truth—3,600—they'd call Chris Hansen. Three seemed reasonable, as it was the number of times I'd beaten off that day.

Then they asked, "How often do you do drugs?" I said, "I don't deal them, but if I'm at a party and there's a doobie going around, count me in." Not only would it seem disingenuous to say "Straight as an arrow," but I was in the middle of an interview for a job with no benefits and no paycheck that I didn't really want in the first place, so I figured, Why lie?

The bad part of being a Catholic Big Brother is that it's a huge time suck. The upside is that if you're a single guy it's better than a puppy when playing the "Aww, that's so sweet" card. Thus I was hoping for a black kid who couldn't get around without his polio crutches. Instead I got paired up with Nate, the kid you saw in the picture at the top of this chapter, a spindly strawberry blond who, worst of all, was from Beverly Hills. Granted, he was poor as hell and lived with his single mom and three brothers and sisters in the cheapest apartment in Beverly Hills. Why Beverly Hills, you ask? Mama wanted to make sure her kids could get the same top-notch education Ian Ziering received.

Since I was also poor as hell and living in an apartment, I'd take him to Taco Bell. That would be our nice meal out. We'd jump into my Isuzu Trooper and head out for some Bell Beefers with him and a friend.

Nate hung around with a chunky Russian kid who would often tag along on our excursions. I have a couple of specific memories of him. First was his thick Russian accent. This is going to be a little hard to translate to the written word, so please forgive the phonetics. When he first introduced himself, he said, "Hello, my name is Teem." I said, "Team? Like in 'basketball team'?" He said, "No. Not Teem . . . *Teem!*" Eventually Nate stepped in and clarified that his friend's name was Tim, short for Timothy. The other interesting thing about Teem was that he learned all his English from gangsta rap of the nineties. For our trips he would hand me a mix cassette of Dr. Dre, Easy E, Ice-T, and so on. Then he would sit in the back of the Trooper holding a bucket of Mountain Dew he poured himself at the 7-Eleven rapping along to the mix. Imagine a Russian version of the fat kid from *Modern Family* with Yakov Smirnoff's voice rapping "Beeches ain't sheet but ho's and treeks/Leek on these balls and suck on thees deek."

Once I took the two of them to Magic Mountain. As the Trooper with the four-banger was struggling to make it up the pass with the added cargo of Teem and his salad bowl of Mountain Dew they were both lamenting their lot in life. They were in their first year of high school, which is miserable no matter who you are. But they went to Beverly Hills High, which made it worse. Both their parents had no money, so they had to go to class every day feeling like poor outcasts among the rich kids who resided in 90210 proper. Nate said, "We don't get any girls," and Teem added, "Yes, those beeches will not talk to us, what is up?" It felt like time for a big-brother pep talk. I turned around and said, "It's all gonna change next year. You'll be sophomores, and you'll have a whole new crop of freshmen coming in, so you'll be big men on campus. You'll be rock stars." Teem interrupted me and said, "Who are you keeding? Nate is too skeeny, and I am too fat."

In 1993 when the Internet was still a new fad, Nate fell in love with some chick he met in an America Online chat room. She was from Kentucky. Nate would call her long distance on his home phone.

People under twenty who are reading this must be thinking two things. What the fuck is an America Online chat room, and what is calling "long distance"? Oh, you kids. Back when I was broke, you used to get charged extra to make a call outside of your area code. Now it's all cell phones, Skype, and texts. I've said it before and I'll say it again, there has never been a better time to be poor.

Eventually his mom got wise and cut him off. He was in love with his Kentucky Woman but was heartbroken by their Communication Breakdown: She was the Wind Beneath His Wings. (Sorry, let me turn off my iPod.) He wanted me to drive him to see her. I didn't even know where Kentucky was, never mind have a car that could get us there. He pleaded about how much he missed her and wanted to talk to her. Taking pity, I gave him my calling card and told him I'd separate the Kentucky calls out of the bills and he'd have to pay me back. I told him to use it but not abuse it. Three weeks later, I got my phone shut off. I didn't receive a cancellation letter or anything. One day my phone just stopped working. I went down in person to the phone company, and they said I owed them $375. Nate rang up a nearly $400 bill ringing up a chick neither he nor his penis would ever meet in person.

Occasionally people come up to me at my live stand-up shows around the country or call into the podcast wondering what happened to Nate. I've completely lost touch with him. He came around once to see a taping of *The Man Show*, but that was the last time I heard from him. It's weird. Contrary to what you think would happen, he sort of cut me off after I got famous. I'm not a huge believer in karma, but it does strike me that things started working out in my life after I mentored him for a year or two. Nate, if you're reading this, two things: First, you still owe me for that phone bill. Second, say hi to Teem for me the next time you visit him in prison.

12

THE BEGINNING OF THE BEGINNING: THE LA CRESCENTA HOUSE

LA CRESCENTA, CA

YEARS RENTED: 1992–1995

RENT: $1,500 A MONTH

1,900 SQUARE FEET

THREE BEDROOMS

TWO BATHS

NO HEAT, AC, OR SMOKE DETECTORS, *BUT A HOT TUB AND TWO POOL TABLES—REGULAR AND BUMPER.*

197

LA CRESCENTA was a weird, sleepy little community on the outskirts of Pasadena (technically the foothills of Glendale). It felt rural, like a Mayberry-esque town. There was a little market and a place to get shoes repaired. I literally got my shoes repaired. Who does that anymore?

There's a guy by the name of Ralph Garman that you SoCal natives may know from the Kevin and Bean morning show, and others of you may know from doing some voices on *Family Guy*. I know him as one of my roommates from La Crescenta. Ralph and I met through the Acme Theatre in 1991. We did sketch and improv and even played on the theater's softball team together. We immediately hit it off and later decided to shack up together. We had another roommate named Courtland Cox, who's gone on to produce all of those VH-1 "whores-in-a-house" shows. Unlike me, with no middle name, Courtland ended up with a worse scenario. His middle name is Downs. Cox is a tough last name, but putting "Downs" in front of it makes your name an activity: Courtland Downs Cox.

Like all of my preceding abodes, this house had no central heat or air-conditioning. Seeing your breath in your own room is pathetic. In the winter I used to go to bed in a thick wool sweater and ski cap. For the hot summer nights, I resorted to a tried-and-true technique from the time in my dad's garage: I'd run out, jump into the pool, then run back in without drying off and hop into bed. This killed two birds with one stone because it also accomplished my biweekly bathing.

Having a pool was great, except for that first day of summer. Confused? Why wouldn't the first day of summer be the best day to own a pool? Let me explain. The first day of summer meant it had been exactly eight months since Ralph skimmed it, ran the pool motor, or put in a drop of chlorine. A little lesson on Human Nature 101.

Ralph slept in the master bedroom, yet the rent was divided equally three ways. So in order to justify having the master suite, Ralph was in charge of the pool and the lawn. This worked out all right during the summer when he *wanted* to be outside, but when it was a little bit colder, he didn't perform his due diligence. One year I had to take it upon myself to drain the pool and clean it. And as I recount this story, keep in mind that this was a large pool. Not quite Olympic size, but as big as you'll see in a residential application. That particular year, Ralph was so derelict in his duty that the pool had turned into the Black Lagoon. I rented a bilge pump and drained off the first several thousand gallons of swamp water. But the last three feet that had congregated in the deep end was a sludge so thick and viscous it wouldn't go through the pump. It was the consistency of crude oil and comprised of decomposing leaves and possibly a decomposing hooker Ralph couldn't be bothered to dump at the park. I, wearing supermarket slip-on shoes and cutoffs, proceeded to remove it with a flathead shovel, one scoop at a time. I was using an over-the-shoulder chuck technique, so half of the putrid swill made it out of the pool and the other half rained back down on me. It was a terrible day made worse by the fact that Ralph was sitting in plain view watching TV the whole time.

We had a hot tub, too, but that was always well kept because it was the ultimate destination when we'd bring home the ladies. We had enough naked hot tub parties that Ralph started referring to the place as Chez Nude. We must have had deaf neighbors, because we would throw long, loud parties. They would go until four A.M. I have to assume there were no kids in the neighborhood, because the sounds Ralph would make with his ladies in that hot tub could have easily gotten us on the Megan's Law registry. In a hot tub, you have to elevate your voice over the sound of the jets and bubbles, so you end up shouting stuff like "DUDE, YOU DON'T HAVE TO EAT HER PUSSY . . . JUST LET HER BLOW YOU." Yet nothing, never even a polite note on the door from the neighbors.

1993—La Crescenta. Me in the hot tub with a friend and a number of floating venereal diseases.

We lucked into the house because Ralph was working at a bar called Tequila Creek and the owner of the bar was also the owner of the house. While I was swinging a hammer for $15 an hour before taxes, Ralph was slinging drinks. He'd come home after a five-hour shift with $200 in cash and eight phone numbers. I'd be reading plans, driving a beat-up truck with a bed box, sweating all day, and he made twice as much as me, tax-free and getting digits. I'm going to tell my son, "Look, I'd like you to turn out to be a doctor or a journalist. But if you don't, move to the beach and become a bartender. Your job will be getting hot chicks drunk while you look over their shoulders at one of the many flat-screens with the big game on in high-def as the next Dave Matthews is jamming onstage."

But the guy who owned the house was cool and laid-back, and we basically had an agreement that if we didn't ask him to repair stuff or install central heat and air, we could throw our Caligula-esque parties. And he even left behind some cool shit like a jukebox and two pool tables—one bumper, one standard. I don't think much pool got played, but one morning while cleaning up after one of our parties

I did find a spent condom in the corner pocket. No heat and no air but a jukebox and two pool tables. A few years ago I had Ralph on my podcast and he humorously noted that we had "all the luxuries but none of the necessities."

When I moved in, I didn't have anything as far as furniture. Well, I did have one piece. It was a large Craftsman rolling tool chest that I used as a dresser.

Ralph's room was outfitted with a nice bedroom set that included a dark oak nightstand which contained a .44 automatic, handcuffs, porno mags that Larry Flynt would think crossed the line, and a French tickler or three. I frequently joked with Ralph that if he ever got T-boned by a drunk driver or shot by a jealous boyfriend, I would get to that nightstand before his parents did. And conversely, if I died on his watch he would place a couple Kurt Vonnegut novels and a Tony Robbins cassette on my nightstand so my next of kin wouldn't know what a lowlife I was. This concept later became the inspiration for a *Man Show* piece about a service called Rest Assured that would rush a SWAT team to your bachelor pad upon your death to remove the stack of porno tapes, bongs, and S&M devices and replace them with Shakespeare, scented candles, and inspirational posters to create the illusion of a wholesome lifestyle.

Let's backtrack for a moment to clarify further why I needed to move from Santa Monica out to La Crescenta. It's a quick, semi-inspirational story about how I became a boxing instructor and eventually a radio host. I had always been interested in boxing, and more interested in getting out of construction. My friend Robbie went to college with a guy named Bruce who owned a chain of "executive boxing gyms" called Bodies in Motion. (If you saw my movie *The Hammer*, it was shot at one of his gyms.) One Saturday afternoon I walked into the

West L.A. Bodies in Motion, announced Robbie Levine sent me, explained my amateur-boxing background, and then asked, "When do I start?" Bruce told me to buzz off. They only hired champions and ex-pros as instructors. You should all know the only reason I'm sitting in a big house, paying a guy to type my second book right now, is because I said to Bruce, "I may not be a boxing champion, but I do hold one belt and it's got a hammer hanging from it." I offered to hang the speed bags that were sitting on the floor in the back and generally spruce up the place, and all I wanted in return was a chance to teach a boxing class. Bruce agreed that if I did some work on the place I could assist one of the regular teachers. Since the gym hours were six A.M. to ten P.M., I would start after closing and often work through the night and into the morning, with the radio as my only companion. One of the programs I most looked forward to was *Loveline,* at the time hosted by Dr. Drew and Riki Rachtman, long before syndication. If somebody would have tapped me on the shoulder and told me, "Two years from now you'll be hosting this show, syndicated in more than one hundred markets and making hundreds of thousands of dollars," I would have punched them and blown them simultaneously. But back to La Crescenta. After a few months of apprenticing in West L.A., Bruce hit me with a proposition. If I built out his new location in Pasadena and only charged him ten bucks an hour, I could start teaching the Monday, Wednesday, and Friday six A.M. classes as well as a Sunday noon class. Here's the point of this story. He gave me an opportunity to have my own class, and I seized it. And at the time it wasn't even an "opportunity." It was "Construct a gym at the hourly rate of a busboy for the privilege of making twenty bucks a class and set the alarm for five A.M. three days a week." Either way, at ten bucks an hour the commute from Santa Monica to Pasadena would have used more in gas than I was making. So when a room opened up at Chez Nude, it was time to make the move.

. . .

I began work at the Pasadena Bodies in Motion. One of the drawbacks of this gig was that the owner had a macaw, which is like a giant blue-and-yellow parrot.

As I said in my last book, birds are mean. They're the only pet that, when they escape, the owners are relieved. You can tell a species is evil by doing this simple math. If my blond lab Molly was the size of a T-Rex, that would just mean more kibble, more work for the gardener in the backyard, and a harder time moving her to my wife's side of the bed at night. If birds were the size of a T-Rex, the streets would be littered with human remains.

This horrible thing lived at the gym and would hang out on its perch. Every now and again it would come down and drag its big black claws along the floor and let out a bloodcurdling screech that would scare the shit out of you. The sound of the macaw's voice is made to travel for miles across the canopy of a rainforest, so when that thing crept up behind you and let one out, you'd jump out of your boxer briefs. I would be in the ring, training students with the punch pads, and this bird would get down off the perch, scratch its way across the floor, and hop up on the apron of the ring. Now, as you know, all boxing rings have ropes, but this one had a sleeve of canvas draped around them that dangled down just enough to give the bird a handle to bite onto and pull itself up to the next rope. It would climb rope by rope until it could walk along the top rope toward the corner pad. The first time this happened, I didn't think anything of it. Maybe it was coming over to say hi or to pick up a little technique from the master. Until I heard the crunch. I turned to see a beak crushing the face of my expensive digital stopwatch. Then again, when you're making three hundred bucks a week, Pez dispensers are expensive. I replaced the stopwatch, and the next time I saw the bird hop down off the perch I thought, I'm gonna keep my eye on that damn macaw. I heard the familiar sound of its talons dragging across the linoleum. The next time I looked over, it was on the ring apron. Keep in mind I was in the middle of trying to turn a tax attorney into Earnie Shavers, so I was a little distracted. Before I knew it, I heard another crunch. It was destroying my new stopwatch. This happened to me three times. Three times I was outwitted by this fucking bird. But as the old saying goes, "Fool me once, shame on you; fool me twice, shame on me; fool me three times, what the fuck is wrong with me?" After three busted stopwatches, I wised up and started putting out the old ones as decoys. It felt amazing to intellectually triumph over a prehistoric animal with a brain the size of a garbanzo bean. Of all my accomplishments in the ring, this one was the most satisfying.

I had another animal-related incident at Bodies in Motion. While I was working there I dated a hot but high-maintenance blonde named Beth. She was a bikini model and her dad was a tool distributor for Black & Decker, so with her I was in hog heaven.

But Beth had a dog. It was a little white lapdog named Sushi. She loved this dog more than me or anything else in the world

1993 - La Crescenta. Me, Beth, and "Tushi" (out of frame, yapping incessantly).

and obnoxiously called it "Tushi." As if Sushi wasn't nauseating enough. One weekend she went out of town, probably to fuck another guy, and she asked if I would watch Sushi. Like all hot blondes, she got her way and I was stuck minding Sushi for three days. I had to go in for my early-morning class at the gym, so I brought Sushi with me. She was running around yapping while I taught my class. What I didn't know was that at some point Sushi scampered out and went down the hall to one of the neighboring businesses, I believe it was a travel agent. Someone there picked up Sushi, read her collar tag, and left Beth a message saying that they had found her dog, which was obviously lost. This is where it got absurd; this is the kind of thing that could only happen to me. The person then put the dog back down when they went to answer the phone or something, and it left and came back to the gym. So when I finished my class and saw Sushi sitting by my gym bag, I had no idea what had just gone down. I left Bodies in Motion blissfully unaware, lapdog in hand. Cut to me back at home, receiving an angry call from Beth. "Where's Tushi? *What have you done with Tushi?*" I said, "She's right here." Beth shouted, *"DON'T LIE TO ME!"* I was totally confused. I had no idea she got that call and therefore no clue why she thought I was lying. I just kept repeating that Sushi was right here, I was looking at her right now, and I never lost her. Beth just kept calling me a liar. Unlike in Colombian kidnapping situations or reruns of *Charlie's Angels,* there's no way to put a dog on the phone to prove they're unharmed. I'm still pissed at that travel agent. What kind of maniac calls someone, tells them their dog is lost, and then lets it go?

Beth and Sushi eventually wised up and moved on to a guy with two pieces of kibble to rub together. I ended up with another girl named Cynthia. She was an ex–Minnesota Vikings cheerleader with a crazy sense of humor. I'm giving you a few background details because Cynthia figures prominently in the next and final story of this chapter.

1994—With Cynthia at a KROQ singles party on a boat to Catalina.

THE WORST WEEK OF MY LIFE

The La Crescenta house was the location of the worst week of my life. It was January 17 at 4:31 A.M. Cynthia and I were sound asleep in my freezing, tiny bedroom. Ralph was from Philly, Courtland was from Denver, and Cynthia was from Minnesota, so nobody but me was prepared for what was about to happen—the Northridge Earthquake. The house rolled up and down violently for what felt like a lifetime. Dishes broke and the house creaked like an old wooden ship in a storm. The next thing you know, we were all standing in the kitchen shocked at what had just happened. I, as the lone Californian and with a background in earthquake rehab, explained to everyone it was no big deal. We'd just sweep up the broken plates and get back to our lives. Cynthia said, "What about my apartment? What about my stuff?" I said, "It's stucco and lath with two-by-four framing and no subterranean parking. You're in the clear. Maybe the refrigerator rolled away from the wall a couple of feet. You probably won't be able to tell the difference." When we got to her apartment in Sherman Oaks, it was cordoned off with red tape. The building was condemned, and the cops wouldn't let people in even to retrieve their pets. It turned out that her building ran along a stretch of the L.A. River that acted like a conduit for the quake's fury; all the buildings and businesses along that stretch were red-flagged, including the nearby restaurant she worked at. So she needed to crash with me. And just for good measure, on the way back to my house her twelve-year-old Nissan Sentra blew a head gasket.

So let me set the stage—her apartment was condemned, her work was condemned, my work was out of commission for the next several weeks, her car didn't run, and her mom had already purchased a plane ticket to come out from Minnesota. I was living with a woman I barely knew and about to have a woman I didn't want to know on my sofa. We were both broke, so we had no way to repair her car or get a hotel room for her mother, who had planned to stay with her for a whole week. I know this doesn't seem like it could get any worse, but it does. A day before her mother was scheduled to arrive, I woke up in the middle of the night with my sheets soaked in sweat. The following day I had lesions on my face and in my mouth and a 102-degree temperature. It's still a mystery exactly what I had. At the time there was speculation that the earthquake had kicked up some stuff into the air that was causing various ailments. Later Dr. Drew announced it was herpes. But that's Dr. Drew's answer for everything. He thinks Abe Lincoln was killed by herpes. No matter what it was, I had no insurance and no money, so all I could do was ride it out. But I'll never forget the look on Mama's face when I answered the door in a tattered bathrobe, covered in sweat and festering boils. She took one look, was horrified, and started in on me. I was in no mood after what I'd been through and fired back. We had it out in the doorway before she even set foot in the house. You can only imagine what the next seven days were like. I had officially hit rock bottom.

But before the year and the lease would be up, I will have met Jimmy Kimmel, convinced him to put me on the radio, and be well on my way to fame and fortune. But before that there was one last apartment.

13

A FAREWELL TO APARTMENTS:
TOLUCA LAKE

TOLUCA LAKE, CA

YEAR RENTED: 1994

RENT: $1,125

975 SQUARE FEET

TWO BEDROOMS

TWO BATHROOMS

ONE NEW BEST FRIEND

THE La Crescenta house we were renting got sold out from under us. Ralph went his way and Courtland and I set sail for Toluca Lake, a nicer part of the Valley on the edge of L.A. next to Burbank. It was a two-bedroom, one of which was a master with its own bathroom and a small balcony. Courtland and I decided that to be fair we'd pay the same rent, but a coin toss would determine who got the master. The winner would occupy it for six months and then we'd swap. It won't surprise you that I lost the toss. It also won't surprise you that Courtland never relinquished the master suite. In fairness to him, I never asked for it. I was working in radio now, and around the six-month mark I was starting to get some career traction. At that point I didn't want to move into a bigger rented bedroom. I wanted a place of my own.

Until that was possible, I was stuck with Courtland and a friendly but nosy landlord. You know those old people who have nothing to do so they constantly monitor the neighborhood for stuff to complain about? That was her. If you pulled into the wrong parking spot at three A.M. on a Tuesday night, left your car running, and sprinted to your unit to grab a ball cap that was hanging on the front doorknob, when you popped up after your shoulder roll into the subterranean parking you would find her there leaning against your car wanting to know what was going on. I wouldn't be surprised if she hid in the ivy with opera glasses waiting for shit to happen.

I've never really understood or been one of those guys who make the entire focus of their lives the Red Sox or Kobe Bryant, living or dying on their latest success or failure and allowing it to cause alcoholism and an emotional rift with their sons. Even more inexplicable than that are the people whose attention is solely consumed with the civilians living within rock-chucking distance. Do you not have a television? There are events in the world more pressing than whether my hedge is too high or my music is too loud. Who are these people who've made you their life's work? You've become the Moby-Dick to their Captain A-hole. I want these people fined for using the cops as their own personal Republican Guard. You always hear that we don't have enough cops to patrol the ports or bust gangbangers, yet these assholes feel free to call them because my recycling bins were out on the street for an extra day while I was out of town. What we need is to ship them off to their own high-walled triple-gated community. Ass-wipe Acres. That would be the greatest payback, making them live amongst themselves. It would be like *Escape from New York*, but with pussies. They'd all be calling the cops on each other then eventually go insane and start calling the cops on themselves.

I told the story of meeting Jimmy and getting into radio in my last book, so I won't include it here. If you need a refresher, I suggest you download several hundred copies of the audio book. But let me share with you some more Kimmel tales dating back to our early radio days on the Kevin and Bean morning show for KROQ.

Jimmy telling me to create a character (which I did, in the form of Mr. Birchum) was a good piece of advice. He also gave me another great piece of advice. At a certain point I thought I could be more present at the studio and a bigger part of the show if I drove the van for the station. I'd always be around and I could make a few bucks while I was at it. Jimmy said no. If I drove the van, then I'd just be the van driver. He was right. But he also told me that I could really become essential to the show if I could cut and edit tape. Back then, to produce a commercial parody or some other comedy bit you had to physically take a razor blade to a piece of audio tape, cut out the chunk you didn't want, and then Scotch tape the two ends together to make your edit. The device you used to perform this was slightly less complicated than a joint roller. Jimmy thought this was a skill I should possess. I blew it off. What seemed like a week later, everything went digital and I never had to waste my time with that nonsense. Lots of books and movies follow the theme of missed opportunities and ignoring advice and the repercussions of that. Nobody ever touts the virtues of saying "Thanks, but no thanks," or blowing off homework assignments. But as important as it is to recognize the opportunities when they arise, such as Jimmy telling me to come up with a character to get on the radio, it's also important to realize when shit's a waste of time. Let's face it, life is short, and the more time you devote to your Beta-recorder repair business, the less time you'll have for your Mr. Birchum.

One of the first times it hit me that Jimmy's advice was paying off was at the 1994 KROQ Acoustic Christmas, a concert with some of the biggest rock acts of that year. It still takes place every December. The '94 lineup had, among others, Weezer, Stone Temple Pilots, Seal, and two kinds of Crows—Black and Sheryl. Mr. Birchum

1995—At a KROQ event. The name placards read "Mr. Birchum" and "Jimmy the Sports Guy."

was just taking off, but I continued to work as a carpenter and boxing instructor. Even with Birchum's growing popularity, I was still only making fifty bucks a bit. I was walking backstage past a group of coworkers when someone from the group called me over. To my surprise and delight, one of the people in that group was Henry Winkler. That's right—one of the producers of *MacGyver*. One of my KROQ compatriots said, "Henry, this is the guy who does Mr. Birchum." He said, "You're Mr. Birchum?" I said I was. He then gave me that super menschy two-handed handshake and said, "Nobody can do what you do. No one can improvise that fast." It was surreal: Here was the Fonz himself, kissing my ass. It got even weirder later at the same event when I was chatting with Duff from Guns 'N Roses and he mentioned that Axl had recently been talking about me. The Fonz and Axl Rose knew who I was. That was enough; I should have just killed myself right then and there.

When the morning show would wrap up, it was time to get some breakfast. (Remember what I said about fucked-up hours and how you compensate with shitty food?) I did odd construction jobs around the station while I was getting paid per appearance to do Mr. Birchum. One of the things I built, other than a ten-thousand-CD storage rack for Bean, was a wheel, like you'd see on *Wheel of Fortune*. Except instead of dollar amounts, it had the names of local breakfast joints like Bob's Big Boy and Denny's. After the show we'd gather around the wheel, someone would take a spin, and fate would decide where we'd eat. Now what makes this interesting is that there was also a spot for a restaurant we all hated—the Tallyrand. Every couple of times we'd end up on the Tallyrand and get pissed off at whoever had spun the wheel. This is something only guys would do. It was Russian roulette with bad omelets instead of bullets. Where's the fun if there's no risk?

. . .

Just because it was radio doesn't mean I didn't have a dickhead boss like on my construction sites. Our boss at the time was named Frank Murphy. Frank was super-uptight and would freak out if you put food in his trash, even if it was just a peach pit or a candy wrapper. And God forbid you took his newspaper. He'd literally threaten your life if you slid the sports section out of his *USA Today*.

In Frank's defense, this may not just be his particular personality disorder, it may be a symptom of working at a radio station. The only thing I miss about radio are the bitter notes on the vending machines. "To the person who maintains this machine: On December 9th I inserted in a dollar for a sixty-five-cent Pepsi Free and got no change in return. PLEASE CORRECT!" The time it takes to write and follow up on that note is worth much more than a dollar. And the community kitchen is a nightmare. The next project I do with this publisher is going to be a coffee-table book entitled *Radio Station Refrigerators* and will contain pictures of all the angry notes left on break-room fridges. Sure, every office has those snarky Post-it notes left on the office fridge by coworkers about not eating each other's lunch. But the fridge at KROQ brought it to a whole new low. I would often find long, vitriolic manifestos taped to the door of the Frigidaire. "To the person who feels it is their right to take other people's property: I left half an egg salad sandwich in this refrigerator. I went to enjoy my lunch today only to find that much to my chagrin it had been *stolen*! If you are going to continue to have reckless disregard for your fellow coworkers I will have no recourse but to take it up with Human Resources." There'd be thirty-year-old scratched-up Tupperware with two-week-old Chinese food in it covered in angry-Sharpie scrawl: "This belongs to Cheryl, AND ONLY CHERYL, if you are not Cheryl DO NOT TOUCH!" And I'm not exaggerating about half-eaten food being the breaking point. At

KROQ I literally saw a can of Chef Boyardee ravioli with a moistened paper towel stuffed into the mouth of it protecting the single ravioli clinging to the bottom. Literally, one goddamn ravioli. These are adults whose average age was forty-one, average education was three years of college, and average salary was $77,000, practically getting into knife fights about food that seagulls wouldn't pick off a garbage barge.

There were other characters around the studio like Michael the Maintenance Man, Jimmy's boxing opponent and the impetus for our fateful meeting. He was an angry brother who thought everyone was a racist, eventually became a Muslim, and got busted selling T-shirts he was supposed to be giving away at KROQ sticker stops. There was also a weird homeless guy who became a regular character on the show named Booger Man. One morning after Jimmy went into great detail about Booger Man's girth-enhancing penile-fat injections over the air, I walked into Frank's office to see Jimmy with his back against the wall while Booger Man vigorously strangled him. You'd think with all my boxing training and my love and allegiance for Jimmy I would have thrown a big left hook to the back of Booger Man's head. But all I could do was stand there and watch. This is how you know everything in this book is true. I stood there like a coward and did nothing. Eventually Jimmy fought him off and Booger Man was fired. Ironically, not for attempting to kill Jimmy: He gave away a cheap mountain bike to a friend instead of caller number thirty-five. Rules are rules. It was a real island of misfit toys.

One of the perks of the job was that Jimmy and I used to occasionally travel together. We'd do remotes from New York for the MTV Movie Awards, Vegas for station-sponsored singles parties, and so on.

It was at one of these singles parties when I had the following incident. After a night of boozing it was time to go back to the hotel, take a piss, and get some sleep. I staggered into the lobby and toward the elevators. I was ready to burst. I'd been drinking all night and the line at the event had been too long, so I thought I'd wait until I returned to the room Jimmy and I were sharing. All the guys reading this understand this feeling. Our bladder has a backward-counting clock, like a timer on a bomb. We can hold it for a long time when it's unarmed, but once you flip that switch, you're past the point of no return. You start to ache. Eventually after what seemed like a lifetime, the elevator arrived on the lobby floor. By the time I got out on my floor, I was ready to explode. I hustled down the hall to my door and . . . the key didn't work. I was locked out. I quickly surveyed the scene and, like on one of the trips to Tijuana in my younger days, I found myself resorting to an ice maker. In my defense, I didn't piss on a bunch of ice: I just saw a drain and an opportunity.

I hate hotel key cards. How about a real key? Is that too much to ask? I have a couple of beefs with those magnetic-stripe key cards. First, they don't have the room number on them. I know you might think this is a safety risk if the card is lost. Let's just say it fell out of your wallet at an Applebee's. What are the chances that the guy or girl who found your key card would think, Somebody's staying in room 824 at the Ramada: Get my ski mask, duct tape, and water-soluble lube? I'd gladly run that nonrisk in order to be able to find my room after I've blown into town, run up to splash some water on my face, done ninety minutes onstage followed by a few beers, and then stumbled back to the hotel exhausted and not remembering if I was in room 914 or 419.

My second beef is that they all need to have the arrows clearly printed on them showing which direction to slide them in. If there are arrows at all, they are impossible to find and are tiny little half-assed pyramids. Are we so lazy that we've removed the dick and left just the tip? I spend twenty minutes, probably at the wrong room, sliding the damn thing in backward and being mocked by that little red light on the door handle. The same guys who are in charge of arrow clarity must also work on rental-car dashboards specializing in not letting you figure out which side the gas cap is on.

My third complaint is that half the time they don't work. And when you go down to the desk the chick says, "Did you put it in your wallet? Sometimes the magnetic strip on your credit card screws it up. But don't put it in the same pocket as your cell phone." Unfortunately I'm one of those maniacs who insists on traveling with his wallet and cell phone. What am I supposed to do, duct tape it to a broomstick and hold it above my head?

Plus sliding a card to a chick at the hotel bar is way less cool than handing her a key. And finally, is this the future? When I'm formally presented with the key to the city of Santa Monica after stopping another purse snatching, are they gonna hand me a giant foam-core key card?

Another time Jimmy and I were up in Seattle doing a remote because UCLA had made the Final Four. We were in a shitty motor lodge, one of those places where the lights from the cars pulling into the parking lot shine directly into your room. And when I say "Seattle," I should be clear: We were twenty-five miles outside of Seattle. This place shared a parking lot with a 7-Eleven and looked like the motel from *No Country for Old Men,* except with more rain. Jimmy and I had to be up at four fifteen in the morning even though the show didn't start until six. We were a good hour away from the sports bar we were broadcasting out of, across from the old Kingdome. This sucked especially hard because we had been at a strip club until past two A.M. the night before. By the way, getting loaded at a strip club for a couple hours before you slide into the bed you're sharing with another dude is not necessarily the best move for straight guys. So the alarm went off after an hour and a half of sleep, and Jimmy got up first to take his shower. We had one of those tubs that didn't drain right, so at 4:30 I stepped into a shin-deep pool of tepid water and Jimmy's back hair. After a minute or so Jimmy did that backward knuckle tap on the outside of the hollow-core door and said, "Oh, FYI. I beat off in the shower. So look out for that iceberg." I didn't know if he was kidding or if I needed to jump out and vomit. It's ironic to have to take a rape shower for something that happened in a shower.

And on the topic of beating off, every year when we made the pilgrimage to New York for the aforementioned MTV Movie Awards, we went armed with needle-nose pliers and a universal remote. Jimmy had figured out that you could use needle-nose pliers to outsmart the sheet-metal shroud that was supposed to prevent you from undoing the coax. Then you could flip-flop the cables and use the universal remote to get the free porn. It was an ingenious plan with only one flaw. We were so cheap we had only one universal remote, so if during your refractory period you changed the channel to the news station and the remote ended up in the other guy's room, you couldn't change it back to the Spice channel.

Quick side note to that Seattle story. Bean now lives there because of that trip. I was walking around with him, breathing the clean air and seeing the green trees, and remember Bean saying, "Wow, this is really amazing." I didn't know he would end up moving there. Being from L.A. is like being in an abusive relationship. When you get outside of it, you don't know what to do. It's like a battered wife who leaves her man and finally goes on a date, and when the guy goes to stroke her hair, she flinches. She doesn't know how to handle it; she can't believe there are gentlemen out there. You go to a place like Seattle and ask, "Where's all the graffiti? Where are all the gangs?" A couple years ago I was doing a stand-up gig at the Moore Theatre in

Seattle and I stopped by to visit him. When I arrived, he was outside and said he was waiting for the wife and kids. I thought, Kids? Bean hates kids. I hadn't seen him in years, so I thought maybe I missed something. Ten minutes later his wife pulled up with two potbellied pigs and it all made pathetic sense.

One of our other trips was to Vegas for Kevin Rider's bachelor party. Technically this may have been later, after I had left this apartment, but it's travel and it's Kevin and Bean so fuck it, this is where it should go. We rented an RV and loaded it up with me, Jimmy, Bean, Lightning (the show's current producer), another couple guys from the station, and five of bachelor Bean's buddies. It was a tight fit, and the heat was in triple digits, but we decided that it was still time to light some farts. For four straight hours, the entirety of the journey to Vegas, I was holding a lighter up to my asshole and entertaining the troops. Actually, my biggest laugh of the weekend was later at the bachelor party itself. One of Bean's drunken buddies was lying down on the carpet of the suite we were attempting to destroy. The stripper squatted over his face and poured beer down her chest so that it followed the contour of her body and eventually dropped off the end of her lady-parts into his mouth. She explained this was called the "golden waterfall." As this was happening, I yelled, "Forget the golden waterfall, give him the mudslide." It's disgusting and not really that clever but to this day it is still the hardest I've ever made Jimmy laugh.

At this time I was still dating Cynthia (thank Christ her mom went back to Minnesota), and there's a funny story that combines her, my gig at KROQ, and my incompetence as a boyfriend. Cynthia's favorite performer was Tori Amos (I guess I should have seen our impending breakup coming just based on that). One day Tori came by the studio. A fan had sent her some flowers, but Tori left them behind. So I took them home to my girlie. I walked in and said, "Here's some flowers." She said, "Oh, my God. That's so sweet. It's not even my birthday. Let me put them in some water." I said, "Hold on. It gets even better. Guess who these flowers were for?" She looked at me with a "Huh?" and I said, "They were for your favorite—Tori Amos. A fan brought them and she left them behind." Cynthia's mood changed instantly and she tossed out a "fuck you" as she left the room. This was another lesson in the difference between men and women. If someone gave me a sack of beef jerky that was meant for Mike Ditka, I'd sleep with it under my pillow. I was thinking like a dude, not a chick. I learned that it's about the effort, not the flowers. Every chick loves getting flowers, but not if they're free. This must suck for guys who work as florists. When the anniversary hits, they must have to show their wives receipts from a competing floral shop.

Eventually I would graduate from doing periodic bits for Kevin and Bean. I had a little something called "it," and Dr. Drew recognized that. But he was currently partnered with a guy named Riki Rachtman. The good news was that Riki wasn't very good. The better news was that he didn't know it. He walked out of the pilot for the syndicated TV version of *Loveline* at the last minute, demanding more money. His demands were not met, and the casting process began. Drew recommended me based on my Mr. Birchum bits.

When the producers came calling, I was in New York with Jimmy, Kevin, and Bean. We were doing a week of broadcasts from there, leading up to the MTV Video Music Awards. The plan was to head out to Little Italy every night for some real Italian food, then hit the bars. (Because of the time difference, we didn't have to get up at the crack of fuck to do the morning-show hungover.) It was gonna be a party and KROQ was paying for the whole thing. We had arrived just the day before and were on our way to get some gelato when I got the call. They needed me to fly back for the audition. I'm a poor reader, as you know, so I'd never been much good at the audition process. And when I say "not good," I mean Mariah Carey–in-high-heels-throwing-out-the-first-pitch not good. This was the second time I'd been to New York in my life, a romantic getaway with Jimmy I'd been planning all year long, and I was being asked to fly back across the country so some producer could flip a coin, nay, a golf ball, and hope it landed on my dimple. I was dying not to go so I asked the producers in all seriousness, "What's Mark DeCarlo doing? He'd be good, he has a lot of experience in TV, he did *Studs*. Why not give him a shot?" They said, "Real funny. Now get back here." With encouragement from Jimmy and the guys I went back the next day (on Tower Air, which doesn't exist anymore, it was such a cheap, shitty airline), and headed over to Hollywood Center Studios for the audition. It was a blazing-hot bright day at high noon without a cloud in the sky. I went from that into a pitch-black studio with a table and some folding chairs to answer fake phone calls. When I was done I thought, That actually went pretty well. It was improv, which is my strength. At the end of the audition the producers said, "You'll be hearing from us." So I was actually feeling confident. As I strutted out of the studio I went to push the door and it pulled away from me. Someone was entering as I was exiting. As the door opened I got hit right in the eyes with a shaft of sunlight and all I could see was the person's silhouette. A second later I literally bumped into Mark DeCarlo as he was coming in to audition. I guess the producers took my note. Thankfully, my nervousness about the audition and thus the suggestion of DeCarlo didn't fuck me. I got the gig and filmed the pilot. I then spent a few uncomfortable months doing *Loveline* on the radio with Drew and Riki not mentioning that I had done the pilot. Drew and I felt like a wife and the coworker she's been banging in the copier room chatting with her husband at the company picnic. Awkward.

. . .

It was a very short time after that when another major life change was about to come out of nowhere. There was a KROQ event at a sports bar, one of those shitty Monday Night Football "come and meet Jimmy the Sports guy" things Kimmel had to do because Kevin and Bean were too big-time. I decided to tag along. The place was dead. With the notable exception of two good-looking ladies. They approached us and introduced themselves. It was a woman named Suzanne and her friend Lynette.

Lynette told me she worked for the company that did the pilot for *Loveline*, New World Entertainment. It was originally supposed to be syndicated, airing mostly on Fox affiliates. Lynette worked in their syndication department, had seen the pilot, and had fallen instantly in love (at least that's what I tell myself). I don't remember exactly what I said to her after she mentioned who she was and that she was a fan. Lynette swears my line was, "Are you a single gal?" She also recalls asking me if I was tired because I was more low-key than on the pilot. Apparently I said, "As a performer I'm a seven, but in real life I'm a four." We exchanged numbers and made plans to meet up because I hadn't seen the finished pilot and she said she could get me a copy.

We began dating, and two months into the relationship she found out that the show didn't get picked up by the Fox affiliates. She was coming to my apartment for a home-cooked meal. (Believe it or not, I used to regularly cook linguine for two early on in our dating.) Eventually the subject of the pilot came up, and Lynette had the very uncomfortable task of telling me it wasn't picked up. I continued cooking and said, "Eh, something else will come along. Let's eat." Within the year I was right and it was on MTV.

Loveline started on MTV November 11, 1996. My hatred of executives, publicists, and dickhead celebrities began shortly thereafter.

One of the first things we had to do was record promos. Promos are one of those bullshit things that take up massive time and energy that celebrities never get credit for. In fact, they get points deducted for them. Every one of you has seen a terrible advertisement with a corny tag line for a show that is probably very good, but you wouldn't know it from the crap churned out by the promo department. Please understand this. That shitty slogan on the bus bench was not produced by the creators, talent, or the writers of these shows. It was farted out by a hack who isn't good enough to write on an actual show but found his way into the network's promo department. The boneheaded nonsensical promo line that Dr. Drew and I were forced to record over and over again was "You need a brain vacation." I still have no idea what the fuck that's supposed to mean.

If you think "You need a brain vacation" is bad, a year earlier when the show was supposed to be syndicated we visited our Chicago affiliate to glad-hand and record some local promos. When we went down to the affiliate station, they unveiled their new ad campaign. We were supposed to say, "I'm Adam Carolla. And I'm Doctor Drew. Watch us on *Loveline* every weeknight at eleven thirty on channel thirteen, the Dubba-Dubba-Dubba-Dubba-WB." This is one of the many, many times over the course of my career that I've said, "This is not going to work." Three days earlier, I'd been remodeling people's kitchens for a living. These people had been working in television for years. Why is it that I was the only one who knew this was a horrible idea? It took the guy a half hour to teach it to us and I kept saying, "Do you really think this is ever going to catch on?" Drew reminded me recently that when I'd get into blowouts with executives and other idiots over their stupid ideas, I used to always shout at them, "History will not be kind to this decision," followed with a super-insulting "Let me save you from your horrible idea."

I should make a living as a corporate "insultant." Not a *con*sultant. An *in*sultant. I would travel from company to company and explain to them why their new product or ad campaign was retarded. I'd circle the boardroom desk with a baseball bat, ask whose idea it was, and take them out Al Capone style. That way we would have never found out What Brown Could Do for You, and we all could have avoided the Noid. Are you listening, Airbus?

Another colossal waste of time/gigantic pain in the ass I had to deal with early on in *Loveline*'s run was "media training." This is the kind of thing I'm sure they had Sarah Palin do before she hit the press circuit after getting the VP nod. You have to sit in front of a camera while fake interviewers throw out made-up questions so you can "refine your message." They'll ask something like, "And what do you say to teenagers about having sex?" And you'll reply, "Well, young people . . ." and before you can finish your thought, they'll stop you and say, "Don't say 'young people.' Say 'young adults.' " They have a bullshit list of buzzwords they want you to avoid.

Drew and I had been in show business for about ten minutes at this point and didn't know what the fuck we were doing. So we went down, on a beautiful Saturday, to Bragman, Nyman and Cafarelli on Wilshire Blvd. BNC is the big public-relations company out here. We went upstairs to a conference room with a long table, and there were about twenty people sitting around it. They had hired a guy to come in and do fake interviews with us to hone our skills. Later Howard Bragman himself would sit down to play interviewer.

First off, I don't like killing a Saturday. The weekend is Miller time. Not Retarded Gay Jews Wasting Our Time time. At a certain point I just looked at everyone and said, "Come on. This is completely unnecessary. Let's go and enjoy our weekend." But they said no, we needed to do it again. By then we had already done four fake interviews. So I took a stand. I didn't say a goddamn word. Not one fucking syllable. Drew, being the team player/pussy that he is, answered every question dutifully. He had the "Let's just get this done and get out of here" attitude. But I had to make a point. For the entire interview, Drew answered every question and I was Marcel Marceau. And at the end, the seals at BNC slapped their flippers together and said, "All right. But if you could answer *some* of the questions . . ." Obviously I was being a dick and going on strike, but that didn't seem to resonate with them. After not moving my mouth the entire interview I opened it to say, "Okay, now let's get out of here." Their response? "Let's keep going." The whole miserable affair was capped off when one of the fake interviewers asked my opinion on one of his many fake questions. I asked, "Do you want to know what I really think?" He said, "Yes, I would." I broke character and shouted that my opinion was that this was all a fucking waste of time.

Another exercise in futility, tedium, and frustration is the satellite tour. This is the mind-numbing experience of sitting in a studio and rolling through thirty-three back-to-back interviews with the interchangeable perky blonde chick and handsome-twenty-five-years-ago, thinks-he's-funny-but-isn't guy duos from *Good Morning Tampa, Good Morning San Francisco, Good Morning Milwaukee, Good Morning Burbank, Good Morning Poughkeepsie,* et cetera.

Loveline was getting some national attention, and Drew and I were scheduled on one of these tours. Keep in mind that because we were on the West Coast and these tours started in the East, they began at five A.M. for us. The only thing that could make trying to be quick-witted, engaging, and funny at five A.M. worse is having a job that ended at midnight the night before. The studio where they did the satellite tours was in Culver City, literally across the street from the studio where I was five hours prior, but across town from where I lived.

On this particular tour we were about twenty-seven back-to-back interviews into our scheduled thirty-two, I was exhausted, and the questions were wearing thin. We were talking to *Good Morning*

Tucson, and before we went on the air the chick reminded us over and over that it was a "family show." She was apparently nervous that we were the "wild sex-talk guys." Partway through the interview, the male half of the morning-show combo asked us how *Loveline* worked. This was a question that had come up a thousand times in the press we were forced to do, so I had an analogy ready to go. I would always explain that on *Loveline* Dr. Drew was the pill that you had to give your dog and I was the Gainesburger it was wrapped in.

So inevitably the question came up and Drew jumped on it. In true Drew fashion, he messed it up. He said, "We liken it to giving an animal a medication . . ." I jumped in. "Hold on, Drew. You're screwing it up. It's not an animal, you idiot." Then I said to the team from Tucson, and this is verbatim, "You want your dog to take an antibiotic because it's got the worms, right? Now what do you do? You give the dog the antibiotic, you put it in its mouth, then it spits it on the floor and doesn't eat it. But you need it to take this medicine, so what do you do? You take the pill—" At this moment the cunty blonde with too much blush interrupted in the most sing-songy and fake-laughy tone she could muster, "We appreciate that Adam very much . . ."

I don't know if she thought I was going to go on some bestiality tangent in the middle of her "family show," but I couldn't finish my thought. Drew then stepped in to defend my point and finish the analogy. He said, "No, this is gonna be legitimate. You put it in some Gainesburger. . ." Drew turned to me, hoping I'd pick the analogy back up. I just leaned back and said, "No. Just go ahead with your interview. Let's get this over with." I went to bed at one thirty in the morning after *Loveline* the night before and got up at four A.M. to deal with a parade of teeth-whitened wannabe weathermen and overcaffeinated survivors of incest, and I couldn't take any more.

That's not to say I didn't have problems during the actual tapings with the in-studio guests. *Loveline* TV was the beginning of my love-hate relationship with celebrities. I've run into some hilarious, great guys who always bring it—like David Alan Grier. I've also run into some incredible assholes. Everyone loves Rodney Dangerfield, but I know him as a douchebag. I wasn't a stand-up, so I didn't have the reverence for him that other people do. But I went into his dressing room to just say hi and thanks for coming on before the show. I'd give every guest the same speech: "Just go out there and have fun, say whatever you want, and if the show sucks, it's my fault." But when I got to his dressing room he was wearing a bathrobe and smoking a joint. I addressed him as Mr. Dangerfield and came in politely but he rudely shot back, "Who are you?" I introduced myself as the host of the show. He said, "So. What are you doing in here?" I said I just wanted to introduce myself and say thanks for coming on. He very dismissively replied, "All right." The show went okay, Rodney didn't have much to add. Then after the show we had to shoot promos. This is when the guest looks at the camera and says, "Hey, I'm Lou Bega. Watch me on *Loveline,* coming up next." Then a version where they say ". . . tonight" and ". . . this week." So the stage manager asked him to do the lines and he said, "No. I have to get a haircut." So we asked him again. "No." The camera was set up, the audience was in place, and the cue-card guy had the lines ready to go. The promos would have taken less time than it took him to tell us he had an appointment for a haircut. We'd just done an hour plugging his piece-of-shit movie *Meet Wally Sparks,* yet he couldn't find thirty-five seconds to record a promo for his episode. Total dick.

Drew got into it with the guests as well. I only mention it because it spilled over and affected me. We were doing four one-hour shows a day for $800 a show because MTV is supercheap and we didn't know any better. It was grueling. That particular day, Jon Favreau was sitting in and a very chemically imbalanced caller was on the line. Jon was telling him, "Don't let anyone tell you you need to take medication." Drew started to freak out a little bit because he really thought this was a dangerous situation and that the guy did need to be medicated. Celebrities are such blowhards and are so used to getting their asses kissed they eventually decide their opinions are as valuable as those of people with actual expertise. Drew started mixing it up with Favreau, and the intensity got to him. Mercifully the show ended. But halfway into the next episode Drew was sweating and couldn't breathe. He stopped the taping and went back to his dressing room. He was having a full-blown panic attack. Yes, even the great Dr. Drew has a chink in his shiny armor, ladies. That and the botched circumcision. We had the audience sitting there and were only two shows into our four tapings. So I entered his dressing room, took a deep breath, and said in my most caring and delicate tone, "Get your shit together, asshole. I'm not staying here for one goddamn minute longer than I need to. I don't care what kind of attack you're claiming to have. You and your flop sweat need to get back out on that set. I will drive this ship. I will handle the calls. You sit there doing nothing, like you always do." Coach Carolla had come through. Drew sprang up, returned to the set, and we proceeded to make another $800 apiece.

THE WORST FORTY-EIGHT HOURS OF MY LIFE

The worst weekend of my life involved, not surprisingly, Jimmy Kimmel's ass. It was April of 1996. We were going to Vegas for the twenty-first birthday of a guy named Big Tad Newcomb. He was an intern/punching bag on the Kevin and Bean show. Tad later found his way to being a production assistant on *The Man Show* and in 2006, when I started my morning show, against my better judgment we took him on as our "chunky flunky." By that point the humor of a dim, overweight, goateed eighteen-year-old who lived with his mom in Fullerton had given way to the pity of a dim, overweight, goateed thirty-one-year-old who lived with his mom in Fullerton. Big Tad had become Big Sad. When you watch NASCAR, see Mountain Dew commercials, or hear Korn songs and wonder, "Who is this shit for?" the answer is "Big Tad."

Big Tad had a big brother named Tim who would be joining us for the Vegas trip. But he was a male stripper, so he called himself "T. Chance Thrasher." He also had a son named Blade. I'll give you a moment to let that sink in. This is who I'd be partying with.

Jimmy, being Jimmy, decided he was going to make our trip miserable the best way he knew how—gas. As soon as we got in the van Jimmy declared that he had loaded up on canned clams and cauliflower, which he had through extensive research in his secret underground fart laboratory deep within Cheyenne Mountain, determined to be the key to his weapon of ass destruction. Apparently the two cans of clams are for the smell and the cauliflower is the propellant. I think his goal was to make us have to get out and hitchhike before we got to the Bun Boy and the world's largest thermometer in Baker.

We were just barely merging onto the freeway when Jimmy let his first salvo go and said, "Boys, it's gonna be a long trip." It was not the worst Jimmy gas attack I've experienced, but a good, solid 6.5. On the homeland security fart chart it would be orange. But then T. Chance pulled the move that Indiana Jones does in *Raiders of the Lost Ark* when the guy comes out spinning the sword and Indy just half-heartedly shoots him. He casually said, "Oh, it's on?" He didn't know us and he probably would have held his gas, but Jimmy drew first blood. Just like the sheriff in the original Rambo movie.

In that movie when they say, "We've got to clean you up for the judge," do they really have to chain him to a wall and hit him with a fire hose? I've been arrested before and no one put me up against a wall and reenacted a civil rights demonstration in 1963 Selma, Alabama. How about I just put on a fresh T-shirt for the judge? Is there something in the lost and found I could slip into?

Anyway, Jimmy drew first mud, so T. Chance responded with an appalling fart. It was horrifying and majestic at the same time—like a great white shark. We were all simultaneously disgusted and impressed. And not only did T. Chance have quality, he had quantity. He was breaking wind nonstop for the entire trip. He was a farting machine with an unlimited fuel supply. He was like the sun. I kept turning to Tad and asking when he'd run out, and Tad said it would be generations from now.

In between lighting matches I kept asking Big Tad, "Is this an everyday occurrence?" He said it was. In fact he said this was better than usual. It was a light flow day. If this had been a period, T. Chance would be merely spotting. If only someone had rammed a tampon up his ass. It was unrelenting. Even Jimmy, the reigning champion, couldn't keep up and had to beg for mercy. He put up a good fight, he has the ass of the tiger, but the clams weren't kicking in. In fact, they gave him a terrible stomachache and he ended up nearly shitting himself and had to destroy the bathroom at a McDonald's in Barstow.

It didn't stop once we got to Vegas, either. We all shared one room at the Continental Hotel, which was a dump. It was probably a story and a half tall. The in-house entertainment was Cook E. Jarr and the Crumbs. He had hair like Cher from the seventies, and you couldn't tell if he was a light-skinned black guy or a dark-skinned douchebag. This was also the hotel where Jimmy lost his virginity. And by "hotel where Jimmy lost his virginity" I mean the hotel parking lot where Jimmy lost his virginity. Our room was small and had two beds, Jimmy and me in one and the brothers Newcomb in the other. The gas-passing didn't stop, even when T. Chance passed out and the sound of Tad's snoring added rhythm to his brother's symphony of stink. Jimmy managed to fall asleep only because he's a narcoleptic. He could nod off on a donkey in a hailstorm. Meanwhile I was staring at the ceiling all night praying for a good old-fashioned Vegas hotel fire.

The olfactory assault continued for the whole ride home. And then just for good measure, as we dropped T. Chance off, he farted into the open door of the van before waving good-bye.

Let me end with one extra detail that makes it just a little more hilarious/pathetic. For the entire time that the Fullerton Fart Machine was blowing wind in the back of the van, he was reading one of those *How to Be a Successful Entrepreneur* books from the fifties. I'm sure he's parlayed his God-given ass-ets into a multinational corporation by now.

Every so often I turn to Jimmy and remind him about that trip to Vegas and ask, "How much to do it again? Two hundred and fifty thousand dollars? Would that be enough?" I've yet to offer him enough money.

It's hard to believe that a guy who spent a weekend sharing a bed in a shitty hotel and being marinated in farts would soon purchase a house in the Hollywood Hills. But things quickly heated up with *Loveline,* and *The Man Show* would soon follow. I looked at a couple of houses and found a nice one that needed a lot of work and was in my price range. I then accomplished something I never thought imaginable even just a couple of years prior. I was no longer a renter.

14

MOVIN' ON UP:
THE BEACHWOOD HOUSE

BEACHWOOD CANYON, CA

YEAR BOUGHT: 1996

PURCHASE PRICE: $350,000

2,400 SQUARE FEET

THREE BEDROOMS

THREE BATHS

ZERO ROOMMATES

THE end of 1996 began an odd period when I was a both a renter and a homeowner. With *Loveline* sailing along and me starting to make some real bread, I decided it was time to buy. After looking at two other places, I stumbled across a dilapidated French Normandy–style house in the Hollywood Hills. And when I say Hollywood Hills, I mean this thing was directly underneath the Hollywood sign. If a suicidal actress tossed herself off the *H,* she would have landed on my hibachi. That said, I don't think it was glamorous. It was a serious fixer-upper. It had major structural damage. The living-room walls were leaning out on both sides about four inches at the top. This might not sound like a lot to you laymen, but trust me, it's a ton. It was way out of plumb. The walls were bowing out and the steeple style roof was sinking. Left alone it would have collapsed under its own weight. I had to take out the ceiling and use chains and come-along ratchets to pull the house back together. That wasn't the only problem. In fact, at a certain point the place was completely gutted. Of course, this was when Jimmy came by and asked innocently if it wouldn't be easier just to take the thing down to the ground and start from scratch. This was demoralizing. The remod took over a year, so I continued to live in Toluca Lake with Courtland while I renovated.

The house had an old stone wall around the property that leads to yet another story of a peon trying to ruin my life. When shit like this happens with a private business it's troubling, but when it's done to you by the city, it's that much more egregious because you feel like your tax dollars paid for the bowling pin you're being violated with. In the process of the renovation of my new bachelor pad, I had to go to the Department of Building and Safety in the city of Van Nuys to pull a permit. My choices were either the Van Nuys office or the downtown L.A. office, which was much farther away. So with my plans in one hand and checkbook in the other, I headed out to get my permit. When you arrive, the first thing you do is pull a number and the second thing you do is wait. Think of a bakery, except replace the smell of cookies with BO, and you've got the Department of Building and Safety. Finally it was my turn. The plan check went well, everything was moving along, and I was nearing the point where I got the privilege of writing a big fat check for the honor of having a city-appointed asshole show up at my house and tell me what I could and couldn't do on my own property when the guy said, "Wait a minute. I see a red X on your plot schematic. That means your house has been designated a historical landmark and you need to go to our downtown office to get okayed." I said, "The house isn't a historical landmark. The retaining wall around the property, however, is. Thus the red X on the plot schematic. But since my plans are only to remodel the kitchen, that shouldn't affect us." He said, "You're gonna need to verify that at the downtown office." I replied, "If you call them, they could verify it over the phone and we could move on with the permit process." He said, "We don't do that. I'll see you when you get back from downtown."

I got in my car and headed toward downtown L.A. An hour and a half later I was looking for a place to park and a half hour after that I was in the historical-landmarks office of the downtown building. And forty-five minutes after that I was stepping up to tell my story to a guy behind a counter and fifteen seconds after that he said, "Why did you bother driving all the way out here? Why didn't the guy just pick up the phone?"

This, in a nutshell, is what's gone wrong with our society. That fucker in Van Nuys wouldn't spend ninety seconds of his time to save three hours of my time. But the story does have a satisfying second chapter. Two years later I had go back to Van Nuys to pull a second permit to add a new roof. When the guy pulled out the schematic, he said, "You've got to clear this with downtown." I said, "Pick up the phone and call them." He said, "I can't do that." That's when I came at him like a wolverine with Tourette's. I said, "Bullshit you can't call him. Now get the fuck back there and call downtown." He once again resisted. I said, "How about you guys try to be a little bit better at your jobs? How about instead of just hoping everyone goes away, you actually provide the people that pay your goddamn salaries some semblance of service?" He was a younger guy who said, "Wow, my first argument on the job and it's with the guy from TV." I said, "Just pick up the phone, call downtown, and let's put an end to this." So he finally agreed and walked back to call the other office. Two minutes later he returned and said, "They didn't pick up the phone, come back first thing in the morning, they should be in the office. I'll call them then." I said, "I'm not coming back. I'm gonna write you a check for the amount I owe you. You can call the guy tomorrow morning, and when he verifies it over the phone you can send me the permit in the mail." He said, "That's impossible." I said, "The hell it is. If I lived on the roof of this building I would not come down here tomorrow fucking morning to waste more of my goddamn time. Now I'm gonna write you the check, fill out an envelope with my address on it, and leave." He made the mistake of yelling over to his cashier, "Can we take a check this way?" She made the mistake of saying, "I guess." And that was the end of that. I was a total asshole to that guy behind the counter, but my asshole was being used for good. My asshole is looking out for yours. It was one of the best days of my life. This poor schmuck got hit with a tidal wave of righteous indignation.

One of the nice things about this house was that it had a living room with big cathedral ceilings. Keep that in the back of your head as I tell this next tale.

One night I had watched that horror movie *The Ring*. Quick refresher on the premise of the movie, because it affects the story. In *The Ring* there is a videotape that shows a bunch of disturbing shit. Immediately after you watch the tape, you get a phone call and then die within seven days. So after watching a movie where people die after staring at a screen with a montage of macabre imagery, I went to bed. At three in the morning I woke up startled. There was a booming male voice bellowing from my living room along with flickering lights. I crept down the stairs to investigate. This is where the big cathedral ceiling comes in. Because I used to work out in there, I had mounted the TV high above the entrance to the step-down living room so I could watch it while skipping rope. But it faced away from the stairs I was currently descending. So as I crept up on the room, prepared to have my soul swallowed by a demon, I could only see a flickering light and hear a big voice coming out of the TV. The really creepy part was that I hadn't left the TV on. It had turned on by itself. With trepidation I walked into the room and I saw on the forty-two-inch screen an old white-haired preacher shouting about Satan and fire and brimstone.

I had a Gateway TV with one of the stupidest features imaginable. After a power outage, when the electricity was restored the TV turned itself on. Even if it was off when the outage happened. So if you were out of town, made sure to turn your TV off before you left, and there was a power outage, it would start up and be running until you got back from Branson, Missouri. Apparently at some point in the night the power had gone out momentarily, and when it returned, the TV started up and happened to be on the late-night cable preacher yelling in tongues. But just to be sure it wasn't haunted, I pulled an Elvis and shot my TV. Can't be too safe.

I'm not a nervous guy and I don't believe in ghosts, but I was thoroughly freaked out for that couple of minutes. First, let me say this about ghosts. Why are there a million ghosts in New Orleans but none in North Hollywood? Do ghosts not reside in the Valley? I wouldn't blame them, by the way. Has no one in North Hollywood ever died and wanted to come back? And why do they want to come back? It's always this "unfinished business." I'm pretty sure when you're dead your business is done. You can clock out. What's your "unfinished business"? Did you forget to clean out the trunk of the Volvo? Plus ghosts are never scary dudes. They're always old women in shawls or little girls looking for their dolly. There's nothing threatening about that. What would be scarier? Which would keep you up at night more—the four-year-old girl in turn-of-the-century knee socks, or a merchant marine who did some wrestling in college, was gayer than shit, and was a top?

There was a good kebab joint right down the street from my new home. It wasn't the Zankou Chicken that I ranted about in my last book, but I did have a similar run-in with the delightful Armenian behind the counter. As I've said, no culture loves the word *no* more than Armenians. You know how Eskimos have seven words for snow? Armenians have seven words for no. The place was called Al Wazir, and they made a hell of a falafel sandwich. Cheap, too. It was only $3.99. But that was the problem. I ordered the sandwich, they made it, and then when I opened my wallet to pay, I realized I had no cash. So I apologized to the guy and took out a credit card. "No. Ten-dollar minimum." I thought about it for a second with the smell of falafel tantalizing me and said, "Just charge me ten bucks." He said again, "No. It is three ninety-nine. Ten-dollar minimum for credit card." I said, "Let me be clearer. Just charge me ten dollars for the three-ninety-nine falafel. Do you understand?" "I understand. No. Next!" He put the *awful* in *falafel*. The guy turned down more than double the price of the sandwich for the pleasure of telling me no. The impatient woman waiting in line behind me tapped my shoulder and said, "Add some baklava." She wanted me to pad my order up to the ten-dollar minimum. But as much as I wanted that sandwich I had to take a stand, drop a "No" of my own, and leave.

You'd assume being a celebrity might help out in a situation like that, but it didn't. You might think, "Maybe they didn't recognize you." That's probably true, but it doesn't explain the next story. You may be familiar with the multiplatinum band System of a Down. They are from the L.A. area and used to appear on *Loveline* regularly. What you may not know about them is that they're Armenian. One night me, Dr. Drew, and the band, about eight of us in total, went out to a nice Armenian restaurant in Glendale that the guys from the band recommended. They'd been there a bunch of times. When they walked into the restaurant it was like Stan Lee at Comic-Con. They were greeted like they owned the joint. We sat down and John from the band started ordering for the table. The excited and somewhat nervous waiter answered each time with a "Yes sir, right away, sir. An excellent choice." Until John got to the one item he'd been talking about on the drive in—the mini-chicken-sandwich appetizer. The waiter said, "Sorry. That's for takeout only." John said, "Well, bring us two orders and we'll eat them at the table." The waiter said, "I can't do that. That's a takeout item." I then chimed in, "So if we ate them in the parking lot, that would be okay?" He repeated one more time that it was a takeout-only item. At this point John raised his voice and said, "Just bring them to the table." The waiter looked the drummer in the eyes and said, "No."

To this day I have no idea why they told the hottest band from their country to fuck off. This is the equivalent of ABBA walking into an Ikea, ordering Swedish meatballs, and being told to hit the bricks.

While I'm on the topic of swarthy folk who drove me nuts while I lived in this house, let me tell you about my neighbors. (Lynette, fortunately, hadn't moved in yet and was spared.) You'd think a better neighborhood would buy me a better class of neighbor. Not so much. The neighborhood was beautiful, but the neighbors were shit. Across the street were the friendly but nosy alcoholics who made the grave error of inviting me over for a drink and a tour of their *Star Trek* room featuring Spock's lute. And next to them was an elderly couple who would constantly yell up at me and my crew to move our cars so the wife could swing into her garage. This had less to do with our parking and more to do with her driving. She couldn't enter into the garage because one end of the street had been closed by the city and this bitch couldn't just pop it into reverse and back in.

But the worst was the woman next door. She was a sixty-year-old Israeli who was the queen of all coozes. She had an old white wrought-iron fence, which always says "class," attached to a peach-colored stucco pillar adjacent to my property. At a certain point she insisted that I pay the cost of repainting it. It was so old that where the wrought-iron was bolted to the post it was rusty and the paint was bubbling and decomposing. This created an ooze of rust and paint the consistency and color of bird shit running down the side of the stucco. She insisted this was paint from my house. Needless to say, I did not pay.

This wasn't my only run-in with her. One night in December of '03, my buzzer rang. I was just hanging out in a towel. This was at eight P.M. I answered the door and it was her. She started ranting about "the water. The water is coming from your house." Somewhere up the street a pipe must have broken, so a stream of water was running down the hill. But it certainly wasn't coming from my place, and I told her as much. Not surprisingly, this answer was not good enough. As no answer ever was for this cunt. In her best broken English she said, "No, I show you, I show you." Against my better instincts I fought through my irritation, put on clothes, grabbed a flashlight, and followed her down to the street. She showed me the water running down the curb and asked, "Is not from your water?" Yeah, you caught me. I was lying before. But now that you've dragged me out of my home at night to the scene of the crime, I confess. What is that impulse that people like her have? I don't know whether she thought I didn't know or that I was lying. I have to hope she thought I was lying, because otherwise she would have to assume I was a complete idiot. Did she think I wouldn't notice that I had zero water pressure?

Secure in the knowledge that I was a thousand times smarter than her and not a liar, I said that I didn't know where it was coming from, but that I assumed it was from up the street and that she needed to call the DWP. She said, "Let me show you what is happening at my house." I replied that I knew what was going on—water was running down the street from higher up the hill, past my house and down to hers, there was nothing I could do about it, and she needed to call the DWP.

At seven P.M. the next day I drove home and saw the poor DWP guy outside her house. My heart sank for this son of a bitch. I knew she must have been driving him nuts.

So as I drove by pulling up to my place, she sprinted toward my car. I've never seen her so spry. As I got out, she started grabbing my elbow and ranting about how the DWP guy said the water was coming from my central air unit. That is simply impossible. There's no plumbing hooked up to an air-conditioning condenser. The only water source was a condensation drip pipe that produces about a tablespoon an hour on the most humid of days. So I called the DWP worker over. I told him it was not coming from my house. She chimed in again about the air conditioner. I could see the praying-for-the-sweet-relief-of-death look in the eyes of the DWP guy. God knows how long he had been there and what she had been putting him through. I walked away and into my house.

As soon as my ass hit the sofa, the bell rang. I could see through the window that it was the city worker saying he needed to come in and check the AC. I shouted at the door, "*You* have to check or *that cow* is making you check?" What I didn't realize was that she was standing right there with him. I let him in. Twenty minutes later she was knocking at my back door to tell me that he couldn't find it. No shit.

She thought she was living next to an evil prima donna. What she didn't realize is that I'm just a normal guy with some good solid common sense who has zero tolerance for those with zero intelligence.

The only thing worse than her was the zaftig pussy that sprang from her pussy. She had a son who was one of the worst people I've ever met. He was an entitled, overweight junior-college student. The best word I can find to describe him is *soft*. He was a doughy asshole who was completely ruined by his horrible mother. Once I ran into him during the construction on the house and he asked what I was going to be doing on Friday. I told him I'd be sandblasting the stucco. He said, "No. That's bad for me. I have a big test on Monday and I'm going to be studying." First off, can't you go to the library? How about you just go in your room and close the door or put on headphones like a normal person? Nope, the plan is to get the neighbor to shut down his entire construction project. Second, I can only imagine what he was studying for. I'm sure his junior-college degree has since gotten him as far as my mom's Chicano Studies degree. Third, I wasn't just a neighbor. I was a celebrity. Low-level, but a celebrity nonetheless. I couldn't imagine a twenty-two-year-old version of myself going next door to Peter Scolari's house and telling him to shut it down.

During another phase of the renovation, we had to do some painting. Some overspray apparently had gotten on his piece-of-shit '84 Honda. You'd need a fucking jeweler's loupe to find it but he claimed it was there, and his mother claimed she had some paint on her car, too, so in an effort to avoid dealing with them I offered to pay for their cars to be buffed out. He called me on a Saturday at eight o'clock and said, "Hey, man, I got the car detailed today. It was a hundred and twenty dollars. I could really use the money, so if you could drop it off." I said okay, that I was heading to dinner but I'd put a check in his mailbox on my way out. He said that he needed cash. I told him I didn't have that amount of cash on me, but that I was going out and I'd hit the ATM and leave it in his mailbox when I got back. At this point I had been more than reasonable. But he insisted that he needed the cash now. I asked, "So you want me to go down the hill, go to the bank, and drive back up to drop off the cash?" Not sensing—or more likely ignoring—my sarcasm, he said that would be good. That's the sense of entitlement this pudgy bastard had. As example #122 of why I'm not the problem and have no self-esteem, I still went down the hill, got his cash, and dropped it off for him.

You'd think that would end the saga, but that's the thing about people like this: They're relentless, like the Predator. In fact, I think I just came up with a great movie premise—*Israelian vs. Predator.* The Predator moves into my old neighborhood and hunts that prick for sport. He called me about some other petty complaint. What makes this particularly dickish is that he called me at nine forty-five on a Saturday night. I had already gone out for the night, so he left a message on my home answering machine. I went out, tied one on, came home, and passed out blissfully unaware that he had called. He called again at nine the next morning, Sunday, and left another message. When I got up I listened to it. In the most put-upon tone he could muster he said, "This is now my second time trying to get hold of you. In the future, I would appreciate it if you would show me the respect of giving me your home number instead of routing me to an answering service." Can you believe that shit? *An answering service!*

After a few years living next to these two I found myself thinking, "I'm not completely behind the Palestinians, but they do make some valid points."

I wish I could call them out as the only nut jobs on my new block. But there was another crazy yenta who lived down the street. This was more of the New York rather than Tel Aviv variety of Jew. Think

George Costanza's mother from *Seinfeld*. She had that bizarre red hair you only find on crazy old women. It falls more into the orange category and is thin enough that you can see their scalp. She looked like Mr. Heat Miser from *The Year Without Santa Claus*.

After I got married, we received a lot of gifts in the mail and thus ended up with a garbage bin full of boxes, wrapping, and packing peanuts. Well, inevitably, as the robotic arm lifted the can and dumped it into the truck, a gust of wind kicked up and the peanuts went everywhere. It was packing peanuts as far as the eye can see. It looked as if they were dumped on my street like fire retardant from a C-130. Now, technically this wasn't my fault: I blame the garbage men for not getting their asses out of the truck and dumping the garbage by hand the way they used to when I was a kid. I also blame the packing-peanut manufacturers of America. But if it was anyone's responsibility to clean up, it was mine. So I grabbed a broom. But that didn't work. The peanuts were too light and scattered like pigeons as I tried to sweep.

As I was doing this, of course Mrs. Heat Miser came walking up the street. She started in on me. "We've got quite a mess here. Who's gonna clean this up? You know they don't break down. You can't just sweep them into the garden. They'll be there forever."

At that point I would have traded all of the wedding gifts that packing material protected to not have to deal with it, but I decided to cut my losses. I told her I was going to take care of it, put the broom back, and grabbed a five-gallon bucket. Over the next two hours I picked up every individual goddamn packing peanut by hand. They had blown all down the hill and were littering several hundred yards, caught in planters, underneath cars, and mired in the muck of the gutter running along the curb. Using my thumb and index finger as the world's worst set of tweezers I extracted every soggy, dirty, sewage-covered peanut on the block.

The following day, I walked out of my house and instantly ran into the Red Menace. She brought the peanuts up. "They're all over the place. Come look at my lawn." Now, I couldn't deny that some might have gotten away in the wind, but they couldn't be "all over." I told her so and she said, and this is verbatim, "It's like snow. It's like it snowed on my lawn." I told her I'd go look. She said she wanted to finish her walk but gave me her address. What I soon realized was that she was not interested in coming down there with me so I could prove her wrong. When I arrived at her lawn I found, literally, one packing peanut.

This is the thing that drives me nuts: the exaggerating to make spurious points. But in the end it was my fault. I engaged. Just like with the other neighbor and the "flooding" coming from my air conditioner, I should have stopped it early on. The first time she came to the door about the water I should have said, "Shut up and get in your house." With Mrs. Peanut I should have told her to keep walking and that I hoped she got mauled by a mountain lion. That's what we need to tell all of these people. That's my sincere wish. I hope you're enjoying this book and find it funny and inspiring, but even more than that I want it to be a call to action. I want it to motivate you to tell your shitty neighbor to shut the fuck up and take a hike. We don't need to protect these people. They're not California condors. They deserve the worst we can offer.

So I had a home of my own and I was finally starting to make some real money. *The Man Show* was in full swing, and *Loveline* was on the radio and TV. But don't worry, my family was not going to let me enjoy my success. My mom's birthday came around, and we all took her out to a Thai restaurant. Somewhere in the middle of dinner she announced to the crowded table, "I got another one of these flyers for cable in the mail. Fourteen ninety-nine. I don't know." And then she said, "Can anyone give me one good reason why I should get cable?" *One* reason. She actually said *one*. Her son had *two* shows on cable at the time. The worst part was that the entire table of Carollas could not provide an answer. Someone said, "There's gardening shows. You like gardening." Here's how brainwashed I'd gotten by the Carolla cult—I didn't even think for a hot second about defending my honor and bringing up my two shows. I actually piled on and said, "They have cooking shows, too." It didn't hit me until the drive in to *Loveline* what had just happened.

My relationship with Lynette continued to chug along, notwithstanding a few minor hiccups. When you get into a serious relationship and get married, for better or worse you get a new family. You might think from what I've shared about my family that this would be a good thing, but there are also some cuckoo birds making their nest in Lynette's family tree.

Lynette has a schizophrenic brother who, when medicated, is perfectly stable; you wouldn't know he had any kind of condition. Minus one factor. His hat. He wears a UCLA ball cap with the two plastic snap-ons undone that looks like it was backed over by a cement truck and then mashed onto his head. I saw the hat get progressively worse over the years until one day I finally said something. Of course I ended up looking like an asshole, but I was just trying to save my brother-in-law the judging stares of strangers.

One of the longest and worst nights of my life was when Lynette's mom (who, like my grandmother, was named Helen) went off her meds. She was bipolar. I had just pulled in from an exhausting four-show tape day for *Loveline* on MTV when Lynette greeted me, upset, saying that her mom was having an episode and was refusing to take her pills. So I had to schlep forty-five minutes on a Friday night out to Canoga Park to try and talk her into the ambulance that had been called to take her to the psych ward before she was forced into it.

I tried reasoning with her and said, "I'm tired, you're tired, Lynette's tired, the ambulance drivers are tired. You need to get into that ambulance or we'll have to sit here and wait for the cops to show up and force you into the ambulance in handcuffs." In not so many words, she said, Bring it on.

Helen was a scrappy seventy-one-years-young fourth-degree black belt. She had 7 percent body fat and went to the gym every day. She was tough. So when the cops showed up, she went into her kata. She was pulling moves like Ralph Macchio on the pier pylon in *The Karate Kid*. The straight-out-of-a-movie black cop and white partner showed up and started to approach Helen, still in her bathrobe but acting like an extra from *Bloodsport*. They followed her into her room and I couldn't see, but could definitely hear, what happened. Down the hall poured the sound of a cartoonish maelstrom: furniture smashing, glass breaking, and Helen screaming, "Why did you do this to me?" at Lynette. She tore the watch off one of the cops and managed to break it, along with what little spirit Lynette had left. She collapsed in a heap of tears.

This wasn't Helen's first episode; she'd had many before this. In fact so many that Jimmy came up with a novel idea on how to deal with it. Helen was born-again, so we had one of the *Man Show* writers call her and as Jesus command her to take her meds.

About five years later, we were sitting in the kitchen preparing for dinner when Lynette called her and she didn't pick up the phone. Lynette immediately assumed the worst—she was having another incident. I tried to keep everything calm and said, "She's probably just at the Olive Garden." Lynette wanted to call Helen's neighbor, a big guy named Stan, but I kept insisting everything was fine and she didn't need to bother him. Like most people, she didn't listen to me and called Stan. While she asked him to go next door and check on her mom, I went for round seven of "Everything's okay. She probably just went to the gym. Hell, she goes three times a day. You don't need to bother Stan. Let him eat his dinner." Less than two minutes later, Stan got back on the phone. This is the end of the conversation I witnessed: "Hey, Stan. You got into the house?"

As I was gesturing for Lynette to let him go and get back to his life, I heard, "She's dead?"

I'd never been shut down so fast in my life. It was an emotional e-brake 180. Right in the middle of my saying, "She'll live to a thousand, she's a tough old broad. She'll outlive us all," Lynette found out she'd taken a nap before her workout and died in her sleep.

Sad, but I know Helen would want me to honor her memory by complaining about inconsequential shit from my road trips with Dr. Drew and Jimmy.

Drew and I had a horrible manager at this time. I was smart enough to drop his fat ass; Drew is still a client. Drew is the only person in showbiz who has worse self-esteem than me. We used to do a lot of the college circuit, going around to various schools, talking to the kiddies and doing a little Q&A. But it wasn't luxury travel, and again, our manager sucked. For example, we would do a gig in DeKalb, Illinois, and then take a short flight down to Kansas City. Our manager would arrange for us to get picked up at the airport. But because he was a cheap dimwit, we'd get picked up by some student from the college, one of the kids who worked with the student council who chose Drew and me to come and speak. More often than not, they'd pick us up in something wholly inadequate. Two-door hatchback Toyota Celicas and things like that. Drew and I would have a week's worth of luggage and have to cram in the back. And half the time it wasn't even the student's car, it was his roommate's. On a campus visit to Northern Iowa, the kid picked us up in his roommate's two-door shitbox and there was a full basket of dirty laundry in the back. I was in the front with my luggage on my lap (the hatchback was full of other assorted crap) and Drew was in the backseat, getting a lap dance from his luggage and resting his arm on someone's dirty socks. After the gig, with Drew still smelling like some sophomore's spent underpants, we went out for pizza with some of the students. This was kind of how it worked—the student group would book us, and after the show we'd have dinner with them. I suspect they never gave a shit about the lecture or question-and-answer session; they just wanted to hang out with a celebrity. We always obliged because we were staying at shitty motels anyway, so what was the rush to get back to the Iowa Econo Lodge.

The same gent who was toting his roommate's laundry was our driver again. I remember that it was snowing and the guy wanted to stop at his apartment first so he could change his pants. Seriously. My zero and Drew's negative-one self-esteem levels allowed us to agree. While we were sitting in the car, which was parked on fraternity row, people kept coming up to us and banging on the window, saying, "Hey, *Loveline*." The pathetic punchline to the whole affair was that when the kid came back down he had changed from a pair of black jeans to a pair of blue jeans.

It got to a breaking point in Kansas City when we almost died because the two ditzy chicks picking us up had a shitty old Pathfinder that was not roadworthy. Plus the driver didn't know where she was going. As soon as we got in the car, she asked, "Do you guys know where the hotel is?" As if I'd say, "Yes, sure. I could get you there blindfolded. I've been to the Kansas City Red Roof Inn many, many times." How the fuck was I supposed to know? I've never been to your godforsaken city before. After calling her boyfriend and getting directions, she agreed to meet us out front at seven to drive us to the venue. She and her girlfriend were twenty minutes late. Apparently they had decided to go out to eat and then do a little shopping. She then couldn't find the venue. The show started a half hour late.

To top it all off, we were in Kansas City, so we wanted some good K.C. barbecue. Ribs are one of those things that when you want them, you've got to have them, and after a long journey and a long show, we *needed* some ribs. But since everything got fucked up because they were late and got lost, by the time the show ended everything was closed and we ended up at a place that ranked somewhere between a Waffle House and a Sizzler.

I'd love to say this has changed, but I did a live stand-up show in Kansas City in 2011 and we were picked up by runners for the promoters. We actually had two cars because one guy I travel with needed to go right to the venue and I needed to go to the hotel. Initially, I was to ride in the car he ended up in, but upon first glance I knew it wouldn't do. I got lucky and only ended up in a Kia that was filthy and covered in bird shit. Seriously, you could see where the windshield wipers had just moved and coagulated the dirt. The other guy ended up being driven by a kid who was twenty years old in a car that was twenty-seven years old. It was a piece-of-shit Toyota Tercel with no headliner: It was his friend's car, which was inconvenient because his friend was the only one who knew how to get the broken *Best of Eric Clapton* cassette—yes, a cassette in 2011—out of the player. This car had covered more miles than the space shuttle. I'm not trying to pull a star trip. I don't ask for much: You can see my tour rider, and all I ask for is a couple of beers and a cup of coffee before I hit the stage (and usually that gets fucked up, too). But for the love of Christ, before you pick me up at the airport, please remove your roommate's spent tube socks.

Another time Drew and I were flying to one of our college gigs out of Cincinnati going to Alabama. Our plane was one of those twenty-five-seat turbo-prop planes. I was already nervous as I boarded the late-afternoon flight, but then the pilot announced that there were electrical storms and that he was going to attempt to fly around them. The next announcement we heard was that the plane was overweight and that either someone needed to volunteer to have their bags removed or they would remove them for us. We must have had a lot of gamblers on the flight who thought about their one-in-twenty-five shot, because no one volunteered. By the way, if the plane is overweight by one rolling backpack and you take that off, all of a sudden at twenty thousand feet dodging thunderclouds you're cool? That's the difference maker?

They went out and removed what I hoped was Dr. Drew's luggage. To tell you the truth, at the time I was less concerned about losing a piece of luggage and more concerned about losing a wing if we didn't get out ahead of that storm. Then they shut the hatch and the pilot fired up the engines. Out of the left-side engine came a giant plume of black smoke. The pilot noticed it and shut the engine down.

Again we waited while he called maintenance. Once the maintenance guy arrived, he fired it up a second time and a bigger plume of black carbon came from the exhaust pipe. At this point I was seriously considering getting off the plane. I was a nervous flyer back then because outside of the aforementioned Hawaii trip I'd never been on an airplane. The Carollas, as you know, were not part of the jet set. So here we were on a tiny, overweight prop plane with smoke coming out of one of the engines and a storm approaching. Needless to say, I wanted off. At this point I was hoping the maintenance guy would red-flag us and spare me the humiliation of raising my hand and announcing I was a pussy. But he did something much worse. He told the pilot to turn it over one more time, for the third time in a row a big puff of black smoke belched out of the engine, and he gave the pilot a thumbs-up and told him he was good to go. I was mortified and didn't think things could get worse, but they were about to. The woman in the seat in front of me innocently turned the page on her *USA Today* to expose the most frightening image I'd ever seen. It was a full-page color ad for *The Roberto Clemente Story*.

Roberto Clemente was an all-star Pittsburgh Pirate who died in the seventies in a plane that was probably manufactured long after the one I was sitting in. Let's review. I'm in a crop duster that's overweight with a blown head gasket, we're flying into a thunderstorm, and I'm staring at a picture of Roberto Clemente. I don't know how the universe works, but the great magnet in the sky only gives you clues. There's no magical force that unbuckles your seat belt, lifts you out of your chair, and pushes you out the door. I was freaked. I pictured a bunch of guys sitting on a cloud with harps and wings yelling, "You idiot, what else do we have to do? Get off of this flight already." And then the song "Chantilly Lace" came over the intercom. (Just kidding. Go to Wikipedia, dummies.) If you'd like to peer into my troubled psyche, this story is all you need to know. I was convinced I was going to die on that plane that day, but I was way too embarrassed and self-conscious to stand up and ask to be let off.

In 1999 we were scheduled to do a weeklong shoot for an episode of *Dawson's Creek*. They taped that show in North Carolina, and we were due on set that Monday. The producers called me and told me there were only two flights leaving L.A. for North Carolina that Sunday, one at eight A.M. and one at two P.M. Ironically, there were only two flights to the birthplace of aviation. They insisted I take the eight A.M. flight because if I missed the later one, I would be liable and would have to charter a private plane to get me there in time for the shoot. I couldn't see why I had to get up at the crack of fuck on Sunday morning if I didn't need to do anything until Monday morning. It's not a twenty-four-hour journey, why should I make it into one? So I ignored their pleas and took the path of champions by sleeping in and booking the afternoon flight. The show was sending a car to pick me up and bring me to the airport. I usually try to cut it close with the car service: I hate when they show up three hours before the flight ringing the doorbell while I'm still in my boxers trying to pack. But I knew the consequences if I missed that flight, so I included plenty of time to get to the airport and had them send the town car at noon. What I had failed to factor in was the fucking L.A. Marathon.

In recent years the L.A. Marathon has gone in a straight line from Dodger Stadium to the Santa Monica pier, and hopefully off of it. This is disruptive to the flow of traffic, to say the least. But in '99 it went in a giant circle around the city like a tremendous, sweaty Berlin Wall, shutting down the entire town from five in the morning to nine at night. L.A. already has a world-famous traffic problem, but the mayor and city council will not rest until it's a full-blown pigfuck. I don't know what percentage of Los Angelenos participate in the marathon, but I'm going to go out on a limb and say way less than 1 percent. This is yet another situation in which the majority has to pay the price because the minority wants to prove something to themselves. By the way, when I say "minority" I mean smaller group: There's no brothers or Mexicans participating in the L.A. Marathon. Just so you don't think I'm a total douchebag, I'm not saying we should cancel the marathon. I'm just saying we should modify it so the entire fucking city isn't forced to participate. How about you head down to the Fontana Speedway? It's got a lovely two-mile oval. First guy to make it around thirteen times wins. It would be the first time a Kenyan won anything on a NASCAR track.

Also, let's add a time limit to it. If you can't complete a marathon in under six hours, you shouldn't be running one. The entire town gets closed down for fourteen hours so some asshole can prove something to himself. But ultimately what did you prove? You're a horrible marathon runner? And according to your "It's not about the time, it's about the distance covered" plan, then technically we're all marathon winners. I ran a marathon between my den and my kitchen. It only took fourteen months to complete. Again, the point is that the marathon fucks up the lives of hundreds of thousands of Los Angelenos who don't have anything to prove, but do have somewhere to be.

Back to my trek to *Dawson's Creek*. The entire city was gridlocked, and getting out of my part of Hollywood was impossible. It was as if the marathon planners had sat down with a map, put a pushpin into the spot where my house was, took out a Sharpie, drew a big circle around it, and said, "This is the marathon route." At about twelve thirty the driver called and said he was running a little late because of the marathon traffic. That was the last time we'd speak. At one o'clock I decided to go out front with my week's worth of luggage and wait for the town car. At one fifteen it became apparent that he wasn't showing up. While delighted over the prospect of not having to tip the driver, I was horrified at the idea of having to charter my own flight to North Carolina. I'd be the first guest star in history to do a week on *Dawson's Creek* and lose nine thousand dollars. I ran up the stairs and screamed at my wife, "We're going to the airport right now. Let's go." We jumped on the 101 freeway and it was a parking lot, so we turned around and got on the 405. I drove like Vin Diesel on three Red Bulls toward LAX. As I approached the United terminal, I told my wife we were only going to be able to slow down to shoulder-roll speed, and that when I jumped she was going to have to take the wheel. Sweaty and out of breath, I hit the ticket counter at about 2:05. I knew there was almost no chance of making that last flight to North Carolina, but maybe it was delayed or they had to pull a drunken James Van Der Beek off the flight after he defecated on a drink cart. So I took a deep breath and asked the woman behind the counter if the flight had left. She said yes. My heart, nay, my wallet, sank. Why didn't I take that eight A.M. flight? Why didn't I listen to the producer? Then I realized I was doing something I promised I would never do—internalize. So I turned my ire toward my asshole driver and the motherfucking marathoners and the city officials that had put me up Dawson's Creek without a paddle. Even though I knew what the answer would be, I decided to ask the woman behind the counter if there were any other flights going to North Carolina that day. To my surprise, she said, "Yes. The last one is at three thirty." That's the only time I've ever been happy a producer's lied to me. I caught the flight, and my only recollection of *Dawson's Creek* was a week's worth of *Loveline* from one A.M. to three A.M. (with the time difference), followed by seven A.M. call times. The only saving grace was that *Perfect Strangers* was on at three thirty A.M. every night when I got back to my hotel.

Jimmy and I did a lot of traveling for *The Man Show* as well. We were invited to be the grand marshals of a Mardi Gras parade. This was a great compliment, and we were happy to accept. That was, until we realized why we had gotten the call. Originally the parade planners had locked down a much bigger celebrity than us, but he had to cancel and we were the backup. I'm sure the Mardi Gras revelers were quite disappointed and confused when they saw the guys from *The Man Show* tossing out beads and commemorative medallions featuring the likeness of the original grand marshal—Tommy Lasorda.

Of course, we made a *Man Show* bit out of this and filmed our time in the Big Easy. One of my favorite moments wasn't actually captured on film. We were doing one of those guided tours and we were in the van motoring along the highway, headed for our next stop. The speed

2001—New Orleans. Not the first time Jimmy and I have been together in pirate costumes. I've said too much . . .

limit was thirty-five and we were going forty-five. I know this because up ahead, going our direction in the next lane over, I saw a cop. I shouted at the driver, "Cop! Cop! Cop!" Because all they do is hand out chickenshit tickets, this is standard operating procedure when you're driving in Los Angeles. One guy drives while the other works as a spotter. "Six o'clock—motorcycle cop!" So I started yelling at the driver, but he didn't slow down. I said, "You're gonna pass him!" In L.A. if a cop does twenty-eight on the freeway, no one will pass him. It'll be a wall of drivers like he's the pace car at the Indy 500 and is gonna pull in to pit row. I shouted, "Cop on the right!" but the driver just blew past him. I said, "I can't believe you just drove past that cop." He said, "They've got real crime to worry about." And I thought, Wow, how liberating: You live in a place where the cops aren't trying to rape you. As a native Los Angeleno, I can't get my mind around this idea of cops stopping crime instead of fucking with motorists. Apparently that's what goes on in these other cities.

Jimmy and I traveled to Canada early in the run to try and pitch *The Man Show* for syndication there. This story doesn't involve him as much, but it's worth telling. Before we left, I got the speech from everyone that you should tell the people from customs that you are there for pleasure, not business. If you tell them business, you're screwed. So I was going through and I told her "pleasure." But they said, Okay, let's look at your briefcase. Besides the *Juggs* magazine, they pulled out an itinerary. In addition to selling *The Man Show*, we were also doing *Good Morning Montreal* and all that stuff. My argument was that I wasn't getting paid for it. It's promotion, so it's not business. I said to the customs agent, "When Michael J. Fox does *The Tonight Show*, he doesn't get paid." And the woman said, "Who's Michael J. Fox?" And the entire tone changed from my business-versus-pleasure argument to How the fuck does a Canadian not know who Michael J. Fox is? And this was in 2000.

What is the deal with customs agents? Who's attracted to that job? I'll tell you. Assholes who want power. They wear a shitty uniform and get paid a little less than a garbage man, but they get to fuck with innocent strangers on a daily basis. But ultimately they're pussies who won't confront anyone who poses an actual danger. They're not going with the LAPD to gang-infested neighborhoods, they're fucking around with Whitey. I told her I was not a criminal there to run drugs, I was just going to promote a show, drop a little money at a strip club, and be on my way. What I don't understand is when everyone tells me to suck it up and take it up the ass from some jerk. These guys allegedly work for us. I didn't barge into her house and demand she blow me. But I spoke up for myself. So they took me to a separate office and made me wait for an hour for someone to come out until I finally realized I was being punished.

Another infamous *Man Show* road trip was one where we didn't travel that far, just a couple of miles to the City of Industry and the Spearmint Rhino strip club. One of the writers was getting hitched, and Jimmy threw him a bachelor party. Jimmy usually spearheads these events because of his own bachelor-party experience. Jimmy got married young and broke, and thus his bachelor party was pathetic—a couple of buddies from high school, a twelve-pack of warm Stroh's, and they would have been lucky if they had the bra section of the Sears catalog for the "entertainment." Plus Jimmy grew up in Vegas, so it wasn't even like they could say, "Hey, we went to Vegas for the weekend."

Just a quick riff on bachelor parties and what they've deteriorated into. The bachelor party used to be about getting drunk with your friends and lying down with one last chick before settling down with another. Over the years it's turned into a fraternity hazing. Now the bachelor is the one having the least fun. He's been duct-taped to a chair and is getting beer dumped on him while his friends beat him with flashlights. And a quick tangent within a tangent: The bachelor-party selection process is important. No inviting the brother of the wife-to-be, and no inviting the buddy of the buddy. That guy who no one at the party seems to know is always the one who gets too loaded and ends up doing some lines and then crossing some lines with the stripper. Bachelor-party crews should have a better vetting process than vice-presidential candidates. There should be full background checks on everyone in the party van.

But back to the story. The bachelor party was the day of a *Man Show* taping, and we were going to hit the road in the party bus Jimmy had rented and stocked with booze right after the recording wrapped. As usual on taping days, we had a catered lunch—that day's special was clam chowder. Everyone had a couple of bowls, Jimmy's tally probably cracking double digits. What makes this notable is that about a spoon and a half into my first bowl I said, "This doesn't taste right." Jimmy insisted that the clams in the chowder were smoked and it was supposed to taste that way. He then slurped down another bowl. I ate a bit more, knowing something wasn't right but that as usual I was. The clams weren't smoked, they were spoiled. Unfortunately, my suspicions weren't confirmed until we were at the strip club. There are a lot of terrible places to have diarrhea, but the champagne room of the Spearmint Rhino in the City of Industry is one of the worst. Throughout the night, in between lap dances, the guys were running into the bathroom and decimating the toilets with explosive ass mud. The night was a disaster only made worse by the fact that the bachelor refused the lap dance and Jimmy wasn't having any of it. He had paid for the party, he felt a writer for the *Man Show* shouldn't be refusing a lap dance, and let's just say he had mixed emotions about the bride. It became an argument, then a scuffle, then a brawl. He was cursing and scratching and he was physically held down for the lap dance. Not surprisingly, he was not hired to come back for another season.

That story reminds me of another travel tale, and you'll soon understand the connection. So we'll flash back slightly to 1997. *Loveline* was humming along, and I was asked to come out to Washington, D.C., for the HFStival, a big nineties alternative-music fest at RFK Stadium. WHFS was a *Loveline* affiliate and one of the first to put us on. They were huge fans because we were number one on their station, so I was flown out on a corporate jet with producer Ann and Tripp Reeb, the then–general manager of KROQ. Tripp was the guy who yelled at me for calling Mountain Dew "the nectar of the tards" on the show. When I informed him that Mountain Dew didn't advertise on *Loveline* and that it shouldn't be a problem, he told me that their parent company, Pepsi, was a sponsor, at which point I offered him a hearty "Yeah, but still."

When we landed in D.C. I went out with Tripp, producer Ann, and the GM of WHFS. I enjoyed some delicious Maryland soft-shell crabs for the first time ever and then hit the 9:30 Club, a famous D.C. rock venue, where I saw Ben Folds Five play and did a couple of shots with Andy Dick. It was a great night, after which I retired to my hotel room.

The following day, I was slated to go to RFK and step in front of fifty-five thousand people to bring out one of the bands. It was a great lineup of nineties rock—Luscious Jackson, Squirrel Nut Zippers, Soul Coughing, the Verve Pipe, and Ben Folds Five among others. It was my job to introduce Beck.

At six A.M. I awoke and instantly began violently throwing up. This happened every half hour thereafter in between curling in the fetal position on the bare hotel bathroom floor. When you're so feverish that the cold tile of a bathroom floor is sweet relief, that's a bad sign. I had gotten food poisoning from the crabs. It was miserable. I would have preferred to get crabs than what I got from those crabs.

I doubled over in agony and thought there was no way I could get in front of a packed NFL stadium and shout out Beck's name, even though Beck is one of the few musicians whose name you could actually say while vomiting. The only better vomiting band name is Blur.

I spent the next four hours violently removing any liquid or solid that had passed my lips in the past seventy-two hours. I felt horrible that the station had gone through considerable expense to fly me across the country and for the fans who made *Loveline* number one in D.C. And who was going to break it to Beck? So I made a promise that if I could string together sixty minutes without vomiting, I would get on the subway and head to the venue. I managed to stop vomiting and decided to go to RFK even though my head hurt worse than JFK's.

When I arrived, I could barely stand. Thankfully, in the bowels of the stadium they had a makeshift tent city for each band—think of the Red Cross setup in a high school gym after a tornado. The first set of cots I passed belonged to the Mighty Mighty Bosstones. I was greeted by Dicky Barrett, who took pity on me. He opened his beach-towel door and invited me in for some Gatorade and a nap. Later we would become great friends, but at the time I barely knew him. That just goes to show what a great guy he is.

An hour later I was out onstage introducing Beck, and six hours after that me and the rest of the Bosstones were in the gay section of town enjoying one of the best steaks I'd ever eaten.

One last travel story again related to Jimmy—this time going to Vegas. In 2000 Jimmy's grandfather passed away, and the memorial was in Las Vegas (that being where the Kimmel family resided at

1997—Washington, D.C. On stage at the HFStival. And they said Squirrel Nut Zippers wouldn't stand the test of time . . .

the time). As Jimmy's best bud I was invited, as was our producing partner Daniel Kellison. Like always, I tried to get to the airport as close to my flight as possible and not waste my life (and remember, this was pre-9/11, so you could cut it a lot closer). But on this sunny Saturday, for no particular reason, LAX was crowded. I pulled into the parking structure and drove around for more than forty-five minutes looking for a spot to no avail. I was already cutting it close, but the added time searching for a nonexistent spot meant I was very likely going to miss my flight. I gave up hope and decided to leave the structure and go to one of those Park 'N Fly lots and take the shuttle. As I pulled out of the structure, the bitch in the booth (by the way, *Bitch in the Booth* is my favorite Dr. Seuss book) took my ticket and asked for eight dollars. I protested that I couldn't find a spot and shouldn't have to pay. The argument continued and I decided that my time was worth more than that, threw eight bucks at the chick, and sped off to the satellite lot.

I got to the check-in counter and had missed my flight. I booked myself on the next plane into Vegas. I landed and was already pretty beat, but Daniel wanted to hit the strip club. I told him no, I was tired and starting to feel a cold coming on, so it was one more hand of blackjack and then off to bed.

Cut to me at Paradise at one A.M. doing that drunk-guy unrealistic math. "Just one more shot of Jaeger, I'll be out of here by one fifteen, hit the hay, and still feel okay in the morning." It was seven A.M. and fully daylight when we left the club. I stepped out into a bright, hot Vegas morning and got myself back to the hotel. The funeral was in less than three hours.

I lay down knowing I couldn't get any real sleep but hoping for something a little longer than a nap. As soon as my head hit the pillow, the hotel phone rang. It was a couple of jag-offs I had met on the flight who I made the mistake of telling I was staying at the Hard Rock and who wanted to invite me out for some more partying. I ended up getting twenty-five minutes of sleep, and when I woke up I wanted to puke.

My head still spinning a little and definitely feeling nauseous, I slid myself into a suit and slid out of the hotel. I was greeted by a cloudless, 115-degree Vegas Sunday. I rode waves of nausea through the funeral, and when it was over we all filed out. As we left the grounds of the funeral, despite the fact that it hadn't rained, there was a rainbow. Jimmy's family stared at it, feeling moved. There was a real moment and lots of comforting notions about how it meant something, a message from Grandpa. I spoke up and said, "I know you're all taking this as a divine moment, but they're filming a Skittles commercial down the street." There was a short, tense beat, but then everyone busted up laughing. Jimmy's mom, to this day, thinks this is the funniest thing she's ever heard in her life.

I thought I'd include a section here where I break down all the celebrities I insulted or had some sort of run-in with while I was living in this house and doing *Loveline*.

PATRICK DEMPSEY: Before he was known to every woman in America as Dr. McDreamy, Patrick was known to me as a tool moocher. He lived a little below my new house and used to borrow my stuff. That's the thing with actors and creative guys—they have no tangible skills. I used to go to his house and help him with home-improvement projects, but I'd have to hang out until it was done so that he wouldn't fuck up my tools or kill himself with them. Eventually, I got sick of this arrangement and said to him, "I'm going to make a man out of you. We're going to Home Depot, I'm going to fill your cart, and you're going to buy everything in it." So off we went to Home Depot, and we walked the aisles with me throwing all the essentials in his cart—a circular saw, cordless drill, framing square, all the essentials. A fellow shopper stopped us, saying, "Hey, you're Adam from that MTV show." I said I was, and then introduced my companion: "You remember Patrick from *Meatballs III*."

MARILYN MANSON: He came on *Loveline* in 2003 and was bearing a gift. You can always tell alcoholics because they bring their own booze as a "gift." Marilyn brought a bottle of absinthe from France and sat it down next to me. During the first commercial break he said, "Why don't you give it a shot?" So I opened it—I didn't want to be a bad host—but then he busted out two glasses. The next thing you know, he was on his fifth glass and had plowed through the "gift" he brought me.

CHRIS PENN: You may not know the late Chris Penn by name, but you've seen him in a dozen movies, most famously *Footloose* and *Reservoir Dogs*. He's the only guest I ever hung out with after *Loveline*. The show ended at midnight, and that usually meant it was time to just head home, but in April of '99 he asked if I wanted to go out for a beer and I obliged. He said there was a cop bar down the street from our studio in Culver City. Why cops need their own bar, I have no idea. Maybe so they can take turns busting each other for DUI and make their ticket quota.

I later became friends with his brother, the lanky musician Michael Penn. At that moment I realized there are no two brothers, in fact no two human beings, who are more different than Chris and Michael Penn. Chris was a big, hard-drinking guy who'd get in your face. He'd fill a room. Michael is a soft-spoken history buff. Sean is probably right down the middle. He's smart and kinda reclusive like Michael, but if he feels like it he'll tap into his inner Chris and punch you in the face. Chris was a good guy and is missed.

GWEN STEFANI: In November of 1995, No Doubt came on the broadcast. I had only been doing the show a couple of months; Riki Rachtman was still cohosting. They were sitting around and helping us roll through calls and a young woman from Vegas talked about how her parents were pissed that she was dating a black guy. Gwen said that she could relate because her family had a problem with her dating outside of her race. She clarified that it hadn't been a black guy, it had been an Indian guy. She then went on to talk for a minute or two about the girl's relationship with her parents and them being from a different generation. Being the hard-hitting journalist I am, I decided to jump in and probe a little deeper. I asked Gwen whether her former boyfriend was "American Indian or 7-Eleven Indian." Gwen was stunned. I didn't realize that the guy was in the room. She was dating the bass player from the band, who had been born in England but whose parents were Indian. Who pontificates about their ex and the trials and tribulations of their relationship without mentioning the person they're talking about is sitting in the same room? He then very testily asked what my culture was. I explained I was from the Valley and was raised with no culture. He asked again and said, "I want to know what you are so I can insult you." I explained I was "a Guinea, a wop, and a dago," and moved on. No Doubt didn't return to the show for five years.

ROB SCHNEIDER: There's not too much of a story and I like Rob, but he did cancel a *Loveline* appearance because he had to finish a script and had writer's block. This is a poor excuse under any circumstances, but the movie that was causing the writer's block was *Deuce Bigalow: European Gigolo*. Anyone who's seen that movie can attest that the writing in that movie goes well beyond unfunny and becomes confusing. Watch it and you'll find yourself asking, "Is that a joke?" For example, during the obligatory music montage in the middle of the movie (set, unsurprisingly, to the equally bad "She's a Beauty" by The Tubes), Deuce helps grotesque women throughout Europe get their groove back. One is randomly covered in shit, twigs, and leaves for no reason whatsoever. He tosses her in a canal, gets out a bucket and brush, and begins scrubbing her. When she emerges from the water she is—are you sitting down?—beautiful. Even more jaw-droppingly, offensively bad is the scene in which Deuce is dating a woman who is forced to wear a veil because in place of where her nose should be she has a penis. That's right. And not only did this poor girl have a schlong instead of a schnoz, she was also conveniently allergic to Deuce's cologne. This causes his date to sneeze spooge all over the patrons of the fancy restaurant, including a perfectly timed and aimed spunk shot into a spoonful of consommé about to be ingested by an unsuspecting blueblood. You know what? I take it back. I'm glad Rob took that night off. Sounds like he really cleared that blockage. Just like a beautiful woman clearing jizz from her penis nose.

MARGARET CHO: Since we're talking comedians, I also had some trouble with Margaret Cho. Margaret is a nice and funny but troubled woman. In 2000 she pulled me aside at a party at Kathy Griffin's house and decided to practice the ninth of her twelve steps—making amends. This is always an awkward situation, but it's especially bad when you're plastered at Kathy Griffin's house. A few years prior, when she was in the grips of her disease and was living down the street from me, she walked over to my house. She had a script and said there was a part in it for me. It involved the two of us at a party having sex on a pile of coats on a bed. Moreover, she thought we needed to get together and "rehearse" this scene. Years later at Kathy's, she cornered me to apologize for this behavior. I told her I didn't give a shit or need an apology. Eager to make her ninth step a success, she insisted. I let her finish and went back to the important work of getting shit-faced. That said, I now think I'm owed amends for the awkward making of amends.

HEATHER GRAHAM: One night in 1996, Heather came in to promote her latest project. I can't even remember what it was, it was so bad, and looking at her IMDB page it had to have been either *Nowhere, Two Girls and a Guy,* or *Kiss and Tell.* Either way, you can see why it hasn't stuck in my memory. So I asked her if she had anything else to plug. She started telling me about a movie she was working on. As she described it I thought, This is going straight to video, and even asked her, "Who's your agent? You've got to get a new agent. You were in *Swingers,* you're a beautiful woman, what are you doing in that piece of crap?" She had told me she was playing a roller-skating porn star named Rollergirl opposite Mark Wahlberg and Burt Reynolds. Obviously I didn't know it was going to be my favorite movie of the year—*Boogie Nights.* But you have to understand the context of the time. Mark Wahlberg was still the washed-up rapper/underwear model Marky Mark, and the last thing Burt Reynolds had done was buy a new hairpiece: The last movie Burt starred in had been *Cop and a Half* (not counting a stellar performance in the Demi Moore movie—nay, *film—Striptease*). Throughout my five-minute rant about how she was shitting on her career and then lighting that turd on fire, Heather never stopped me or defended the movie. She never came on *Loveline* again, and *Boogie Nights* eventually went on to earn millions of dollars and multiple Oscar nominations.

DAVID ARQUETTE: The guests for *Loveline* on November 3, 1999, were Spike Jonze, Catherine Keener, and Orson Bean, who were promoting their new movie *Being John Malkovich*. It was the top of the show, and we were discussing John Malkovich and I was asking if he was truly as nuts as he seems. I was making the point that actors who play bizarre people are actually bizarre in real life. But I was also pretty clear that I was impressed with actors who could be that nutty and yet still hold down the job of showing up on set and memorizing lines. The first example that popped into my head was David Arquette. He'd been on the show before and I thought he was a nice guy, but he'd always left me with a distinctly nutty aftertaste. I piled on a little bit, suggesting that it was impressive that he didn't fold his script into a Napoleon hat and then eat it.

Drew told me to watch my step because if David was as much of a lunatic as I was saying, he could hunt me down. I laughed and told Drew he was too crazy to find the studio. But I moved on and we took a call.

We were still in the midst of this call five minutes later when David Arquette burst through the studio door. I was stunned, and the pathetic life you've been reading about flashed before my eyes. Everyone in the room was shocked. I remember saying over and over again, "This is the worst day of my life." It was as if I had summoned a crazy genie from a lamp. Like if you say "Beetlejuice" three times. If you talk shit about David Arquette, he'll pop up wherever you are.

Turns out David was driving home from the Lakers game, flipped on the show, and heard me making fun of him. Contrary to my belief that he was too crazy to find the studio, he remembered it from past appearances and walked right by the security guard and into the studio. He could have easily stabbed me, no problem. Remember, this is the same security guard who used to fall asleep on the sofa next to the studio while we were broadcasting. I inadvertently got him fired after the time I ran the mike-cord extension and broadcast him snoring just to prove a point.

Interesting tidbit: I've actually pulled off the Uncomfortable Arquette Trifecta. Alexis Arquette came by the radio show in early '07 and got testy when I tried to talk about her testes. She stormed out of the studio. Then in '09, when I was casting my CBS pilot, Rosanna Arquette came in to read for the role of my wife. After a flubbed line or two, she looked across the big oak table to me, my writing and producing partner, a couple of casting chicks, plus some useless executives and had a breakdown. She just stopped, cried, and said, "You know what I can do." Then she looked at me and said, "Adam, nothing personal, but I just don't feel like I need to do this." I agreed with her, by the way. I still have no idea why she was auditioning to be my sitcom wife. Throughout her apology, she kept looking at me and saying my name. The whole time I was thinking, Why do you even know my name?

KELLY OSBOURNE: Speaking of famous families, I also got into it with Ozzy Osbourne's daughter. Somewhere during the height of Osbourne MTV mania, she was our guest. During a rant, I made the proclamation that women didn't know anything about war. Kelly declared that not only did her father live through the Blitz, but her favorite thing to do was watch World War II documentaries with him. I thought for a moment that maybe the snot-nosed teen with the fake British accent might be the exception to the rule and that I was going to look like an ass on national radio. But just like MacArthur returning to the Philippines (ladies, you can Google it), I stuck to my original point and stayed the course. I decided to do it *Who Wants to Be a Millionaire?* style by starting with the most basic questions first. "Kelly Osbourne, for $100, which countries fought in World War II?" She started stumbling through her answer, and it immediately became apparent that she didn't even know who was on the Allied side and who was on the Axis side. And I don't mean she didn't know what team Hungary or Spain was on, I'm talking about the big four. I said, "Well, this proves my point." She answered with,

"That wasn't a fair question." I said, "Are you high? That's like you saying you're a speed reader but it took you a weekend to get through *The Cat in the Hat*." I said, "Thank you for proving my point. Now if you could just admit that you don't know anything about World War II, we could get on with the show." She stuck to her guns and insisted she was an expert. At this point Drew jumped in, said this was uncomfortable, and asked, Could we move on?

I've gotten into hundreds of arguments with people on and off the air in which they've made some sort of proclamation, turned out to be wrong, and pulled the let's-just-agree-to-disagree bullshit. I then end up coming off like a dick because I'm not willing to leave the subject until they admit that they were wrong. I don't think this makes me an asshole; I think it makes me a champion of justice.

I said to Kelly Osbourne as soon as she admitted I was right about women knowing nothing about war, we could move on to lighter fare, like genital herpes and dry anal rape. She never did give in, and that night I got home and prayed that one day there would be a show called *Dancing with the Stars* and that she would be second runner-up.

Chicks pull that it-was-before-I-was-born shit all the time, especially when it comes to war. I think it's out of convenience. If they saw all the footage of the kamikazes diving at the aircraft carriers and our grandfathers going up in a ball of flames, and if they knew about the hundreds of thousands of men who died in defense of this country, they wouldn't be able to say no to a blow job or a Denver omelet for the next thousand years.

CELEBRITY BASEBALL: Since the fifties or sixties, the Dodgers would have the Hollywood Stars Night games with real celebrities like Burt Lancaster and Rock Hudson. Nowadays I'm out there with the guy who played the corpse from *Weekend at Bernie's* and Mini-Me. Many years ago, during *Loveline* and before *The Man Show*, about ten minutes after I became a "celebrity," Dr. Drew and I were invited to play.

I was very excited. Back then they played hardball, and I even thought that maybe if the wind was just right, I could jack one out of there. I'd taken some batting practice that day and had hit some to the track. I can swing a bat. Unfortunately, I noticed that not only was the roster deep, twenty-plus guys on each team, but that we only had about forty-five minutes to play. I looked up at the scoreboard clock and saw that the Dodgers were due on the field a little after six, and we were starting after five. So I said to the coach, whom I'd never met before, "Coach, I just want to let you know some of the guys, like Dr. Drew, aren't that interested in playing. Other guys, such as myself, are. Also, I've got some game." He snapped back, "Don't tell me how to coach this team. Now sit down." I hit the bench and said to Kevin Frazier, the black guy for *Entertainment Tonight,* "He's gonna punish me." Eventually he started weaving people into the game, and none of them were me. I looked up and saw that there were nine minutes left in the game and I wasn't getting in. I was pissed because I went to the batting cages and oiled my mitt the night before, I got there two hours early, took batting practice, and yet I was stuck on the bench watching Elayne Boosler run to third from home plate. Eventually it was coming to the end of the game and the coach turned around looking for Stephen Baldwin, who had already been up several times. He was nowhere to be found. I realized this might be my only opportunity to get in the game, so I picked up a bat and I started heading for home plate. The coach grabbed me and said, "Where are you going?" I replied, "I'm going up to hit. Baldwin's not around—" Before I could finish the sentence, he said, "Sit down." I was done. I turned around to him and I said, "Fuck you, Pops. Fuck you. Kiss my ass." Again, I thought he was just a Triple-A coach from the Toledo Mud Hens or something. Unbeknownst to me at the time, it was Jack Gilardi. He was a high-powered agent at ICM who basically ran show business. And he was pissed. This was a guy who hasn't been told to fuck off in at least thirty years. So Esai Morales got up instead and dribbled one right to the pitcher, who barehanded it and tossed it to first for the third out. I shouted sarcastically, "Good call, coach. Way to get us out of the inning." I'm the only guy on a baseball team who ever heckled his own coach from the bench. After that, he freaked out on me. He ran over and got in my face again, at which point I gave him the invitation to bring it on because I would kick his old ass. We had to be separated. I was sent over to the other team's dugout and was banned from the celebrity game. It wasn't until eight years later that I made my triumphant return.

ALEC BALDWIN: Alec Baldwin is one of my few celebrity friends: He even blurbed my last book. Let me share with you why Alec likes me. Alec had a driver who would take him around town to his various gigs on movie sets and TV shows. And this guy was infatuated with *Loveline*. He used to tape the show on cassette and play them in the car while driving Alec around. Well, apparently one particular call, and more important my response to that call, stuck out in Alec's mind. One day I got a call from him on my cell phone and he wanted to talk about the piece of wisdom I had handed out. In 2002 we had a caller named Troy who wanted to convince his old lady to have anal sex. He asked us if there was some medical reason he could use to convince her that it was good for her. Drew said there was "no medical benefit to that behavior." Then I chimed in with my words of wisdom. Alec asked me if I remembered what I had told the gentleman. I said I had no idea. That's the thing with *Loveline* calls, we did so many of them I can't remember any in particular. So Alec, in his deep baritone, repeated back to me what I had said: "You told the guy to shit in a jelly jar, duct-tape a bagel to the top of it, toss it in the microwave for thirty seconds, and rape it." Alec thought this was the greatest piece of advice ever handed down and declared me to be the funniest man on the planet. And yet he's been asked to host the Oscars and I'm writing this crappy book.

PENNYWISE: Many bands came through *Loveline* in the nineties. Some of them were pretentious British assholes (Blur), and some of them were blowhard British assholes (Chumbawamba). But others were just good old-fashioned American alcoholics. I could rattle off a list of the bands that were drunk and belligerent, but they all paled in comparison to Pennywise. The guitarist from the band is a guy named Fletcher, and one night he pulled some shit that would make Keith Moon sit you down for an intervention. A little backstory to show you what kind of gentleman of the upper crust we were dealing with. Fletcher is six foot eight, four hundred pounds. Before I was on the show, in 1995 Fletcher came in drunk and vomited on Drew live on the air. When he returned in 1999 he presented Drew with a Stanley Cup–esque trophy filled with vomit he had generated from a trip earlier in the day to the Cheesecake Factory. He had put resin over the top so you could see the chunks of cherry cheesecake floating in it. Now, bear in mind this presentation happened within the first eight minutes of the show. This was *before* shit got weird.

After the vomit story came up, Drew mentioned my fecal history and Fletcher took it as a challenge. This affront to his dignity stewed throughout the show, and after dropping numerous f-bombs and fellating the microphone, with about twenty minutes left in the show Fletcher stood up, barricaded the door, and threatened to shit in his hand and make me eat it. The *Loveline* studio was smaller than your average walk-in closet, there was only one way out, and the biggest, drunkest human being on the planet was blocking the door. (A surreal side note: When reviewing the tapes to refresh my memory on this story, I noticed that while Fletcher was threatening my and Dr. Drew's lives and shouting, "We're going to Poo-Poo City!" a long PSA on the dangers of airline turbulence was playing to the unsuspecting radio audience.) This went on long enough that six Culver City cops were dispatched and arrived on the scene. But neither Drew nor I wanted to press charges, so Fletcher was not taken away in extra-large handcuffs. This despite the fact that he dropped a couple of references to Ice T's "Cop Killer" and claimed to be holding a live hand grenade.

Perhaps my most infamous incident with a celebrity—or in this case, celebrities—was in February of 1999, a few months before the Pennywise incident. Jimmy and I shared an office at *The Man Show* and had desks that faced each other. Yeah, I know, that's kinda gay. We were working there one day during the first season when, out of the blue, I got a call from our aforementioned horrible manager, who had received a strange offer. He'd gotten a call from Natalie Maines, the lead singer of the Dixie Chicks, who wanted me to escort her to the Grammys. I was baffled. I wasn't sure why I'd been chosen for this. I asked my manager, "Why me?" It turns out that Natalie was a big fan of *Loveline* on MTV. One night I was telling the following story. I was driving in my car with my girlfriend at the time, who is now my wife and will probably be my ex-wife by the time she's done reading this book. Hey, that's the circle of life. Anyway, I was driving with Lynette. We had pretty much just started dating. As we were rolling down the road, I had to break wind. I farted, and without thinking about it, out of pure male instinct, cupped my hand and wafted the fart toward my nose. I can't overstate how powerful this urge is in guys. This is something chicks will never understand. If I died and let out some gas a few days afterward, my cold dead hand would instinctively waft it up toward my face. After about three wafts, Lynette glared over at me with a look of disgust that I have come to know well in the ensuing years. She was horrified. It was the look of a woman who had just moved in with her fiancé, opened his desk drawer, and found a pile of pictures of kids with their eyes erased. An "Oh my God, what kind of monster am I with?" look. She said, "Do you have to do that?" Knowing that the best defense is a good offense, I got deadly serious with her and said, "Sweetie, I'm operating a motor vehicle. What would you like me to do, put my head between my legs? We'll drive into an oak tree. Think about it."

Natalie heard me tell that fart tale on *Loveline*, thought it was hilarious, and decided I was the gentleman who needed to escort her to the Grammys. She hates George Bush and loves fart humor. I found out afterward that Natalie actually had to pitch me to the rest of the group before the date would be approved. Fortunately, the rest of the band liked me too, or at least didn't give a shit.

I accepted the invitation and decided to go to the Grammys, since it would probably be my only chance to ever do so. It's not like I'll ever have an R&B single heating up the charts. The problem was that I didn't know how to break it to Lynette. I knew she wouldn't be cool with it. I had even asked my manager (or his gay assistant Chip, I can't remember) how it would work and he said it would be cool, that kind of thing happened all the time in show business. He said she'd understand.

Well, she didn't understand a fucking syllable. I responded with two points. First, I told her there were pros and cons to being with a guy in show business. The upside is you get to go to a lot of parties and there are gift baskets and things like that. This was one of the downsides. That didn't get a great response. The second point was that I had to do *Loveline* right after the Grammys, so it wasn't like I could do a couple eight balls and fuck her in the limo afterward. Maybe a quick handy in the bushes outside the auditorium, but that's about it. I left out that last part about the handy, but still Lynette was not thrilled. I went anyway.

Cut to the night of the Grammys. I'm sitting at the Shrine Auditorium next to all the Dixie Chicks with their Dixie Husbands. It was time for their category, Best Country Album. They had been nominated for *Wide Open Spaces*. I knew if they won, the cameras would cut to us, there'd be hugging and kissing and excitement, and it would all be broadcast to Lynette, who was watching angrily at home. She's full-blooded Italian. I pictured her spinning a whetstone wheel, sharpening a machete, and chugging red wine. I must have been the only person in the row rooting for Shania Twain. But alas, Martina McBride and the Backstreet Boys opened the envelope, called their name, and the Dixie Chicks won their first Grammy. I knew the cameras were on me so I stayed in my seat and awkwardly patted Natalie on the back, followed by an even more awkward "Hey, up top!" high-five moment. Ladies, you know that uncomfortable minimal contact you give the creepy guy at the office Christmas party? It was somewhere between that and a Howie Mandel fist bump.

At the end of the night, I said good-bye and went to do *Loveline*. The next day I arrived at the *Man Show* office and I must admit I was preening. I was talking to production assistants I'd never spoken to before, dropping Natalie's name into conversation. In my defense, I couldn't really keep it a secret. When I arrived at the office that morning there was a huge bouquet of roses on my desk. They were from Natalie. The card said, THANKS FOR LAST NIGHT. YOU'RE SO SWEET. CALL ME. Jimmy thought it was weird that she sent me flowers and said I should call her and tell her I had a girlfriend. So I decided to give her a call that night on the way in to *Loveline*. It was about ten o'clock. Natalie picked up, and when I told her who it was, she said, "Oh, my God. I'm watching you on MTV right now." So I was thinking, "Jeez, this chick has it bad for the Ace man. Can't blame her, she's only flesh and blood. Probably using that guitar pick in ways God never intended. Just strumming that bean." I said, "Thanks for the flowers." She said, "No problem." I added, "You should know, I have a girlfriend. But next time you're in town, come by and do the radio show." She said okay and we hung up.

Unfortunately, the next day a giant Mrs. Fields cookie arrived at the office with something like THANKS AGAIN. CALL ME. I MISS YOU written on it in frosting. Jimmy said, "You've got to call her and straighten this out. You've got a girlfriend." On Jimmy's insistence, I called her on my way to *Loveline* that night. I said, "Thanks for the cookie, too. It's all very flattering, but I've got a girlfriend so—" This was followed by an awkward silence. I filled the gap by saying, "But seriously, next time you're in town, come in and do the show."

By the way, you have to appreciate how difficult this was for me. Men aren't wired to turn down eager, available pussy. Especially when it's hot blonde millionaire Grammy-winning pussy. It's not in our DNA to say, "Take your perky boobs and your nice ass, your Grammy and your Brinks truck full of cash, and hit the bricks. Shoo! Go on, git!"

The next day I got to the office and Jimmy asked if I had called her. I told him I had and that it was all cool. But the day after that it was not so cool. I walked in and was greeted by a six-foot sub sent by Natalie. By the time I got there Jimmy had eaten two feet of it—I could tell by the chalk body outline of shaved lettuce on the wooden plank. On a large sign stuck into the sandwich was written in mustard, I WILL NOT BE IGNORED! —NATALIE. I decided to brush it off, thinking it was probably her just showing she had a sense of humor. She was embarrassed and was trying to make a joke. Jimmy was skeptical: He thought she was a home wrecker. But I blew it off and thankfully no presents were greeting me the next morning.

But about a week after the sub arrived, I walked in to find a box on my desk. A little gift box. I opened it up and inside was a pair of panties. And they were not new. They were what I would call spent. I could tell by the smell. Panties are one of the few things that smell better as they age. You can't say that about Indian food or car interiors. Anyway, the spent panties were accompanied by a note. It read, I NEED TO FUCK YOU TONIGHT. NATALIE. At first I paraded around the office, showing off the underwear. I was in love with the idea of a celebrity being in love with me. But when I was done

Jimmy pulled me into our office. He was outraged. He said, "You have a girlfriend. This bitch is nuts. You've got to put a stop to this. You man up and call her." I said I'd call her on my way in to *Loveline,* but he said, "No, you call her right now. You've been too nice. She's not getting the message. This is a crazy person. You need to call her and lay into her." I asked, "Now?" Jimmy said, "Right *now!*" I thought, Jimmy's right. Enough was enough. I was fired up. I grabbed the phone, dialed with purpose, called up Natalie, and had the following conversation. "Hey, Natalie, it's Adam." "Hey, Adam, I'm in Nashville at a Pottery Barn with my mom." I interrupted, "Listen, I'm flattered, I know you're into me and you want to get it on, but I've got a girlfriend. I don't know how many times I need to say it. This has gone on long enough. I don't care how badly you want to fuck, you can't be sending me panties." Natalie cut me off. "What are you talking about?"

I said, "Don't play dumb." She shot back, "I didn't send you any panties." I asked, "Well, what about the six-foot sub?" She replied, "No." "What about the cookie and the flowers? I thanked you for the flowers, and you said, 'No problem.'" She said, "I just figured my agent sent them, what was I gonna say?" (She's right, by the way. If I got a call at four A.M. and a big black guy was on the line and said, "Hey man, thanks for the flowers," I'd say, "No problemo.") At this point my head was swimming. I was sweaty, confused, and embarrassed. And then I looked up.

Jimmy was standing on his desk. And he was holding a video camera.

As it sunk in that I had been the victim of Jimmy's all time greatest prank, I started to hang up. My recollection is that I just said

"Sorry" multiple times before I slammed the phone down, and even then apologized to the hung-up phone. Jimmy says that I asked Natalie, "So how's the album going?" The adrenaline rendered the memory a little fuzzy, and unfortunately Jimmy's videotape of the moment has been lost somewhere along the way. Perhaps you could ask the writing staff of *The Man Show* what happened, because Jimmy invited them all into the office to witness my humiliation.

It had been Jimmy the whole time. As soon as he found out I was going to the Grammys with Natalie, his diabolical wheels started turning. The next day after the awards he had called Teleflora and had the flowers delivered. He had sent the Mrs. Fields cookie. He had the six-foot sub delivered. I should have been suspicious at that point, because the sub came from my favorite place, Giamela's. I remember thinking, How could Natalie have known that? I also should have thought, How could she have warned the writers to not bother ordering lunch that day?

There was a detail I never knew about this prank until it was revealed last year when I was in front of eighteen hundred people at a sold-out Wiltern Theater in L.A. and invited Jimmy to come on stage and retell the story. When we got to the part about the box containing the panties he asked, "Do you know where we got them?" I said no. He replied, "Do you remember our receptionist, Angela?" I said I did. Her name was Angela Box—that was her actual last name, and she was really hot. He said, "Those were her panties." Jimmy had commandeered an actual pair of panties from our receptionist. He then reminded me that after I had gotten the panties from "Natalie," I was strutting around with them, wearing them on my head and talking through the leg hole, sniffing them like a wine cork, hoisting them like the Stanley Cup, while poor Angela was standing there watching me the whole time, attempting not to throw up in her mouth.

The Dixie Chicks came on *Loveline* a couple of months later. I recapped the whole story for them, and we all had a nice laugh about it. And the next time they came on Natalie arrived bearing a six-foot sub.

THE BEST DAY OF MY LIFE

I'd like to close out this chapter with one last wonderful memory of my Beachwood Canyon house. I was thirty-three years old, October 17, 1997: the greatest day of my life. I had a poker night with the fellas: Kevin (but no Bean), Kimmel, his brother Jon, and some other buddies were there. The night had two highlights. The first was when Jimmy stood up and very casually walked away, like he was going to the kitchen for some more Doritos. Moments after leaving the table, he jumped through the open window into the room completely naked. To add to the weirdness, he ran through the room saying, "Look out!" as if he was being chased.

The second highlight was not just of the night but of my life. The game wrapped up and at one A.M., like an old gay couple, Jimmy and I found ourselves alone cleaning up. Jimmy was at the sink doing dishes when I felt a big fart coming on. Jimmy adores fart jokes. So I grabbed one of those cylinder-style Trader Joe's whole-bean coffee cans. It had about four beans rattling around in the bottom of it. I popped off the plastic lid and put it up to my ass. I even twisted it a little bit to create an airlock. I then released a long, warm, silent fart into the can and quickly sealed it back up. Then I said to Jimmy, "You want to smell some fresh-roasted Sumatran beans?"

Now, you have to remember that when you ask people to smell things, they're usually tentative. If you say, "Hey, smell this milk," they're not going to go all in. They're going to think it's spoiled or something. But not with coffee. People bury their face in that. You see those commercials where people open a can, push their nose into the opening, and the smell wakes them up. People suck that in like it's their last breath. So I handed Jimmy the can with a picture of a rain forest on it. He popped the lid and put his whole face in it. He took a deep inhale of pure, uncut, end-of-a-long-poker-night Carolla ass. Guys talk about unforgettable moments like winning the Super Bowl or scaling Mount Everest. All of those would pale in comparison to that moment: the part where Jimmy's brain had to catch up to what had just happened. At first his look was puzzled, but that was quickly replaced by horror.

And here's the best part. On top of the brilliance of that moment I was stoned, so it made it all that much more amazing. I've never laughed so hard in my goddamned life. It was far and away the greatest moment of my existence. (Sorry, Lynette, Sonny, and Natalia.)

15

A GRAY AREA AND THE BIRTHPLACE OF NO SELF-ESTEEM:
GRANDMA'S HOUSE

NORTH HOLLYWOOD, CA

YEAR BOUGHT: 1955

1,100 SQUARE FEET

ONE BEDROOM

ONE BATH

NO GARAGE. NO AIR-CONDITIONING.
(STREAK INTACT.)

NOW that you've gotten to know me, let's flash back to where all the trouble began. This is the home of my grandmother Helen, my mom's mom. I never formally lived here, but I had so many memorable moments throughout my life in this house I thought it warranted its own chapter. You might remember my dad's medallion from the picture in the opening chapter. Well, big amber beads and whatever the fuck Helen is wearing were as egregious a fashion choice. I also enjoy the picture on the previous page because Grandma, in her quest to look like an extra from the first twenty minutes of *Coming to America,* managed to combine both tacky leopard print and flower print. It also should be noted that my dad is wearing clear, nonprescription glasses.

Among the many atrocious features of this house were the cheap wooden knockoff Greek columns. As if you'd be driving by and think, Classy—it's a little slice of the Acropolis right here in the San Fernando Valley.

What you can see in the previous picture is the kitchen I added on to my grandmother's house. My table saw is in the foreground. That kitchen was a piece of shit. I put it on in 1985 for ten bucks an hour under the table when I had only been in construction for ten minutes. With Grandma helping, or at least looking over my shoulder critiquing every step of the way, it took me a year to finish. She was a tough, brassy old broad who didn't take no for an answer. One day in July, toward the end of the job, I was in the kitchen rolling on primer when she walked in and offered to help paint. She was wearing a blouse, underwear, and nothing else. I asked her why she wasn't wearing any pants and she said she was a grandmother and didn't have any painter's pants, she just had weird long grandma skirts with sunflowers on them that she didn't want to mess up with paint. I said, "Okay, but for God's sake, stay off the ladder."

In order to connect the new plumbing to the sewer line, it had to be found and unearthed. Turns out the old clay pipe was six feet under the lawn, so I dug a ditch just wide enough for the plumber, Bob, to crawl down, cut a section out of the crumbling old pipe, and splice in a Y for the new waste pipe to connect to. Bob was at the bottom of the hole carefully trying to cut the pipe, but it was so old that it was disintegrating as he was sawing into it. He managed to remove the top section, creating a trough filled with chunks of seventy-year-old red clay. Meanwhile I'd forgotten Bob was down there, and as the old saying goes, Out of sight, out of behind. I went to use the bathroom and moments later heard screaming coming from the hole in Grandma's lawn. I had floated a log down the rustic clay flume that settled on the debris right where Bob was working. He made me get in the hole and manually move it along. Later my grandmother fell in that hole after we'd covered it with a tarp like a Burmese tiger trap.

Grandma Helen grew up in Los Angeles before it was even really a city. She would tell me stories about Wilshire Boulevard being nothing but bean fields, and how she used to go and get chickens from a ranch that occupied the plots now housing the Comedy Store and the Whisky A Go Go on the Sunset Strip. When she told me this, my expression had the appearance of interest but inside I was a ball of rage, thinking, "You couldn't have bought one acre when it cost a dime? It would be worth millions today."

She lived with her mother, father, and older brother in Beverly Hills before her father's paving company went under during the Great Depression and they had to move to one in a long line of San Fernando Valley shitboxes. Years later after her mother had died her brother and father were living together. They literally were best friends. They would go hunting and fishing in the presuburban North Valley. It was a weirdly close relationship. He lived with his father well into his adulthood in that home, up to the point when his father died in his sixties of natural causes. This was not the case with her brother's death. Within a week of his father's passing he sat in the home they shared, put a shotgun in his mouth, and pulled the trigger. He just couldn't live without dear old Dad.

Here's the telling thing about Grandma. She and my step-grandfather promptly moved into that house without a moment's hesitation. I asked her once if she ever felt weird about living in the eight-hundred-square-foot home in which her brother blew his brains out. She, with zero emotion, asked, "Why?" I said, "A lot of people would have feelings about that." She replied, "What for? It's just a house." When I told her that according to California real estate law, when someone kills themselves in a home within the past three years the realtor needs to disclose it, she thought I was kidding. My grandmother was a hard-assed, tough woman. Up until the end of her life a few years ago, she had veins filled with ice water and Geritol.

One offshoot of her beyond-fucked upbringing was that she, without ever using profanity or calling you stupid, worked very hard at making sure your points got undercut and that you walked away from every conversation feeling bad. One of the best examples is when I was doing *Loveline* all those years ago with Riki Rachtman, formerly of MTV's *Headbangers Ball*. I told her that he cut me off a lot: He wasn't good at the "Yes, and . . ." part of improv, didn't listen very well, and was generally not a great partner to work with. She paused and said, "I bet he'd say the same thing about you." This was based on nothing. She'd never met the man or listened to the show. It wasn't like Riki was her other grandson from a previous marriage. She had no dog in the fight.

In 2005 I was visiting her on her birthday. My mother and sister were there, too. My sister brought up that she had seen a picture of me at a supermarket. I was curious and asked for more details. All she could tell me was that it was me and Jimmy "with some cheese." I had no idea what she was talking about. Did someone hang a head-shot of me at the deli counter? I don't know what was more confusing; the fact that there was an unauthorized picture of me out there hawking cheese or the fact that my sister didn't bother to investigate further. I eventually figured out what she saw. Every year Kimmel and I host the Feast of San Gennaro, a big Italian street fair. We were sitting at our desk one day after we had just gotten back from a trip to New York and were talking about how there's no Little Italy in L.A. We've got a Little Armenia, a Koreatown, and a Little Ethiopia, but no Little Italy. By the way, I'd argue that actual Ethiopia *is* Little Ethiopia. Until you get a building with a third story, you can't franchise your country into "Littles" in other nations. Anyway, as we were lamenting our lack of Little Italy, Jimmy said, "We don't even have a feast of San Gennaro. We should start one." We got the vendors and the permits and have done it every year since. Jimmy and I, but mostly Jimmy, had been running the thing for about five years at the time of this incident, and it had turned into a big deal with lots of vendors, thousands of people, three days of street closures, charity auctions, and sponsors. The feast was, and continues to be, sponsored by Precious Cheese, thus the picture of "me and cheese." I never spoke about the feast in front of my family. It was just part of the Carolla "don't ask, don't tell" policy. But since the subject had come up, after a moment of hesitation I decided to tell them about it, how it had expanded over the years, and the charity aspect of it. I was telling Helen that the feast had raised a good amount of money to go toward college scholarships for kids who couldn't afford it. I was feeling pretty proud. That was my downfall. She had heard thirty seconds of bragging, and like a soldier diving on a self-esteem grenade, immediately yelled that Jon Bon Jovi had raised over a million for victims of Hurricane Katrina. Helen was way out of the Jovi demo; she was ninety-two and had never even visited New Jersey. Yet she was locked and loaded with that piece of information. It's like those tales you hear where a mom gets superhuman strength to pull a car off her child. Grandma was that way, except her power was shitting on points. And my mom and sister completely backed her up, changing the subject to a guy they had never met.

The following year, I was visting my mother and brought up the feast. She asked what I was talking about. I said, "You know, that event I was telling you about last year at Grandma's birthday." She replied, "I've never heard of the Feast of San Gennaro." Mission accomplished, Grandma.

Other people would even suffer collateral damage from the Helen discount. One day we were talking and she said, "I went to the supermarket today and you'll never guess who I spotted—Bill Maher." I said, "You know, Bill's a big fan of mine, he loves *The Man Show*, in fact he's one of my few celebrity friends." That was all she needed. She said, "Oh, do you consider him a celebrity?" I was stunned, thinking, You brought him up—if he weren't a celebrity, you wouldn't have noticed him at the Gelson's in the first place.

Like most things, this trait got passed down through the generations. My mom got the downgrade gene as well. She showed up at my house one afternoon for a visit and had a VHS cassette. In true cheap Carolla tradition, it was one of those tapes that got used over and over and over. Because a new one would cost a nickel, this thing had probably been rerecorded on fifty times, most recently with an episode of *Oprah* featuring Jon Stewart as the guest. She asked me and Lynette, "Have you heard of Jon Stewart?" First off, I was on the same network as the guy at the time. Ignorant of this fact, she continued, "He's really funny, he's on Comedy Central." Lynette's jaw dropped. I got suckered in just the way I did with Grandma and Bill Maher, and said that Jon and I were friendly, had been out to dinner together, and even had the same agent. Her enthusiasm escaped like air from a deflating balloon and she said, "Oh . . . He's a little hit-and-miss." Poor Jon Stewart. Purely by association with her son, he was immediately downgraded from America's greatest comic talent to Pauly Shore.

I'm continually reminded of this attribute. As I write this, I'm working on *The Car Show* for the Speed channel. My mom, to her credit, watched an episode. She told me she had seen the show, enjoyed it, and then came the turn. She added, "Even though I'm not interested in cars." She went out of her way to let me know that she didn't give a shit about my passion. I own cars that transcend gearhead stuff. You don't have to know the displacement on an '84 Nissan ZX in full race trim to be interested in the fact that it looks awesome and was driven to a championship by Paul Newman. In fact, taking an interest in your kids' hobbies even when they're not yours is Parenting 101. I don't give a shit about dinosaurs, but when my son is playing with them I tell the nanny to act interested.

As I said, my grandmother was named Helen. And that's what she was called by my mom for her whole life. She was never once called "Mom" by my mom. That is a horrible sign. Growing up, I didn't really notice it or think it was weird. But then I started hanging around with normal adults and later had my own kids and thought, What the fuck? I didn't address it with her until later in life after doing some therapy and examining how my FUBAR family system affected me. I asked my mother, "Didn't she ever ask you to call her

Mom?" She hadn't. I asked, "Not even when you were in front of company?" She said, "Nope." At no point did my grandmother say, "Look at this shiny new nickel. I'll give you one of these every time you call me Mommy. When we're at home, call me Helen all day long. But when we're out at a store or a party, you call me Mom and you'll get a nickel." That's the craziest part, not that my mom obviously had a shitty enough relationship with her mom that she called her by her first name, but that my grandmother didn't give a fuck if people knew it. I have to assume she never addressed it because it would lead to an uncomfortable conversation about why she didn't deserve to be called Mom in the first place. If one of my kids called me Adam instead of Dad, I would sharpen a mop handle and fall on it.

My mom was a hippie, but my grandmother was a counterculturalist. Basically, if the Man told her to walk left, she'd run right. She needed to embrace a culture that wasn't her own. She married a guy from Europe and romanticized their governmental systems. She said she was a communist, though I'm sure she wouldn't have lasted a minute in a true communist country. She loved anything that wasn't apple pie and Uncle Sam. I never let my dad off the hook for not going to my football games, but my grandmother lived down the street from the field as well. It was walking distance. I played either every Saturday afternoon or Friday night, depending on the year. But she never attended one game. It wasn't like she was working while the games were being played. She had a regular nine-to-five job and never worked a minute of overtime. She just didn't like football. If I had been kicking around a soccer ball with some French kids, she would have been in the stands with a foam finger.

She also had gay and lesbian friends before it was cool. She marched with them back in the day, and during my childhood I would see old cross-dressing queens floating around her house at parties. She used to hang out with a guy named Harry Hay and his partner John. Harry was essentially the Rosa Parks of the gay-rights movement. And slightly more feminine. If there was a gay Mount Rushmore, he'd be on it. Harry was cross-dressing in the thirties and forties, when not wearing a three-piece suit and fedora to walk to your mailbox meant you were a hobo. And in the same way my grandmother loved communism—i.e., a rebellious teenage fuck-you to society—she was wild about Harry. Probably the most pissed my grandmother ever got at me was the time she was telling me stories about Harry showing up at parties wearing a dress and pearl necklace and telling people to fuck off for staring at him. I said, "He sounds like an asshole." She was furious and shouted, "What?" I replied, "He just sounds like an antisocial prick to me." She brought up his queer-pioneer status. I told her I'd done *Loveline* long enough to know the type. He was like that guy who gets facial piercings and tattoos, then is pissed when he gets rejected for the job at Toys R Us. I'm sure my grandmother was disappointed that I didn't turn out to be gay. That would have been something for her to brag about. The same way getting a Prius enhances your liberal-progressive street cred, she would have loved to introduce her grandson and his partner, Troy, to all of her friends.

My grandmother was a sex therapist and was very comfortable talking about the subject. A little too comfortable. Here are four quick stories of conversations a grandmother should never have with her grandson.

- One afternoon at her house—she was about 80 at the time—she pulled me aside and said, "I've been listening to the show, and I noticed you and Dr. Drew say 'cli-*to*-ris.' It's pronounced '*cli*-to-ris.'" I said, "I think you can pronounce it either way." She disagreed. "My friend Emery Kennerick is a doctor. And Emery pronounces it '*cli*-tor-is.'" So I said, "I also have a friend who is a doctor. His name is *Doctor* Drew." So we went into the den and found my recently deceased grandfather's large-print dictionary and looked up *clitoris*. It said you can pronounce it either way.

- In her discomfort-be-damned style, my grandmother also tried to get me to go to one of those nudist camps. She was talking it up saying, "They play volleyball. It's very freeing." I feel pretty free; I don't find cargo shorts to be confining and oppressive.

- When I was nineteen, I was over at her house and out of the blue she asked me if I knew what a rim job was. Someone at her sex-therapy group for veterans had mentioned that he was giving his boyfriend a rim job and she didn't know what it was. Of course, she thought the dinner table with five people on a Sunday over some goulash was the right time and place to ask.

- A couple of months after my grandfather died, I was sitting around with Grandma talking about how she was coping. She was doing okay, but told me it was hard. She said, "Everywhere I look I see something that reminds me of him. I look in the closet and I see his trench coat. I look at the bookshelf and I see his books. I look in the medicine cabinet and I see our water-soluble lubricant." I shit you not. With no sense of irony or embarrassment, she told her grandson the thing that made her wistful for his recently deceased and beloved grandfather was the lube he used to plow her grizzled vagina.

As you know, she was astoundingly cheap. She took cheap to a poetic level. She was to thriftiness what Hendrix was to the guitar. And her shining moment, her Monterey Pop Festival, if we can continue the Hendrix analogy, was my sister's wedding. The blessed occasion was held at my grandmother's house. Nothing says "sacred ceremony" like a one-bedroom in North Hollywood. There was zero pomp and even less circumstance. Grandma was telling me about how Christoph, my soon-to-be brother-in-law, was getting greedy and over the top with the planning. She complained how it went from twenty people to thirty people, then the cold cuts became hot food with chafing dishes, et cetera. She then said, and this is verbatim, "At a certain point he wanted to get rid of the plastic utensils and replace them with real forks, *and that's where I drew the line.*" This would not stand. He had gone too far. He was a madman. On his wedding day he wanted to use stainless steel instead of sporks stolen from a KFC. How dare he?

To bring it all back to houses and launch us into the next chapter, when I bought my next house I told Grandma, "Hey, guess who just bought a five-thousand-square-foot house on a hill?" She brought up the woman who was helping her in her old age—Delia—and said, "Delia doesn't even have a dining room table. She has to eat on the floor." It was a wonderful housecooling gift from Grandma Helen.

16 FROM THE VALLEY TO A PEAK: VISTA DEL LAGO

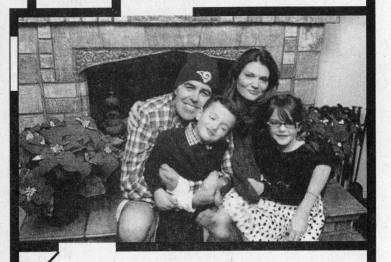

YEAR BOUGHT: 2003

PURCHASE PRICE: $1.6 MILLION

5,500 SQUARE FEET

THREE BEDROOMS

FOUR BATHS

TWO KIDS, ONE NANNY, ONE GARDENER, ONE MAID, ONE DOG THAT PRACTICALLY LIVES AT THE VET *(I.E., THE REASONS I NEED TO SELL A LOT OF THESE BOOKS)*

AND finally we get to my current home. Five miles away from where I grew up, but a million miles away from my first house.

When I bought the place in 2003, it was a mess. I had discovered it driving from my Beachwood Canyon house up to Jimmy's, which was a stone's throw away. It took me a year and a half to turn it from the rats' nest it had become to a habitable human dwelling. And despite what may be reported in some of the architectural and design magazines that later published features on my house, I did most of the work myself. I did not "pitch in" or "help out." It was more than patching plaster and stripping floors. It was a total gut job, like the aforementioned Beachwood house, but on a much grander and more overwhelming scale. And I dug into the minor details, too. I picked out all the vintage hardware, from the period-correct doorknobs and window latches to the stamped-tin ceiling in the kitchen. I stripped the awful white paint that the previous assholes/owners had slopped over the fresco ceiling and the ornate faces carved into the exposed beams.

People have such a hard time accepting that I'm a comedian *and* a carpenter. Comedians are usually so worthless around the house that people generally assume I'm a fraud. Well, I'm not. You know who is? Ty Pennington. He may look better with his shirt off than me, but he doesn't know shit about construction. In 2004 when I was still ass-deep in the renovations of my new house, he came on *Loveline* to promote *Extreme Makeover: Home Edition*. I immediately sensed he didn't know his ass from his elbow when it came to building. I threw some carpentry questions at him and was not impressed. I started off asking what OSB stood for and even mentioned wood as a clue. The right answer is "oriented strand board." His answer? "Obviously saturated board." He then brought up MDF. I asked him what it stood for—knowing the correct answer was "medium density fiberboard." Remember, he brought it up, yet still answered, "Multiple fiber density board." I said, "It's gonna be a long night." For the next question, I dumbed it down significantly—standard door height. Any carpenter worth his bags knows that it is six foot eight, eighty inches. Ty's answer was seven foot six. This is the equivalent of a marine biologist not knowing what a dolphin is. I repeated, "It's gonna be a long night." I tried to save him from himself and turned it around: I told him to ask *me* some questions. His first salvo was asking me to tell the difference between a butt joint and a dovetail joint. This is carpentry 101. He might as well have just asked, "What is wood?" I was very easily able to explain and moved on. His next attempt at stumping the Ace man was to ask the difference between a header, a beam, and a joist. Of course this was answered quickly and without any difficulty. Many uncomfortable minutes later, I prompted him to ask me a blade-related question. He coughed out some confusing nonquestion about metal studs and drills and blade oil. Eventually he just gave up and asked me how many days it took to build the Brooklyn Bridge. It's nothing personal against Ty. It's more an indictment against this business. Ty looks like he knows what he's doing, and that's all they care about. I don't mind him playing the role of a carpenter in a movie, but to put the title "master carpenter" in front of his name is like putting "insurance salesman" in front of Jesus'. It's just wrong.

Not only did I do the work myself, I powered through some pain to do it. In the summer of 2004 I hung full-length, 110-pound mirrored doors on the upstairs closet. What makes this a real feat is that I had hernia surgery the afternoon before. For about eight years I had a bulge in my lower gut, right above the pubic bone. If I sneezed you could see it expand. But for a lot of that time I didn't have insurance, so I just let it be. When I eventually showed it to another doctor that was filling in for Drew, he said I needed to be operated on immediately. A day later when I told Drew I was going in for the procedure, he mentioned that he'd had the same surgery a few months prior and did that thing all dicks do, try to make you nervous: "You are going to be knocked on your ass. It's going to be awful." I told him I was getting it on Friday and that I'd see him at work Sunday night. He said I wouldn't be there. He was actually laughing and saying how much pain I was going to be in.

This is something you should know about Drew: He has no bedside manner whatsoever. It's morbid. I told him about Lynette's best friend who had just been diagnosed at age thirty-four with cervical cancer and he simply said, "Death sentence." Unfortunately, in that case he was right. Jennifer was dead within six months.

Drew actually showed up at my bedside just before I went under and encouraged his friend, the anesthesiologist who was Jamaican, to bust my chops a little bit about how long it was going to take me to recover. He was Drew's neighbor, so I made a joke about Drew moving down the street because he "didn't like the direction the neighborhood was headed" and didn't need "his type." The Jamaican anesthesiologist (also the nickname of my favorite welterweight) said that his wife wasn't black. I replied, "That doesn't balance it out. Drew is a purist. One is too many." Probably not the best move to make a racist joke about the guy who's going to be over your unconscious body deciding whether you ever wake up again.

Drew took delight in the fact that even if I constantly talked about how everyone is a pussy and I was an iron man because I played Pop Warner, this surgery was going to knock me on my ass and humble me. He had the same operation and took seven days to recover and thought I would suffer a similar fate. After my surgery, I went home, drank a couple glasses of wine, went to bed, popped up at six fifteen the following morning, and announced to my wife, "I'm heading to the new house to hang doors." She gave me the "you're nuts" grunt and went back to sleep. The point is this; I powered through because I'm a heavyweight and had a project to finish.

. . .

The home was built in the twenties and has a lot of great architectural details from the era, such as the green bathroom with beautiful art deco tile and fixtures One of the elements of this bathroom was the original toilet. It was jade green and had a tall tank in the back. During escrow, before I even took possession of the house, someone from the city was dispatched to remove the original toilet and install an ugly, standard-issue, low-flow white toilet so it would comply with city code. This toilet would be fine in any apartment in the San Fernando Valley, but it stood out like a sore thumb in the middle of my mint-green, art deco bathroom. It was like hanging a cat-shit ornament on my beautiful green Christmas tree.

Los Angeles is what I would call ground zero for the anti–Patriot Act people. Yet they are the same ones who fully condone someone from the city coming into your home and enforcing their agenda without your consent. They raise holy hell because they're afraid George Bush is listening to their phone calls, as if the government gives a shit about you telling your wife when to pick up the kids at soccer practice, but some douche with a Members Only jacket, a clipboard, and a Mike Ditka mustache can come into my home while I'm not there, take a green art deco masterpiece, and install a white Home Depot master–piece of shit? I want a formal apology from all of you dicks.

And how about the hypocrisy from the city? They enforce this low-flow code and ticket you if you hose down your driveway, but every day on my commute to the morning show, my car would get sprayed by the sprinklers on Wilshire Boulevard. A sprinkler head every three feet was gushing a ten-foot arc of water in both directions. Occasionally this would even happen in the rain. All of this to wet a two-foot patch of grass on the median. I drove through Niagara Falls while listening to a taxpayer-funded radio PSA about water conservation.

Anyway, you'll be pleased to know I removed the porcelain pimple and reinstalled my emerald commode.

Not too long after I moved into the house, James Van Praagh was a guest on *Loveline*. You may know him as a celebrity psychic, but I like to think of him as Gay Larry Csonka. I'm not saying he *is* gay, I'm just saying he looks like NFL legend Larry Csonka *if* he chugged cock.

After busting his chops, essentially calling him a fraud and delighting myself with the gay Larry Csonka stuff for an hour and a half, the show had one last commercial break. Once we were off the air, James went into psychic mode and started talking about my new house. He seemed to know quite a few details about my new place, even naming specifics like my French doors. (Which I call Freedom Doors, by the way. Fuck those frogs.) It was interesting, a little weird, but not mind-blowing. At least to me. Drew, a supposed man of science, was like a teenage girl and said, "You're describing his house exactly." Van Praagh then asked if the new house had a view of an empty plot from my kitchen. This was true. There was an empty lot of overgrown grass and weeds behind my house. Thinking he was going to tell me to add on a deck or some generic bullshit like "This is a very creative space for you," I told him it was true. He then said, gravely, "There's someone in that field . . . more than one guy. They're watching your house." I was officially freaked out.

Remember this was at eleven forty-five at night and he just finished describing my house in detail that he shouldn't know. (Though the hidden drawer filled with issues of *Milkin' and Poppin'* magazines was probably just a lucky guess.) And Drew was backing him up like one of the brothers in the bow ties behind Louis Farrakhan. Doctorate be damned, Drew was in hook, line, and sinker. Van Praagh then added that the guys watching my house were Hispanic, wearing knit caps, and had tattoos. They looked like gangbangers.

So I was sweating a little bit, picturing my wife at home with some members of MS-13 about to commit a home invasion. Thank God I didn't have the kids yet, I probably would have run out of the studio.

I sped home after the show and took a drive down the cul-de-sac adjacent to the lot and shined my high beams in. I didn't see anything. I crept into my house, trying not to disturb a sleeping Lynette, grabbed a Maglite and a steak knife, and headed out into the windy, rainy, moonless, black-as-velvet night looking for the gangstas casing my joint. Again, no hyperbole, the weather looked like something out of a Stephen King movie. I skulked around the lot prepared to die defending my home.

Nothing.

The next day I casually talked to Lynette about adding outdoor motion-sensing lighting and putting up a fence on the edge of the property and letting some ivy grow over it. I couldn't tell her what had happened. I especially couldn't tell her that I had also purchased a shotgun for protection. She's a chick and therefore looks at that psychic crap as a hard science. *I* was nervous and I'm an atheist who doesn't believe in that nonsense. She would have called movers that day.

Eventually, after the thirty-fifth time she didn't lock the front door and I snapped at her, I had to explain. Fortunately, I never had anyone try a forced entry. Which only makes sense, because if you watch the ads for ADT you know that home invaders aren't Hispanic gangbangers, they're all white guys who look like Corbin Bernsen.

Granted, I would have gladly traded my newest in a long series of horrible neighbors for a pair of cholos camped out in my backyard. He's the old dickwad with whom I had the hedge-related battle I wrote about in my previous book. Long story short, this asshole called the Department of Building and Safety on me multiple times because my hedge was supposedly too high.

I hated this guy. I still do. I feel the same way about my neighbor as the Palestinians feel about theirs. At one point I declared I hated him so much that if his house went up in flames I would not call the fire department. Screw him. I'm an atheist and he's an a-hole.

Two weeks after announcing this to the heavens, I was sitting in my den watching *SportsCenter* when I heard something in the distance. A loud crackling sound. I got up, walked down the hallway, and I saw what appeared to be his house on fire. It was the one wish God has ever granted me.

So I was standing there in my sweatpants, dumbfounded. But I made a promise, and I was not going to call. That's the way I approach life—I'm not gonna fuck with you. I won't start any trouble, but if you get that ball rolling, it's on.

But here's the twist. This is what I didn't factor into my I'm-not-gonna-call-the-fire-department plan. My phone rang, and when I picked up, somebody yelled, "Call the fire department!" Some random person came to my gate, buzzed my phone, and threw a cosmic curveball at me that I could not have anticipated. What were the chances? I still don't know what this person was doing at ten thirty at night just walking up and down the street without a cell phone. My plan had come unraveled. I didn't factor in the potential witnesses to my crime.

After another moment of internal debate, I picked up the phone. As I stared at it, trying to do the math on his address, a fire truck pulled up. It was great because I didn't have to break my word and the neighbor who told me to call must have thought I had a lot of juice to get that fire truck out there so quickly.

But this is about a bigger point. This is the hell we have created as a society. We've become beholden to the narcissistic dickheads we surround ourselves with. This guy was such an asshole to me about my hedge—along with a hundred other petty complaints—that I chose to discard normal human empathy and turn a blind eye to the fact that he was possibly about to perish in a blaze. This guy and many of my other neighbors thought only about themselves, sucked up my life and energy with their bullshit, and therefore when it came time for me to give a rat's ass, I didn't.

I held a benefit at the rental property I bought and renovated in Malibu. It was in the afternoon, and a lot of celebrity friends came out to do some stand-up and raise some money to teach kids Shakespeare or some bullshit. And when I say, "I held," I mean "My wife held and I paid for." Anyway, the property is deep and has a three-tiered backyard going down a hill. The event was held on the lowest level. Yet the neighbor across the street called the cops to come out at two thirty in the afternoon on a Saturday. There is no way he could have possibly been disturbed by it. John Daly couldn't hit a ball to his house from where the stage was. And it was Jay Leno up there, not Jay-Z. But we hadn't cleared it with him in advance, and he had to let us know. That's what all of this shit is about, not hedges or noise. It's about daring to do something without asking their permission. If we had gone to him the day before and asked for his blessing, it would have been fine. But we acted like he didn't exist, so he had to let us know in the most cocksucking way possible that he in fact did. Well, fuck you. We were three-hundred like-minded people trying to enjoy ourselves and raise money for charity. You were one person. You're outvoted. Go see a matinee or put in some ear buds, asshole.

Having a big house and kids means you need people around. And those people cause problems. My place is a constant beehive of gardeners, nannies, and maids. I know, quit complaining about my rich-white-guy problems. But the gardener was warned multiple times about leaving the pool gate open. Call me crazy, but I don't want to come home and find my twins facedown in the pool. There's no amount of richness or whiteness that can solve that problem.

And the maid is constantly moving my shit. Twice a week I play hide-and-go-seek with my hats, keys, and corkscrews because nothing ever gets put back in its proper place. That's the current maid. We had to let the previous one go.

My friend Oswaldo's wife (Oswaldo being my sidekick in *The Hammer*) used to come by once a week to clean the house. She did a decent job of it, that wasn't why we had to fire her. I would come home and my eyes would start burning. It took me a while to figure out that it wasn't some cleaning supply she was using, but rather her perfume. She smelled like she didn't dab it on but rather dumped it on by pulling a chain attached to a bucket like in *Flashdance*. I asked her very nicely if she could tone it down a little bit, but the following week there it was again. We chalked it up to a language barrier and asked the nanny—Olga, a Guatemalan woman—to tell her in Spanish that I was allergic to her perfume and it was hurting my eyes. She showed up the next week fragrance free. But the week after that she smelled like she had been dropped in a carnival dunk tank of the stuff. (I later found out it was that Liz Taylor perfume White Diamonds when Kimmel bought me a quart of it for Christmas as a literal gag gift.)

What the fuck is up with perfume and cologne? Why do we need these strong scents? Perfume, cologne, and deodorant are supposed to stop you from being noticeably smelly, not create a smell so strong and blinding that it masks your BO. That Extreme Red Zone High Endurance stuff is not a deodorant, it's an odorant. It's not really a smell other than deodorant smell. Isn't the Tom's of Maine baby-powder stuff good enough? And the thing where they say perfume "smells different on every woman"? Bullshit. White Diamonds would smell like ass if I put it on Scarlett Johansson or my mom. If you put White Diamonds on Giselle Bundchen, I wouldn't fuck her. That shit smells terrible.

My point is this. We eventually had to let Ozzie's wife go because she couldn't tone down the perfume to the point where I could enter my home without a hazmat suit. What is that instinct? Isn't it everyone's worst fear to have the same embarrassing thing said to them twice? If your friend sat you down and said, "Hey man, as a friend, the last time we had lunch I could really smell your breath. I don't know if you need to go to the dentist or. . ." you'd be embarrassed, and then next time you hung out with that person you'd floss five times and funnel a bottle of Listerine. Yet she got the speech from me, the speech from Lynette, and *el discurso* from Olga but couldn't, or wouldn't, throttle back on the perfume.

I don't have too many complaints about Olga, with the exception that every couple of weeks I'll come home to find fifteen other Hispanic nannies and the thirty white kids they're raising running around my house. She'll host what I have coined "nan-borees." I'm trying to get some work done—such as writing this fucking book—and a soccer team's worth of blond kids are being chased around my house by their south-of-the-border, paid, part-time parents.

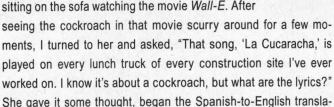

This one involves Olga but isn't really about her. Not too long ago, my wife was out of town. It was getting close to bedtime for the twins. We were all sitting on the sofa watching the movie *Wall-E*. After seeing the cockroach in that movie scurry around for a few moments, I turned to her and asked, "That song, 'La Cucaracha,' is played on every lunch truck of every construction site I've ever worked on. I know it's about a cockroach, but what are the lyrics?" She gave it some thought, began the Spanish-to-English translation, and came up with this. "It's about a cockroach that got its legs pulled off and it was buried on a hill with a mouse and a buzzard." I went crazy. This is the song you play to let us know it's chow time? A song about an amputee cockroach? Oh, a mouse *and* a buzzard? Now I'm starving. Maybe it's one of those Smuckers things where they're so confident in their product they can remind people of cockroaches. What, you guys don't have a maggot song? You couldn't just hit a metal triangle like we do?

Having a big house, a family, some investments, and people to maintain them means you have a big nut. And having a big nut means taking jobs you don't want to take.

One of the gigs I took just for the payday was for Lance snack crackers. They're those little orange crackers with cheese or peanut butter that you put in your kids' bag lunch when you don't like them very much. I was asked to do a series of ads for them. It typically wasn't the kind of thing I would do, but it was what they call a "non-ID," meaning that I wouldn't have to say "I'm Adam Carolla for Lance snack crackers." Second, it wasn't for television. It was a bunch of radio spots where I'd do man-on-the-street interviews with people about the product. But most important, they were coughing up a hundred and fifty grand. So I couldn't turn it down.

I said great, I'd get the DAT recorder, head down to Venice Beach, and knock out some man-on-the-street stuff. They said no, Lance snack crackers was based in the South and they weren't available on the West Coast. Therefore I needed to fly out to Florida and then fly up to North Carolina to do the spots. We'd go to a swap meet, a county fair, a mall, a bowling alley, and so on and record. I asked if we were going to say where we were, like, "I'm here at North Carolina's most famous bowling alley. . ." and we'd hear pins crashing in the background. They said no, it'd be recorded in a separate room, they just wanted a cross-section of people. Being logical, I asked why we couldn't just go to a mall out here and talk to fifty people. What the fuck would be the difference? Just send me a case of snack crackers, I'll head down to Santa Monica Pier and knock this shit out in two hours. Without sounding too grandiose, there is no one on the planet better than me at that man-on-the-street stuff. I could get them fifteen radio spots at any L.A. tourist attraction in the amount of time it took to have the argument about where to record the goddamn spots. This went back and forth through my agent a couple of times, and eventually they said in so many words, "Hey, asshole, we're paying you a hundred and fifty grand. Get on the fucking plane."

I soon found myself in North Carolina touring the Lance snack cracker factory, because how could I possibly do these spots if I didn't understand every aspect of how they were manufactured? As if not seeing the two-hundred-thousand-gallon vat of peanut butter would have rendered those ads unusable. One of the low points of the tour was when the plant manager asked, "You're from Hollywood. Do you know any comedians?" I said yes, as a matter of fact I did, just about all of them. He asked, "Do you know Larry the Cable Guy?" I said no, there was a long awkward silence, followed by the rest of a long awkward factory tour.

Shortly thereafter I was stuffed into a van and driven to a county fair, then a bowling alley, and then a swap meet to talk about crackers with a bunch of crackers.

That said, some of the jobs were ones I desperately wanted to take—namely my sitcom pilots. But because of the process and executives, what should have been a highlight of my life became an infuriating pain in the ass.

Here's how the process worked. In '08 I wrote a sitcom script with my writing partner Kevin Hench that was considered one of the best of that pilot season. There was even a bidding war among the networks for it. It was called *Ace in the Hole* and eventually landed at CBS. We then spent the next seven weeks leading into the pilot taping having the script picked apart by a small army of unfunny people whose claim to fame is they fucked up a bunch of other sitcoms before fucking up mine. The executives, at least when I did my CBS pilot, were women in their forties or fifties who couldn't crack a smile even if their Botox wasn't preventing it in the first place. If you want to know why traditional sitcoms aren't funny, here's one possible explanation. In the eight weeks of preproduction, and what felt like 2,000 notes we got from the network and studio, the phrase "story arc" was mentioned 26,000 times, "C story momentum" was mentioned 19,000 times, "proactive story drive" 16,500 times, but the word *funny* was never whispered once.

After they were done turning my 9½ into a 5, it was time for the network run-through. I'm not saying it was an uncomfortable experience, but I'd rather have been raped on a pinball machine. A network run-through is like giving the best-man speech if the bride and groom were a couple of the heads from Easter Island. I had to perform the script for the humorless decaf-coffee klatsch, a script that was being picked apart up to the very moment I hit the set. This was including character names, which is a particular mindfuck. I spent the three days leading up to the final taping calling my son "Nate," his original name, instead of "Eddie," the name we needed to change it to for no goddamn reason.

As if changing the name wasn't bad enough, the actor changed three times. The casting process on a sitcom is brutal. The boneheads I made the mistake of working with picked a kid to play my son who was way too young and way too Canadian. We never even saw him live, just on tape. Hench was the only one smart enough to raise his hand and say, "We're going to hire him sight unseen? That could have been his fifty-seventh take." Of course he was shut down by the "experts" I would have had to share executive-producer credit with. After the first run-through, we had to send him packing back up to the Great White North. But they looked at Kevin with a straight face and said, "We're gonna have to replace the kid" as if he hadn't raised the red flag and as if they hadn't pulled that red flag down and wiped their asses with it. Leaders of banana republics and Middle Eastern dictators are more willing to say "my bad" than TV executives.

We later held a quick casting session and saw one kid we liked and one we could settle for but weren't in love with. The development executives said that we should take them both to the network for approval. Kevin Hench, being the smartest guy in most rooms he walks into and definitely in this one, asked why we would even give the network the option of picking the kid we didn't want. He was greeted with the usual executive chorus of "We know what we're doing." Well, the story wouldn't be worth telling if we didn't end up getting stuck with the kid we didn't want. Through the whole final pilot taping, he was a combination of forgetful and asleep. He had the energy of a sloth on methadone. Except for one moment. When the taping wrapped, the cast came out to do their bows. Apparently he'd finished metabolizing the bottle of Nyquil he chugged beforehand because he bounded out and did a mock home run swing into the bleachers. In keeping with their MO, after the taping the executives looked at Hench with a straight face and said, "Great taping. But we need to get rid of that kid."

I wish I could say that was the worst story involving my sitcom son. But after kid one had been fired and kid two hadn't been hired, we had another run-through. So they needed a temporary Nate, or Eddie. I can't even remember what the fuck he was called at that point. It was an important day, and there were executives buzzing around. And they don't sit in the bleachers—they hang right on the edge of the fake sitcom kitchen. I could see them eighteen inches away from me staring coldly as I had to do the important scene where my son had decided to quit the baseball team. I got down on one knee, looked him in the eye, and in my best dad heart-to-heart voice said, "When you bail on the Padres, you join a new team called the Quitters."

Except our temporary kid that day wasn't an eight-year-old with TV good looks, it was a grizzled fifty-two-year-old midget wearing a cabbie hat. Yes. You may not know, yet may not be surprised considering how fucked-up this business is, that when they need someone to stand in and read lines for a kid actor, they often use a little person. I was nervous as hell knowing what was on the line if I didn't get this scene right. But across from me in the spot where my cute son was supposed to be stood a four-foot-three guy with cigar smoke and bourbon on his breath who probably did two tours in Nam.

The funniest moment of *Ace in the Hole*, however, did not take place on screen, or on set, but rather at the table read. A table read happens before the full rehearsal. The actors sit at a table and read the script, the director reads the stage direction, and the executives read their BlackBerries. This helps the team figure out the pace and what is and isn't working. Our table read went fine, with the exception of the aforementioned child actor. It was what happened afterward that is the stuff of legend. The show had a producer named Dionne. She was the nicest woman on the planet and one of the few producers who actually pulled her weight. She also happened to be the granddaughter of showbiz legend and philanthropist Danny Thomas. Danny was the Daddy of *Make Room for Daddy*, a sitcom that lasted thirteen seasons. He starred in some movies in the fifties, produced legendary sitcoms like *The Dick Van Dyke Show* and *The Andy Griffith Show*, and most important, he founded St. Jude Children's Research Hospital, which has treated thousands of kids with cancer.

But he's also famous for another thing that he may or may not have done. Or, rather, infamous. A rumor has been floating around for at least fifty years that Danny had a particular sexual fetish. He would allegedly pay hookers to squat over and defecate on a glass-topped coffee table while he was underneath it, looking up.

I've always wondered how these rumors get started. I can understand it now in the age of the Internet, but how did we all spontaneously, at different ages, in different parts of the country, hear that Rod Stewart had his stomach pumped because it was full of semen? I work and hang out with guys who are in their twenties and are from Boston and guys in their fifties who are from Southern California. Every one of them knows the Rod Stewart story. I could parachute into a remote Ugandan village that doesn't have running water or electricity and ask the first tribesman I encountered, "Did you hear about Rod Stewart?" and he'd respond, "Yeah, stomach pumped 'cause it was full of jizz." Here's the documentary I'm going to make and subsequently win an Academy Award for. I'm going to track down the guy who started the Richard Gere gerbil rumor. This shit has to start somewhere. In fact, I'm going to start a rumor in this book and check back in twenty years to see if it has become legend. Here it is. Justin Bieber had to have his stomach pumped because he swallowed a gerbil that was filled with Rod Stewart's jizz.

Danny Thomas's granddaughter adored him and we adored her, so we all avoided the subject. After the table read we were all mingling, snacking, and discussing how it went. I was standing around with Dionne and Kimmel (a producer on the project as well) when up walked Pam Adlon, who played my sitcom wife. Jimmy was heaping praise on Dionne's aunt Marlo Thomas because he had recently purchased *Free to Be You and Me,* which had been dedicated to Dionne. Pam joined the conversation, and Jimmy explained the Danny

Thomas connection. Pam instantly, without a second of hesitation, asked, "What's up with the glass coffee table?" There was a beat of silence that felt like it lasted as long as the dinosaurs roamed the earth. Meanwhile, all of our hearts stopped beating from the pure uncut discomfort. A second later, Pam said, "Oh, my God. What did I just say?" and began profusely apologizing. This only made it worse. The producer then had to address it saying, "Well, I've heard the rumors." I don't know what Pam expected, like the producer would pull out a shoebox full of fecal-fetish mementos or a coffee-table book about her grandfather's coffee table and the many asses it had seen.

Me and Jimmy were beet red from holding in our laughter. Jimmy loves an awkward moment. For him, this was like having front-row seats on the 50-yard line at the Super Bowl of Embarrassment. I later noted as I was telling Dr. Drew this story the irony that it happened at the "table" read.

The next year when I did a pilot for NBC, I made the mistake of working with the same company that produced my CBS pilot. Overall it was a similar experience, an exercise in infuriation. The casting was miserable and included a battle, nay, a protracted war over casting my friend Oswaldo in the role of my friend Oswaldo (who, like Eddie/Nate, was briefly Rogelio and Eduardo). There was also the hilarious moment when we wanted to cast Amy Landecker, who was fresh off the Coen brothers movie *A Serious Man*, as my character's ex-wife. The network wanted her to come in and read for the part. Hench and I said, "Good enough for the Coen brothers, good enough for us." But the suits insisted and she was forced to come in and read *while she was in L.A. for the goddamn Academy Awards.*

Like every other job I've had working for a corporation—such as when I had my morning show on CBS radio—for this pilot I was told I needed to sit through a sexual-harassment seminar. And like when I was on CBS radio, I refused. My thoughts on these time wasters are more than laid out in my previous book. But just so you don't think I'm bullshitting about how strongly I feel about these, I'll share a story of my less than passive resistance to this one. After I put my foot down and said I wasn't going to do it, the network put its foot down and said it wouldn't shoot the pilot until I sat through it and signed a piece of paper saying I sat through it. I still refused, holding up production and scaring the shit out of all the employees who hoped this would turn into a steady gig. The network relented and offered that the chick could come to me at my convenience to do the seminar. I said I had to work on the script and did not have a convenient time. They said they could have her come in while I was working on the script. Knowing that I was going to ignore her anyway, I reluctantly agreed. At this point the rest of the cast, the producers—essentially everyone except Hench—were pissed at me. So one night while Kevin and I were working on the script, the chick came in and started going through her materials. I made it abundantly clear that I wanted this thing to move quickly and that I would probably spend the next half hour ignoring her. But at a certain point she brought up the lawsuit in which a female writers' assistant on *Friends* sued because of the sexual conversation in the writers' room. She asked me if I understood the point she was trying to make. I'm sure she was hoping I'd say to not create a hostile work environment but I said, and truly believe the lesson is, "Don't hire chicks."

On every TV show I've ever done, I've had to deal with the idiots from Broadcast Standards. The NBC pilot was no different. For those who may not know, these are the people who make sure you can see a dismembered hooker corpse on every episode of *CSI* but protect you from seeing a little nip slip on *Survivor*.

Why is it okay to see smashed bodies being pulled from the rubble in Haiti on the six o'clock news, but at eight they have to tile the ass crack on the chick scrambling up the cargo net on the reality show? Though I must admit that if they did start showing nipples on TV, we would just keep going. It wouldn't be too long before you'd hear me complaining, "What, no vag?" And then in ten years I'd say, "You can see people fucking but what, no cum shot? I'm not saying he has to cum in her face, but would it be such a crime to blow a load on the tits? What is this, the Vatican?" Eventually it would get down to, "I don't understand the taboo on double penetration. Why are we such Puritans?"

One of the battles I got into with NBC Broadcast Standards was over smoking. Despite that fact that obesity kills more people than smoking, networks will, without hesitation, show an ad for Hardee's bacon ranch country-gravy strudel, but won't show someone taking a drag. All the *Law & Order*–type shows use the "ripped from the headlines" angle when they do the story about the pedophile murderer, but when I was doing my pilot for NBC we couldn't show a construction worker smoking a butt. Construction workers smoke. This is not an advertisement, it is a fact. And it is hardly a glorification. The character was a dimwit hybrid of every chain-smoking stoner white guy I ever worked construction with. No one would watch him and think, "If that guy is smoking, then I should too. I want to be like him." The network said we could show him holding a cigarette, but not if it was lit. As if that makes a fucking difference. It's not like people out there would watch that and think he was going to eat it. They did eventually concede that if we showed him with the cigarette lit, we would have to say something negative about it. Eventually we just cut that bit because it was too much of a pain in the ass. Congratulations, Broadcast Standards, you've succeeded in making your product 20 percent less funny.

. . .

You'll be pleased to know that my streak of getting into awkward situations with celebrities and the Hollywood elite continued unabated. Here are three of my favorites:

QUEEN LATIFAH: In January of 2009 I did *The Tonight Show*. The guest before me was Queen Latifah. First, how great must it be to be black? Somewhere in your early twenties, you can just declare that people call you Queen and everyone goes along with it? I could never pull that off. If I told all my friends to call me King Carolla, they'd instantly dub me Sir Douchebag. Plus black guys get to wear crazy hats and no one ever says shit.

Anyway, just to set the table for the disaster that was about to befall me, let me say this: I have no idea what Queen Latifah is into sexually. But she's a woman in her forties who's never been married, has no kids, and let's just say there are a lot of rumors that perhaps the Queen isn't interested in finding a king. Queen Latifah's segment focused on her recent trip to Trinidad and Tobago and how she had spent the whole time "limin'." That's slang down there for relaxing. She went on to explain how it came from British people rubbing lime on their skin and proceeded to say the word "limin'" 217 times in a six-minute segment.

Then I came out for my spot. I was doing a bit on kids' toy packaging, since the holidays had just ended. I took out a Hannah Montana doll and had Jay try to open it while I explained how you needed spindly fingers, the jaws of life, lineman dykes, and a cutting torch to extract it. It was a good bit and I thought it went over well. That was, until the commercial.

When we went to break, the band was playing and five producers came scurrying out of the booth and up to the edge of the stage and called me over in a panic. It was three gay guys and two postmenopausal women. They said, "Listen, we've got to put this show up on the satellite to New York in the next twenty minutes, but we don't want to do that." I asked why. They said, "Because you just pointed at Queen Latifah and called her a dyke."

I was confused. I knew I was thinking it, but I didn't say it. I denied that I called her a dyke. One of the producers said, "Yes, you did. You pointed right at her and called her a limin' dyke. You said to get that package open, you needed a limin' dyke."

I figured out what happened. In my list of tools you needed to open the package, I had included *lineman* dykes. But they heard *limin'* dyke. I'd been in the trades too long. I assumed everyone knew what lineman dykes were. Just like everybody knows what an oscillating spindle sander is. Right? I tried to explain to the three gays having cows and the two ladies having hot flashes, "No, No. *Lineman* dykes. Diagonal cutters. The kind *linemen* use. You know, dykes? Just dykes." At this point the lead female producer gestured for me to lean in and said, "Adam, could you please stop shouting *dyke*."

PHIL ROSENTHAL AND SAUL RUBINEK: Phil Rosenthal is the brains behind *Everybody Loves Raymond*. He's a nice, funny guy and has more money than God. Thus he has an amazing home theater and throws movie nights. Phil invites all his showbiz friends and gets the best food, so if you're lucky you'll find yourself sitting around eating homemade pizza with Norman Lear. Phil and I have a mutual friend named Ed who hooked me up with an opportunity to attend one of these events. I asked Ed what time it started, and he said it was about seven or seven thirty. I asked because I had to go and host *Loveline* that night. This was in 2009, long after I'd left *Loveline*—I was just filling in for the night. I did some math and figured out that the *Loveline* studio in Culver City was about fifteen minutes away from Phil's house and that I'd be able to make it. Bear in mind that radio shows start on time, whether you're there or not, so I had to plan this out to the minute.

Phil's theater looks like a regular movie theater with about twenty seats and some pillows to sit on lying on the floor in front of the first row. So before the movie, I flopped down on the pillow with a belly full of red wine and pizza. It was wonderful, except the part where I saw Phil's happy kids floating around and was thinking about my own miserable childhood and how inconceivable this all would have been.

One of the key features of Phil's movie night is that he always brings in someone connected with the movie to talk about it. One time, after the evening I'm telling you about, I was there to watch *Spinal Tap* and Fred Willard joined us. At the end of the movie, Fred got up and said a couple words about what it was like on set. For Fred, brevity was the soul of wit. On the outing when I needed to dash to *Loveline,* we were watching *True Romance* and Saul Rubinek was there. Saul played the role of the coked-up Hollywood producer. The movie had started about twenty minutes late and *True Romance* is a little longer than you remember, and we were watching the director's cut. I looked at my watch during the credits, at 9:33, and decided to sneak out during the intermission I'd envisioned taking place between the movie and the speaker. I'd assumed there'd be a ten-minute break where people would be able to fill their wine glasses and empty their bladders. I started to make my move, but a moment later the house lights were powered up and so were Saul's gums. I immediately sat back down on the pillow. Keep in mind I had almost eleven years of *Loveline* five nights a week, oftentimes from different restaurants and other establishments around town, so I knew exactly how long to the minute it would take to get from wherever I was in Los Angeles to the studio chair. In this particular case my hard-out time was 9:46. This would give Saul more than ten minutes to talk about his nine minutes of screen time.

Saul started talking about the movie in excruciating detail. Unlike Fred Willard, Saul was a little windy. I don't know if that's a shocker, but the Jews can get a little verbose when given the floor. He's a great guy, but you wouldn't want him giving the best-man toast at your wedding. You'd be divorced and have three kids in college by the time he finished. He talked about the film stock they used and the score and the catering but all I could hear was his drone and the ticking of my watch. It was now 9:44. At a certain point he finished a lengthy anecdote about his agent, said, "And that's when I knew I got the part," and took a long pause. I jumped up. As I did that he took a deep breath and started into his next story. I stammered, "Sorry, I have to leave." I then faced the Bataan Death March up the aisle. He said, "What is this? You're interrupting my story?" He was busting my chops and being humorous, but it was still embarrassing. I said, "I have to go host a radio show." Keep in mind this was almost ten on a Sunday night, so he and everyone else in the room must have thought I was just bullshitting. To make it worse, just before I got to the door Jeff Garlin got up and said, "I don't have to host a show but I'm leaving too."

In 2011 I went back to Phil's house to watch *The Ten Commandments.* I enjoyed myself and didn't have to interrupt the post-movie speech by Charlton Heston's son, Fraser, who played baby Moses floating in the basket. Though I did make an uncomfortable "from my cold dead hands" joke that is going to get me shot by Chuck in the afterlife.

TOM CRUISE: I've saved the biggest celebrity for last. Or actually the shortest.

I was over at Kimmel's as usual for football Sunday. Also like usual, I was hitting the kegerator pretty hard.

The kegerator is the greatest invention of all time. I didn't think the keg could get any better, and then they added the *-erator* portion. You put *-erator* at the end of anything and it instantly becomes better. Doesn't matter what it is. Apartheid-erator, cat shit–erator, AIDS-erator. But I don't even need the *-erator* part. You can just stop at *keg* and I'm there. No one has ever said, "Come on over. We've got football on the big screen, buffalo wings, some ribs, a keg—"

And I interrupt: "Aaaannd?"

"-erator."

"I'm in."

Also, I don't want to seem like one of the leeches who goes over to Jimmy's to drain his microbrew, so I'm the asshole who shows up with a skunky sixer of Natural Light and then makes a big deal about it. "Hey, I brought beer. Where do you want me to put this?" Every party has this asshole. The cheap dick who has to do a parade lap drawing everyone's attention to the fact that he brought a warm six-pack of Stroh's before he drains the keg full of Sierra Nevada. "Where's this go? Jimmy, where does this go?" I don't know. The chandelier in the upstairs bedroom? Put it in the fridge, you asshole.

So I was hitting the kegerator pretty hard, getting shit-faced and watching the game on Jimmy's 117-inch plasma TV. Not a projection screen, a plasma. The thing doesn't even use standard household electrical current, it uses 240. That's the shit they run bilge pumps off of. Four Mexicans died mounting it. I say it's a small price to pay.

Jimmy took me aside and whispered, "Keep it down, but Tom Cruise is coming over to watch the games today." Tom had been on Jimmy's show recently and Jimmy invited him over. I thought, Holy shit, I am gonna talk to him about *All the Right Moves* for two hours. Now I was nervous, so I started hitting the kegerator even harder.

The early games came and went with no sign of Tom. I was starting to lose hope. But with about two minutes left to go in the fourth quarter of the late game, and me completely blotto, there was a knock on the door.

I jumped up to answer it. I flung open the door to find Tom Cruise. But he wasn't alone. It was Tom and his mother. And his mom was holding a box of cupcakes. Tom said hi, handed me the cupcakes, and strolled into the living room.

There are a lot of rumors swirling around Hollywood that Tom likes the fellas. I don't know if they're true. Now, I'm no publicist, but if you're looking to squash that kind of gossip, next time you go to the home of the dude from *The Man Show* to watch football with the guys, perhaps you should leave your mom and the cupcakes at home.

I offered Tom a beer, but he said no thanks and would prefer a bottled water. I lost a lot of respect for the man that day, because he had a town car driver waiting outside. If you have a driver, it's your job to get shit-faced. I don't care if you're in a funeral procession or a presidential motorcade: If someone else is behind the wheel, you should be getting wasted.

Tom did a lap around the party and mingled for a couple minutes as the game wound up. Shortly after that, one of the *Man Show* writers and a regular at Jimmy's Sunday football parties, Tony Barbieri, said to me, "Do your touchdown dance for Tom." Because I was drunk I said, "That's a capital idea." When you're drunk, everything sounds like a great idea. Somewhere in America right now, two drunk guys are having this conversation: "Hey, let's go fuck with that cop's horse." "That's an awesome idea. Just let me strip down to my underpants."

Jimmy has a sunken living room. So Tom was three steps up on the landing in front of the door. I told Tom I was going to do my famous touchdown dance, handed him a ball, and told him to throw me a pass. Tom reluctantly accepted the ball, and I stood in front of the big-screen a couple feet away. I shouted, "Tom, I'm open!" and waved my arms. Tom threw me a wounded duck. I caught it and proceeded to do my touchdown dance, which you can learn to do yourself by following the simple illustrated steps on the opposite page.

Tom and his mom were mortified, grabbed their cupcakes, and bid a hasty retreat.

TOUCHDOWN DANCE

1

CATCH
THE FOOTBALL.

2

SWING THE
ARM BEHIND BACK.

3

SQUAT.

4

READ
NEWSPAPER.

5

DROP
THE FOOTBALL.

I want to bookend this chapter with some thoughts about my house. It is a constant work in progress. A couple years ago, I added my super-garage. And during that process I had the ultimate fuckstick screw with me. In order to complete the garage, I needed a bunch of half-inch-thick sheets of tempered glass. Each sheet was eight foot by eight foot, and they needed to go up to the second floor. That meant each sheet, at about four hundred pounds, was going to require a couple of guys and a hand-cranked telescoping lift to get it up there intact. It was hairy. You'd have to crank it up to the second floor, and then the team of guys would get it with suction cups and gingerly put it into place. If one thing went wrong, someone could have easily died. I had a small army of guys waiting at my place and said I was going to jump into the Ford Explorer and go over to Acme rental in Van Nuys on Oxnard and Sepulveda and get the lift. I pulled up in the Explorer and saw three or four of them sitting in the yard, plus I had called ahead to make sure they had one. One of these lifts is about six feet high but collapsible. They're made to fit into the back of a truck or van. I went into the front office and gave the guy a credit card and did all the rental paperwork and liability waiver. He then got on the blower and called Manny. I don't know his actual name but it was a fifty-year-old Mexican guy who looked like he'd been working there for twenty years. I backed the truck up, eager to load the Genie lift and return to the team of guys on the clock waiting back at the house. Manny looked at the Explorer and said, "It won't fit."

After being a carpenter for twenty years, I have tape measures for eyeballs. I can tell sizes and capacities instantly. It comes in handy on a construction site and also when checking out a chick's rack. I can tell a cup size from twenty paces. Anyway, I knew this thing would fit. But Manny insisted it wouldn't. We went back and forth on this for a couple of rounds, talked about folding in the legs, until finally I just said, "Let's give it a shot, I'm here, I'm backed up to the bay, the hatch is open, let's just try it." He said, "It won't work." I was confused. He had gone from it not fitting to it not working. He said, "It's no good. Even if it does fit, I can't let you take it in that vehicle. You need a truck or a van."

Here's where I wanted to go to the sledgehammer section, rent one, and take it to the back of the guy's skull. There was no "I'm sorry, sir," and no explanation like, "We put one of these things in an SUV last year, the chick stopped short, it went through her windshield, and now we have a lawsuit on our hands. Sorry." None. He just said I had to come back with a truck or a van. I told him I could easily put it in the back, close the hatch and drive away. No go. There's a phrase for this on construction sites: "We've got a dime holding up a dollar." Well, this peso with a fourth-grade education was holding up several hundred dollars. So I marched back into the office and said, "Listen, man, you've got a rogue employee out there. I've rented something from your establishment and he refuses to load it into my SUV. You need to go straighten him out." I expected the manager to walk out and settle Manny's hash. "You put it in the back of Mr. Carolla's Explorer and stop arguing." What I got was, "It's his call." They were semiapologetic about it, but apparently their company policy was that this guy was the yard foreman and if he said it was no-go, it was no-go. At that point I started begging. "I have a small army of guys on the clock three miles from here. I'll stick to the surface streets. We've already done the paperwork. Can you please just tell him to look the other way while I load it up?" The guy just repeated, "No."

I then announced, "You've lost a customer for life. This dump will never see my shadow again, and I'm going to dedicate the first hour of my radio show tomorrow to what ass-wipes you guys are." I stormed out and immediately got on the phone with United Rentals a short hop away in Burbank. Out of Genie lifts. "That's all right. I'll call Wannamaker Rents in Glendale. I'm sure they'll have a baker's dozen of those babies lying around." Once again, all rented out. I don't know what the fuck was going on at this point. This is a fairly pedestrian item that every rental yard has at least five of, and the only place in town that possesses one is the one I just got done telling to fuck off.

So I called my buddy Ray and asked him to commandeer a van. He had a friend who owned a motorcycle shop and could borrow it. I told him to go to Acme, don't mention I sent you, get the lift, and meet me at my house with it. A half hour later my phone rang. It was Ray calling from the rental yard. He had the van, Manny was going to allow him to leave with the lift, but Ray did not possess a credit card. Because why would a forty-six-year-old have a credit card? When I brought this point up, Ray countered with an even more pathetic response: "I had a credit card, but when my mom died it was canceled because it was in her name." Touché.

In an attempt to save time and face, I told Ray, "Don't tell the guy my name and just ask him if I can give him the credit-card number over the phone." He told Ray he needed to swipe the credit card.

So I had to return to the place where just forty-five minutes earlier I was screaming "You'll never see a nickel of my money again" with my credit card in hand and tail between my legs, meet Ray with the van, and get the lift. Remember, while all of this is happening the crew were back at the site picking their noses and consequently my pocket.

When it was time to return it two days later I told one of my guys, Gary, to fold the thing up and see if it would fit into the Explorer. He folded it up, slid it in, and the tailgate was completely shut, no tie-downs or bungee cords needed. I was furious. I told him to bring it back and tell Manny to fuck himself with any number of the tools that they rent. He ruined my entire day and cost me hundreds of dollars. Everyone argues with me on this point: "Oh, leave him alone. He's miserable, he probably only makes nine dollars an hour." Fuck him and fuck you for saying I shouldn't tell him to fuck himself.

This year I passed the store on my way to the party-supply place for my kids' birthday. I was delighted to see that it was out of business.

Every day I repair or replace something in this house. Because I take so much pride in it. Of all the homes I've had, this is really my *home*. It's a metaphor for who I am. I built and installed every cabinet in the kitchen, built and installed every custom closet unit, set every piece of tile, hung every fixture, and picked out every antique knob. This isn't me bragging about my aesthetic sense or expertise. It's not about the skill set, it's about the mind-set. That useless second front door on the first house you read about didn't stay there for years because no one had the *skill* to remove it; it was because no one had the *will* to remove it. I came from the least effective group of people to grace this planet, yet I'm a doer. I'm a closer. I get shit done. And that's not something you can buy, or that someone can give you. It's something you have to build into yourself and your life. The ability to take care of business, to focus, to lock it off and knock it off. As opposed to every dump I grew up in, my current house stands as a testimony to that mind-set.

CONCLUSION

Thank you for joining me on this walk down memory lame. In dredging this stuff up, I've surprised myself at just how pathetic it all really was.

But I hope you've gotten something out of it. I wanted this to be more than just a bunch of stories strung together so that you could laugh at my misery. I wanted it to be inspirational. So in that vein, I'll tell one last story followed by one last, and most important, message.

1970—Grandma's patio with Laci. Note my parents in the background.
Hey you kids, get a room!

. . .

I've talked a little about my grandfather, technically stepgrandfather, over the course of this book, but I've never really delved into him. His name was Laszlo Gorog. But we all called him Laci (pronounced *Lotzi*). He was an old-world Hungarian Jew who escaped the Nazis while many people in his family didn't share the same fate. He was a creative guy, a playwright, who came to the U.S. and eventually found himself in the film business. He was nominated for the Best Original Story Academy Award for *The Affairs of Susan* in 1946. He also wrote *The Mole People* and *Earth vs. the Spider*. Not high art, but hey, the man had to put goulash on the table.

And he did. That was one of the things that endeared him to me so much. He was the only member of the clan who knew how to, or gave a shit enough to, rattle some pots and pans. He used to make fantastic traditional Hungarian food, a food I still love to this day. He even made weird shit like beef tongue, and I remember he used to lament that he couldn't get goose liver out here. He didn't care that they stuffed the goose until its liver nearly exploded, he just wanted something to spread on a Ritz. He would even occasionally travel to Hungary and come back with paprika, because he couldn't get the good stuff here. While everyone else would be muling in cocaine, he was the only guy going through customs at LAX with a pillowcase full of paprika. He liked it authentic. One day he saw a sign pop up for a Der Wienerschnitzel right near his place in North Hollywood and thought, "Finally! A place where I can get some schnitzel in this godforsaken town." He was devastated when he found out it was corn dogs and 7-Up.

He was a loving, caring man and an oasis in the emotional Sahara that was the Carolla family. Some of you may know that I was a bed wetter until age nine. While the rest of the family was tuning out or analyzing whether I had latent anger issues (by the way, my anger has historically been anything but latent), Grandpa took the novel

325

approach of actually doing something. He would wake me up in the middle of the night and make me take a leak into a bucket next to the sofa I was sleeping on so I wouldn't piss myself at two A.M. It was a simple, practical solution, and it worked. But more important, it demonstrated more warmth and attention than I had come to expect from the rest of my family.

So, now that I've set Grandpa up a little bit, here's the story. My whole life, my family had known me as a loser. To them, I was the guy from the first thirteen chapters of this book—stringing together construction gigs to pay for beer and rent with a bunch of nut-job roommates. But even when I finally started making some dough in showbiz, it didn't make a difference. Because they were who they were, none of them had cable or really acknowledged the two shows I had on TV. And *Loveline* on the radio was way past their bedtimes. (In fact, one time my dad wanted to come on to plug one of his psychology lectures and I said sure. He replied with, "How about seven on Friday?" The man had no idea *Loveline* aired Sunday through Thursday at ten.)

But I didn't give a shit that they didn't give a shit. Except for Laci. He was nearing the end of his life when I became successful, and I wanted him to know it and to be proud. One day I got that Social Security statement the government mails you, letting you know how much you made that year and how much of it they extracted. I had made $543,453. So I went to Grandpa to brag a little. I said, "Hey, Grandpa. You know, I'm not a loser anymore. I'm making a good living in show business. I'm doing really well. I made a ton of money this year." He looked at me and asked, "Did you make a million dollars?"

I was deflated. I thought, No, you old fuck, I didn't. I sulked out to my BMW cursing my paltry take of more than a half million dollars. "You're such a loser, Carolla. A measly five hundred and forty three thousand. You've devastated your poor grandfather. What the fuck is wrong with you?"

But the next year rolled around and I got my Social Security statement and saw that I had made $1,237,903. I immediately hopped in the car and sped down to Grandpa's. The man didn't have long to live, and I needed to rub this shit in his face. You know, because I loved him so much. So I sat down with him and said, "Hey Grandpa, you know how last year you asked me if I had made a million dollars? Well, this year I made over a million dollars." Grandpa paused, looked down, then looked me in the eyes, and said, "Money doesn't buy happiness."

It was such a Jewey move. He gave a little and then he took it away. He had given me the Jew-jitsu. Used my own momentum against me and choked me out with my own gi.

It was infuriating, but he was right. And that's the point I want to end with. Money *doesn't* buy you happiness. I hope you didn't read this book as "Get rich and successful, and everything will be perfect." It won't.

Don't get me wrong. If you found these pages motivational and took away the idea that if, like a younger me, you have dreams but no support—or even anchors in the form of family and friends telling you to shut up—and no record of success, that it's still okay to try, well, then I'm gratified. Because you only get one go-around, so you should just put your head down and keep moving forward. But there are no guarantees in life. At no point did I ever think when I was hauling shit on construction sites and cleaning carpets, "This will make a great chapter in my book someday. I can't wait to talk about it on syndicated radio or *The Tonight Show*." No. I just kept trying.

But I want you to really absorb this idea about money and happiness. Of course being destitute sucks. Not having enough money to pay your bills blows. I know it: I was there. But as my good friend Biggie Smalls once said, "Mo' money, mo' problems." (I miss you, homie.) There is a sweet spot, and hopefully you've found it. Enough to raise a family and have a modest-sized house. When you get past that, you just start chasing your life and never stop to enjoy what you have.

This year I went to my recently passed-away grandmother's house, the one I put a kitchen on. My mom and my stepdad were remodeling it so they could move from their piece of shit to a slightly better piece of shit. I was looking around and had a flood of memories, having been essentially raised in that dump. I was walking through, looking at what they were remodeling and seeing all the trinkets and shitty carpentry I remember from growing up.

After I came home from the visit, it was a cold night so I decided to take a steam. (I built a steam room in my house.) I put in my ear buds and put on a towel then sat schvitzing and thinking about that house and the lousy memories attached. As I started getting emotional, the steam room got a little too hot. Then just as a cosmic kick in the balls, Kenny Rogers's "Through the Years" came up on the iPod shuffle. So I left the room. As soon as I walked out, I saw my two kids sitting on the edge of my bed. I was covered in sweat and Kenny was blaring in my ears. I looked at my twins sitting on my king-sized bed in a home I built with my own hands, absorbed the juxtaposition, and started bawling. Since I still had the ear buds in when Lynette walked into the room, she saw me sweaty and crying, "Daddy loves you so much" for what appeared to be no reason. But it came from the emotional whiplash of being in my childhood home to see how far I'd come. Or, more accurately, how far I'd dragged myself.

And that's what life is all about. Not super-garages or television shows or hanging with celebrities. If you can get those along the way, then fine. But life is about emotional growth. Humans are the only creatures that get to witness and partake in their own evolution. I love the fact that we can actively change ourselves, but I hate the idea that it's squandered by 99 percent of the population. We appreciate change on a physical level—like before-and-after shots of people on Jenny Craig. But there are no before-and-after shots of someone maturing—a "before" picture of me shotgunning a beer with a pen in my one-bedroom and an "after" picture of me depositing money into my kids' college fund.

That's what this book is about—not getting better houses in the physical sense, but in the symbolic sense. Working hard and using your talents, whatever they may be, to pursue your dreams, whatever they may be, and to get a better life for yourself, in whatever form that takes for you. Thanks for reading, and *Mahalo*.

ACKNOWLEDGMENTS

I'd like to thank Lynette first because I didn't in my last book. I'd also like to thank my agent, James "Babydoll" Dixon, my literary agent, Dan Strone, my editor, Suzanne O'Neill, and the whole team from Crown Archetype.

And I definitely need to thank super-fans Giovanni Peluso and Adam Dristle for their tireless and borderline creepy archiving of everything I do. Without them the writing of this book would have been significantly more difficult. And finally, Mike Lynch, without whom it would have been impossible.

ABOUT THE AUTHOR

ADAM CAROLLA is a radio and TV host, comedian, and actor. Carolla is well known as the cohost of the syndicated radio and MTV show *Loveline* and the cocreator and star of *The Man Show* and *Crank Yankers*. He currently hosts *The Adam Carolla Show,* the Guinness World Record's Most Downloaded Podcast, available daily on iTunes and AdamCarolla.com.

NOT ENOUGH CAROLLA FOR YOU?

The *New York Times* bestseller *In Fifty Years
We'll All Be Chicks* is Adam Carolla's comedic
gospel of modern America. He rips into the
absurdity of the culture that demonized the
peanut-butter-and-jelly sandwich, turned the
nation's bathrooms into a lawless free-for-all
of urine and fecal matter, and put its citizens
at the mercy of a bunch of minimum wagers
with axes to grind. Peppered between
complaints, Carolla shares candid anecdotes
from his day-to-day life as well as his past—
Sunday football at Jimmy Kimmel's house, his
attempts to raise his kids in a society that he
mostly disagrees with, his big showbiz break,
and much, much more. Brilliantly showcasing
Carolla's spot-on sense of humor, this book
cemented his status as a cultural commentator,
comedian, and complainer extraordinaire.